# the Book of
# TARA

To Mark at Tara
June 21, 2003
*[signature]*

Inside the Mound of the Hostages.

the Book of

# TARA

Michael Slavin

foreword by Conor Newman

WOLFHOUND PRESS

*With thanks to editors Frances Power and
Adrienne Murphy, who believed in the project
and made it better; to Conor Newman of the
Discovery Programme, and to the Meath
Heritage Centre; special gratitude to Gerard
Whelan and Mary Kelleher at the Royal
Dublin Society Library in Ballsbridge, and to
Dr Pat Wallace at the National Museum; and
to Michael Slattery at Clarecastle, Co Clare
for his help. Statoil Ireland Ltd., Royal Tara
China, Waterford Crystal and Tara Mines
helped make the colour reproduction possible.
Robert Vance created brilliant pictures of the
hill. Finally, thanks to Katie for her patience,
and to all my neighbours here at Tara, who
keep the quiet spirit of the hill alive in our
small community.*

*Michael Slavin*

**Tara from the northwest.**

First published in hardback 1996
This paperback edition published 2002 by
Wolfhound Press
*An imprint of Merlin Publishing*
16 Upper Pembroke Street,
Dublin 2, Ireland
publishing@merlin.ie
www.merlin-publishing.com

© 1996 Michael Slavin

British Library Cataloguing-in-Publications Data.
A catalogue record for this book is available from the British Library.

ISBN 0-86327-472-2 paperback edition    10 9 8 7 6 5 4 3 2 1
ISBN 0-86327-507-9 hardback edition

*Cover design: Slick Fish Design, Dublin*
*Book design: Ed Miliano*
*Photography: Robert Vance*
*Typesetting: Wolfhound Press*
*Colour Separations: Repro Link, Dublin*
*Printed in the Republic of Ireland*
*by ColourBooks, Ltd., Dublin*

# TABLE OF CONTENTS

**Foreword by Conor Newman • 10**
Director of the Tara Project Discovery Programme

**Introduction •11**

### Chapter 1 / Tara and the Invasion Legends • 13
Tuán's Visions — The Partholóns — Evil Formorians — Fir Bolg from Greece — First Kings at Tara
The Tuatha Dé Danaan — Legendary Battles — Arrival of the Milesians — History or Fable?
New Interpretations of the Legends

### Chapter 2 / The Sacred Hill • 27
Gateway to Mystical Realms— Shrines of the Earth Mother Goddess — Festivals of the Gods — Vestal Virgins?
Patrick at Tara — Battle of Old and New Beliefs

### Chapter 3 / Women of Tara • 41
Named for a Woman — Maeve the Warrior Queen — Search for the Great Bull — Conflict with Cúchulainn
Victory over Ulster — The Love of Étaín and Midhir — Escape to Tír na nÓg — Flight of Gráinne and Diarmaid
Death on Ben Bulben — The Heroine Molly Weston

### Chapter 4 / Home of Heroes • 55
Sreng of the Fir Bolg — Confronting the Dé Danaan — First Battle of Moytura — Lugh, Son of Light
In the Land of the Ever Young — Under Formorian Tyranny — Lugh's Return — Second Battle of Moytura
The Giant Fionn Mac Cumhaill — Chieftain of the Fianna — Oisín, Last of the Fianna

## Chapter 5 / Tara of the Kings • 69

The Roll of Kings — Local Kingships and Tuaithe — Sacral Kings — The Royal Legends
First King of the Fir Bolg at Tara — The Dé Danaan Takeover — Historical Manipulations


## Chapter 6 / Priest Kings and Ancestors • 79

Otherworld Origins — The Taboos — Saviour Warrior — Tax on the Leinstermen — The Triennial Feis of Tara
Birth of Conn of the Hundred Battles — Conn Comes to Tara — Cormac Conceived — Right Judgement by Cormac
A Mill for Cormac's Lover


## Chapter 7 / Rise of the Uí Néill • 91

Origins of the Sept — Niall of the Nine Hostages — Meeting the Hag at the Well — Laoghaire and the Leinstermen
Sín Drowns Muircheartach — Christianity and Kingship in Conflict — King Diarmaid: Half-Christian, Half-Pagan
The Cursing of Tara — Abandonment of the Sacred Hill

## Chapter 8 / Quest for High Kingship • 99

Northern and Southern Uí Néill — The Síl nÁedo Sláine— Kingship at Lagore — Domhnall, King of Ireland
Loingsech Mac Oengusso — Áed Allen, a Warrior King — Religion and Politics


## Chapter 9 / The Munster and Viking Challenge • 105

The Invasion of Turges — Victory for Malachy I — Munster Ambitions — Feidhlimid Attacks Tara
Defeat of a Dictator — The Vikings Remain


## Chapter 10 / Two Kings in Conflict • 111

Malachy II of the Uí Néill — Malachy's First Victory Over the Vikings — Brian Boru, King of Munster
Coronation at Cashel — Allies Then Enemies — Confrontation at Tara — Submission of Malachy
Death of Brian Boru — Malachy Restored

## Chapter 11 / Tara and the Norman Knights • 119

Celtic Concept of Kingship — Norman Conquest — Last King of Tara
New Rules of Ownership — Hugh de Lacy and His Knights — The Barony of Skryne — Tara Owned

## Chapter 12 / Still a Hill of Hostings • 125

A Place of Muster — Meeting of 1641 — Red Hugh Ó Domhnaill — Battle of Tara 1798 — Lord Fingall
The First Lord Tara — One Million on the Hill — O'Connell's Monster Meeting — The Final Hosting

## Chapter 13 / Ownership of Tara • 137

Heart of the Golden Triangle — Stronghold at Trim — Dillons — Prestons — Duke of Bedford
Prime Minister Lord Russell — Nieces to the Cardinal — Inherited by the Briscoes — Bill Tormey
The OPW Takeover — Tara United Again

## Chapter 14 / The Tara Landscape • 147

Legends of the Wells — Birth of the Hill — Tara and the Ice Age — The Outer Ring — Mound of the Hostages
Archaeology at Tara — Seat of Kings — Rath of Laoghaire— Sloping Trenches — Ceremonial Entrance
Ancient Roads to Tara — Rath of the Synods — In the Churchyard

## Bibliography • 165

## Index • 169

## THE OPENING PAGES . . .

*Title page spread:* Inside the Mound of the Hostages. Here there is a stone passage measuring seven feet, which contains a unique decorated slab depicting images of the sun, moon and stars. This could have been a ritual chamber associated with the coming of age of young princes, or with the union between the king and Queen Maeve, Goddess of Sovereignty. It is also a sacred grave mound that contained up to 200 burials in cremated or skeletal form when excavated by Professor Seán P. Ó Ríordáin and his team betwen 1955 and 1959. The Mound of the Hostages is the oldest earthworks on the Hill of Tara; on the outside it measures seventy feet in diameter and nine feet in height. *(Turn to page VII in the second colour section for an exterior picture of the mound.)*

*Copyright page:* Aerial shot of Tara from the northwest. Roughly in the centre of the picture are the Sloping Trenches; above them and to the left are the long rectangular earthworks formerly known as the Banquet Hall. Most experts now maintain that they were more likely to have been the ceremonial entrance to Tara. If so, the structure would have been the converging point for the five roads to Tara, which were said to have magically sprung into existence on the night that the king of Tara, Conn of the Hundred Battles, was born.

**Table of Contents pictures: (1)** *Contemporary illustration of Lugh, the God of Light, as he defeats Balor of the Evil Eye.* **(2)** *Two great Battles of Moytura are described in the* Book of the Taking of Ireland *– first betweeen the Fir Bolg and the semi-divine race, the Tuatha Dé Danann, and then betwen the Dé Danann and the ferocious Fomorians. Modern Irish artist Jim Fitzpatrick created this heroic image of these fierce mythical encounters. Note how the stone to the right of the warrior corresponds to Adamnán's Cross on the Hill of Tara.* **(3)** *Bellinter House, the seat of Lord Tara built in 1750. Its front door faces directly up towards the hill. In 1892 ownership passed to the Briscoe family, and in 1965 the house was purchased by the Daughters of Sion, a Catholic order of nuns. It is still run as a conference centre.* **(4)** *The ruins of Bective Abbey in silhouette.*

**Opposite:** *Painting by Earnest Wallcousins featuring the god-king Lugh, who, according to legend, led the Dé Danann to victory over the evil Fomorians.*

# FOREWORD

In the course of my as yet quite short acquaintance with the place, I have come to realise that Tara is all things to all people. To the romantic, here lie the enigmatic remains of a bygone heroic age, where high kings ruled, warriors sparred, muses composed and lovers embraced. To the naturalist, it is a countryside smoothed by the forces of nature into a perfect midland balance of fertile plains, broad rivers and mature woods, supporting the finest of Irish bloodstock, livestock and wildlife. To the mystic it is a liminal zone, shared with the otherworld and a panoply of pagan deities whose potency is not extinguished, but merely dimmed by time. To the historian it is the prize fought over by our medieval forebears jockeying for political supremacy, for with Tara came the right to claim kingship. To the archaeologist, ever mindful of the fact that it has been invested with all that was dearest and most sacred to our ancestors, it is a palimpsest of prehistoric ritual monuments; a burial ground and meeting place. And to those who live there and have lived there, it is quite simply home. Who better then to reassert that no one party has a monopoly on the truth about Tara than someone who lives there, someone who has daily to reconcile all of these sometimes contradictory facets into a life-narrative? Michael Slavin's love of Tara is palpable and this book, which is a labour of love, is infused with the same contagious enthusiasm, founded on his detailed knowledge of the monuments, the legends and the countryside that combine to create Tara.

*Conor Newman*
*Director of the Tara Project Discovery Programme*

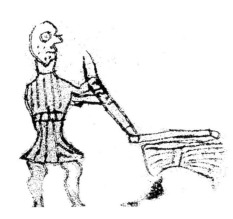

# INTRODUCTION

Tara's story is Ireland's story. Tara's symbols are Ireland's symbols – the harp, the shamrock, the ancient gold. Prominent in our oldest myths and legends, the hill has been at the centre of things Irish since the earliest times. In some mysterious way, Tara touches the very soul of Ireland. While its regal and heroic identity hark back to a legendary time long gone by, as a symbol Tara has survived right up to the present. Thus down the centuries great lovers of this land – like the United Irishmen of 1798, or Daniel O'Connell, the Liberator – have used Tara's grassy banks as a backdrop for their dreams and their messages.

Tara's fame extends far beyond our island shores. Every year thousands of infants around the world are given its distinctively female name. And at the same time, ranches, farms, ships and firms are called after it. One of the most famous mansions in cinematic history is Tara in *Gone with the Wind*.

Thanks to the Office of Public Works' Discovery Programme, initiated in the early 1990s, Tara has been subject to closer scientific scrutiny than ever before. Along with recent historical studies, this research clearly highlights the *imaginative* rather than factual content of the legends surrounding Tara. Many of the stories which have proliferated around this sacred hill are not historically verifiable. Yet at the same time, Tara's deeply ingrained popular and literary tradition is too colourful, entertaining and culturally important to be disregarded. In my telling of Tara's story I have attempted to trace that tradition through the invasions legends, the romantic and heroic sagas associated with the hill, and what there is of written history.

Despite my enthusiastic love for this wonderful place, I have tried to be objective, taking recent academic discoveries into account. In some instances where the evidence is clear, I've had to

*One of five sacred royal seats in Ireland, Tara lies in Co Meath, about 30km north of Dublin city and just 1.5km to the west of the Dublin to Derry road, midway between the town of Dunshaughlin and Navan. It is at the centre of the 'golden triangle' of fertile land that stretches from Ireland's east coast, between Dublin and Dundalk, west almost out to the Shannon.*

*Do not expect to notice Tara from a distance. It is a hill of no more than 155m in height. Yet despite this small size, its unique position at the edge of Ireland's central lowland plain allows it to overlook miles of country in every direction,*

let the critical historians hold sway. But where there is still overwhelming doubt about what did or did not happen here, I felt Tara and its legends deserved the benefit of that doubt.

Above all else, I have tried to portray Tara as a spiritual place. For in the long run it is not exclusively the domain of historians, archaeologists or scientists. It is also a place for dreamers, storytellers and mystics. I invite you to join me there.

*Michael Slavin*
*The Hill of Tara*
*Lughnasa 1996*

# CHAPTER 1

# TARA AND THE INVASION LEGENDS

*'Temair Breg, whence is it named?*
*declare O sages!*
*When did the name part from the stead?*
*When did Temair become Temair?*

*Was it under Partholón of battles?*
*or at the first conquest by Cesair?*
*or under Nemed of the stark valour?*
*or under Cigal of the knocking knees?*

*Was it under the Firbolgs of the boats?*
*Or from the line of Luprachans?*
*Tell in what invasion of these it was*
*From which the name of Temair was set on Temair?'*

(Tenth-century poem)[1]

The fame of Tara is based on legends – magical tales about successive ancient invasions, the exploits of pre-historic kings and the arrival of St Patrick at the sacred hill. These invasion legends are contained in the *Lebor Gabála Érenn* or *The Book of the Taking of Ireland*, which was written down in various versions by monastic scribes of the eleventh to fourteenth centuries. The texts are a fascinating account of the early habitation of Ireland – a mix of oral lore and the Christian tradition of the Middle Ages.

'Tuán son of Cairell was heard:
Jesus gave to him in his sin,
that he spent an hundred long years
in the form of a man under good appearance.

Three hundred years had he, in the form
of a stag deer on the deserts:
he spent an hundred good years
in the form of a wild boar.

Three hundred years had he on flesh
when he was in the form of a lonely bird;
then he spent an hundred tuneful years
in the form of a salmon under a flood.

A fisher took him in his net,
carried him to the king's fortress;
when she saw the pure salmon,
the queen desired him.

So that it was assigned to her, a good course,
and she ate it all by herself:
the very noble queen became pregnant,
and thence was Tuán conceived.'[3]

**One version of the *Lebor Gabála* is found in *The Book of Leinster*, compiled around AD1100, probably in Terryglass monastery in north Tipperary. Another is in the fourteenth-century *Book of Ballymote*, but parts of the text can be found in fifteen different manuscripts and they seem to be an attempt not only to preserve the oral legends, but also to put across the prevailing political and religious message of the time.**

The mythical narrator of the *Lebor Gabála* is a spiritual presence called Tuán Mac Cairill, who many times changes his shape as he tells a story that covers thousands of years. Hovering above the land in the form of an eagle or racing across the hills as a stag, Tuán seems to represent the soul of Ireland and tells of the successive arrivals in Ireland, after the biblical flood, of the Parthalóns, the Nemedians, the Fir Bolg, Dé Danann and finally the Milesians.

Tuán, who would reappear in later legends named Fintan, is said to have been the only survivor of the first invasion of Ireland by the Parthalóns. 'On a Monday plague took them and the plague killed them all except one man – Tuán ... And God fashioned him in many forms in many times and that man survived alone from the time of Partholón to the time of Findian of Mag Bile and to Colum Cille so that he related to them the Taking of Ireland from the time of Cessair, the first who took Ireland to that time of the saints and of Diarmait Mac Cerbaill, King of Ireland. For it is Fintan who arranged the settlement of the household of Temair [Tara] for Diarmait and it is clear that Fintan was Tuán.'[2]

**Tuán tells us that, prior to the invasions, in all of Ireland at this time there were but three lakes, nine rivers and only one great plain – perhaps the Plain of Meath. 'For Partholón found not more than one plain in Ireland before him, the Old Plain of Edar.'[4]**

First, 78 years after the flood in 2678BC, according to Tuán, came Partholón from Greece with his queen Dalny, and their followers. They had to do battle with the ferocious seafarers, the Fomorians, who had a stronghold on Tory Island off the coast of Donegal. The Fomorians derived their name from *fomóiri* which means 'underworld spirits'. But the *mór* part of the name is confused with

*Ancient stone representation of Nuadhu, the first king of the Dé Danann at Tara.*

*mur* or 'sea' — thus *fomhoire* came to mean 'sea pirates'. In Celtic mythology, the northern region was always associated with evil, perhaps because it was colder and more inhospitable to settlers. The Fomorians inhabited this forbidding territory and therefore represented the epitome of evil. In one story they are said to have threatened to use their dark magic to tow the island of Ireland far into the frozen north. They constantly reappear to do battle with each successive wave of invader.

The Parthalóns defeated the Fomorians but were later afflicted with plague. Having gathered on the Great Plain, at what some say was Moynalty, 24 kilometres north of Tara, they all died, leaving Ireland once more with only the spiritual presence of Tuán hovering over it.

In the form of an eagle, Tuán next witnessed the arrival of the Nemedians who also had to fight the Fomorians. Only 30 of the invaders survived; among them was Tailtiu, daughter of the King of the Great Plain. She was later to marry Eochaid Mac Erc, a Tara king of the next wave of invaders, the Fir Bolg. She was foster mother to Lugh, one of the mythical heroes of Tara and originally a Celtic deity (*see Chapter 4, Home of Heroes*). Tailtiu gave her name to the plain of Teltown along the River Blackwater, sixteen kilometres north of Tara, where the annual Tailten Games were held in her memory as late as 1770.

Having taken the form of a black boar, Tuán then watched the third wave of invaders – the Fir Bolg, who are portrayed as a hard-working and not very attractive race. They escaped from slavery in Greece by stealing their captors' boats and sailing for Ireland. Some historians have associated them with a continental group of Celts known as the Bolgi or Belgae (*fir*, meaning 'men', was a common prefix used by early medieval genealogists) who may have taken over Tara and Leinster around 500BC. But in the legends the date of their arrival is pushed back to 1972BC. It is with the Fir Bolg that the myths concerning Tara really begin.

The Fir Bolg had five chieftains: Gann, Genann, Rudraige, Sengann and Sláine. They divided Ireland into five provinces or *cúige* ('fifths', a word still used in Irish for 'province', even though there are now only four provinces in Ireland) with Meath in the eastern midlands as the central province and Tara as the royal seat. A tenth-century poem ascribed to one Caoílte Mac Ronáin states: 'Sláine of the Fir-bolgs of fame t'was he by whom Tara was first raised.'[5] The Hill of Slane, sixteen kilometres north-east of Tara,

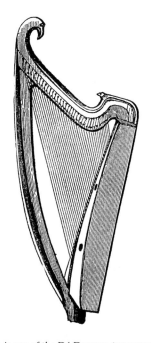

*The harp is one of the Dé Danann treasures recovered from the Fomorians and brought back to Tara. A symbol of Tara, down through the centuries it has come to symbolise Ireland. This drawing of a beautiful instrument dating from the late sixteenth century was included in W.R. Wilde's 1857* Descriptive Catalogue of the Antiquities in the Museum of the Royal Irish Academy.

Above: *Bronze Age cauldron. The cauldron of the Daghdha, or father-god, was brought to Ireland by the Dé Danann. Its power was that it would never go empty.*

Right: *Bronze Age implement, possibly a javelin head, found on the Dillon farm at Tara. Both in the legends and in historic times, many battles are said to have taken place around Tara: at the arrival of the Celts in the late centuries BC, the arrival of the Vikings in the ninth century AD and during Ireland's fight for independence during the second millennium. No wonder many items of war have been found near its now peaceful slopes.*

where St Patrick is said to have lit the first pascal fire in Ireland, takes its name from the king of the Fir Bolg.

Their ninth king was Eochaid son of Erc and *The Book of the Taking of Ireland* says of him, 'It is Eochu s. Erc who was the first king of the Fir Bolg who sat in the beginning in Temair, even though he was their last king: and in his time the Mound of the Three Men was erected upon Temair [Tara], and the Stone Heap of the One Man. Druim Cain was its name before the time of the Fir Bolg at the beginning.'[6] There is no trace of any monument bearing the name 'Mound of the Three Men' or 'Stone Heap of the One Man' at Tara today.

Eochu or Eochaid married Tailtiu of the Nemedians and the date given for his accession to the kingship at Tara is 1904BC. He is said to have been a fortunate and good man under whose rule the land blossomed and the people flourished in great happiness. 'There was no wetting in his time save only dew; and there would be no year without harvest; and falsehoods were expelled from Ireland in his time.'[7] But it was Eochaid who had to face the terror of Ireland's next invaders, the divine race known as the Tuatha Dé Danann. 'In this wise they came without vessels or barks in dark clouds over the air by the might of druidry. Thereafter the Tuatha Dé Danann brought a darkness over the sun for a space of three days and three nights. They were to demand battle or the Kingship of the Fir Bolg.'[8]

Eochaid was forewarned of the Dé Danann landing by a vision. When his messengers informed him that the invaders had landed in the west, he called his chiefs to Tara. The assembly decided that the warrior Sreng should go to meet the Dé Danann (*see Chapter 4, Home of Heroes*).

Following an intimidating one-to-one meeting with the leading Dé Danann warrior, Breas, Sreng returned to the royal seat at Tara and reported that this new race was a mighty force with superior arms and awesome magical power on their side. In order to avoid a terrible battle, Sreng advised Eochaid to accept the Dé Danann offer to divide the island equally with the Fir Bolg.

Eochaid refused their offer outright, believing that half of Ireland would not satisfy the invaders for long. He mustered his forces for battle. Eleven battalions gathered from all five kingdoms of the Fir Bolg and made camp on the slopes of Tara, the Hill of Hostings. Then, marching west across the great central plain to Sligo, the Fir Bolg engaged the invaders in the first Battle of Moytura.

In the *Book of the Taking* the narrative of this mythical encounter tells us that a hundred thousand of the Fir Bolg perished on the field and that after four days of fighting they were defeated. Eochaid was killed, but Sreng survived and made peace with the victors. His people were allowed to stay in the west while the Dé Danann moved east to take over the kingship at Tara. The legends give the date as 1896BC.

Nuadhu, semi-divine leader of the Dé Danann, lost his hand in the battle. According to the beliefs ascribed to this race, their leader had to be without blemish. Thus, Nuadhu could no longer reign.

Breas, who had a Fomorian father but whose mother was of the Dé Danann, had distinguished himself in the Battle of Moytura and was appointed to rule in Nuadhu's place. However, he proved to be a mean and ineffectual king who was willing to collect tribute for the Fomorians. He degraded some of the most revered supernatural beings of the Dé Danann and even set their father-god, the Daghdha, to work digging trenches. Just as offensive was his breach of the important code of hospitality when he refused to offer some of his guests a drink.

When Nuadhu's arm was restored through magic, the Dé Danann asked the disgraced king to step down in favour of their former leader. Breas agreed and went into exile.

Being a godly race, the Dé Dannan had brought four divine gifts with them to Tara, including the Lia Fáil or Stone of Destiny: 'From Falias was brought the Lia Fáil which was in Tara and it would not utter a cry but under every king that should take Ireland. From Goirias was brought the spear which Lugh had: battle would never go against who had it in hand. From Findias was brought the sword of Nuadu: no man would escape from it; when it was drawn from its battle-scabbard, there was no resisting it. From Muirias was brought the cauldron of the Dagda; no company would go from it unsatisfied.'[9]

A stone called the Lia Fáil still stands at Tara today, though no one knows whether it is the same Stone of Destiny described in the legends. It would certainly appear to be

*Page from the* Lebor Gabála *or* Book of the Taking of Ireland, *an eleventh-century compilation of earlier poetic and prose texts going back two hundred years. These in turn were in part based on ancient oral tradition. This particular page tells of the Milesian arrival in Ireland, their going to Tara and the poem uttered by their leader Amorgen, in which he willed 'that there may be a king of our own in Tara'.*

**the stone that was at Tara when the legends were written down in the *Lebor Gabála* and the topographical guide known as the *Dindshenchas*. It is commonly accepted that the author of the latter visited Tara during its composition in the late tenth or early eleventh century. At that time a stone called the Lia Fáil was in place near the Mound of the Hostages. The present Lia Fáil was moved from there to the top of the Forradh or King's Seat after the 1798 Rebellion. Claims have been made that the Stone of Scone in Westminster Abbey in London is the original Lia Fáil, but there is no proof to support this.**

The usual translation of Lia Fáil is Stone of Destiny. *Lia* means 'stone' and *fáil* or *fo áil* means 'the under stone', or the stone that was under the king. It was believed to roar when the true king touched it or drove his chariot next to it. And its obvious phallic symbolism may support this theory – as the true king underwent a ritual marriage with the Goddess of Sovereignty before he could rule.

While the Tuatha Dé Danann were powerful in magic and in war, they were not, according to the mythological tales, very good administrators. Gradually they let their land slip into the grasping hands of the Fomorians, who were always waiting in the wings. Matters deteriorated to the point where the ageing king Nuadhu was himself forced to work as a slave under the tyranny of the grotesque Fomorian leader, Balor of the Evil Eye. (The eye sat in the centre of his forehead; when he was angered its gleam could destroy anything in sight.)

Breas returned from exile with forces gathered from abroad. But instead of joining with the oppressed Dé Danann against the invaders, he revealed their magical secrets to the Fomorians and together Breas and the malign Fomorians soon dominated the island. In a raid on Tara they even managed to take the Spear of Victory and the Cauldron of Plenty as tribute. Gone too was a powerful symbol of Dé Danann supernatural power – the Harp of the father-god, the Daghdha. This magical harp was later to become an emblem of the Uí Néill kingship at Tara and eventually of Ireland itself. Its music could make the crops grow, enemies weaken and children laugh, and its absence from Tara was a bitter blow to Dé Danann prestige. The Sword of Light was hidden away so that it would not be confiscated as well. All that remained to the

*The Lia Fáil.*

Dé Danann was the Stone of Destiny, the Lia Fáil, symbol of their now ransomed kingship.

Thus the scene was set for the dramatic arrival at Tara of a saviour hero – Lugh of the Long Hand (*see Chapter 4, Home of Heroes*). He would lead the Dé Danann to a decisive victory over the Fomorians at the second Battle of Moytura, said to have been fought between the lakes of Mask and Corrib at Cong in Co Mayo.

Such a warrior had never been seen in Ireland before. It was claimed of Lugh, the Superman of these wonder-tales, that on a morning when he stood on the rampart of Tara, people thought the sun had risen in the west, so bright did his countenance shine. The Milky Way he wore as a silver chain around his neck, the rainbow formed his sling. He had a sword called 'the Answerer' that could cleave through any armour or wall; his boat needed no helmsman and he had a horse which galloped with equal ease over land or water.

In preparation for the battle to come, Lugh equipped himself with every magic weapon in the world at that time. Then, with all the powers of heaven and earth on his side, he went out from Tara at the head of a mighty host to do battle with the Fomorians and banish them from Ireland forever. After a fearsome encounter, during which Lugh killed his father-in-law, Balor of the Evil Eye, the Dé Danann were victorious. They returned to Tara bearing the Spear of Victory, the Cauldron of Plenty and the Harp of the Daghdha, and ruled there for the lifetime of nine kings until the coming of the Milesians.

All that had been memorised by the Celtic storytellers and all that was written by the Christian chroniclers of those early invasions was just a prologue to the arrival of their own legendary forebears – the Milesians. Once again Tara was the stage for a new act in the struggle for control over Ireland.

Having come from Spain under the leadership of Amorgen, one of the sons of King Míl, the Milesians first attempted a landing in the east of Ireland at Inver Sláine (near Drogheda today) but were beaten back by the magical power of the Dé Danann. They sailed south and, having landed on the coast of Kerry, made their way north – first to Slieve Mis, then to Slieve Felim in Co Limerick, from there to the Hill of Uisneach in Westmeath and finally on to the royal seat at Tara. 'The sons of Míl and of Bregon went till they were in Druim Cain, that is, Temair.'[10]

*Clonmacnoise, on the banks of the Shannon 70km west of Tara, founded by St Ciaran in the sixth century and one of the major monastic settlements to arise around the time of the abandonment of Tara. Important annals were written here.*

Although some of the ancient documents say that Tara got its name because it was a hill of 'great prospect', the legends dealing with the arrival of the Milesians state that Tara was named after the Spanish princess and mother-goddess, Tea. She was wife of another of the sons of Míl, Eremón, and had requested that she be buried on the most beautiful hill in Ireland:

> 'In the year before the setting of that battle by the two sons of Míl, Tea the daughter of Lugaid Mac Itha died – the wife of Erimón son of Míl of Spain. She had sureties against her husband, namely Amorgen Glúingel and Eber, before they came into Ireland, that whatsoever land she should choose, therein should she be buried and her rampart and her lair dug; and that therein should be every royal dignity and every assembly that should be convened, of the progeny of Erimón, for ever. This is the mound which she chose, Liath-druim; because it was the fairest sod by far which she saw in Ireland. And therein was the dignity of Ireland; and from her is it named, Temair, from her being therein habitually. And she was buried afterwards, and her rampart was raised over her, namely, *Múr Tea*, Tea-Múr.'[11]

The Milesians, along with their leader, Amorgen, met in the palace at Tara with the three sons of Neit, grandsons of the Daghdha – Mac Gréine, Mac Céacht and Mac Cuill, who represented in their names the power of the sun, the plough and the hazel. They were sharing the kingship of the Dé Danann at that time, and to the amazement of the newcomers were quarrelling about inheritance of their father's treasures even though they were surrounded by the great riches of nature on the Plain of Meath.

At this Tara meeting, Amorgen spoke for the sons of Míl and gave the Dé Danann the choice of giving up the kingship or facing the Milesian might in battle. It was agreed that the Milesians should return to their ships, retreat the distance of nine waves from land, and, if the power of the three Dé Danann kings and their enchantments could prevent them from landing again they would return to Spain.

The Dé Danann drew on the power of the wind that blows so fiercely over Tara to force the invaders back out to sea, but failed. In the midst of the tempest they had raised, Amorgen uttered these

*Opposite:* Page from the Book of Kells, *featuring a monastic scribe.*

*Below:* The fourteenth-century Book of Ballymote, *preserved by the Royal Irish Academy, includes one version of the Dindshenchas of Tara, a topographical description of the Hill first penned at the turn of the eleventh century, and based on lore going back into pagan Celtic times. On this beautiful page is a section which includes two poems about Tara by poets Cinaeth Ua hArtacan (d. 974) and Cuan Ua Lothcháin (d. 1024). They are called 'Tara Free From Feebleness' and 'Tara, Noblest Of Hills'. They begin on the bottom left of the page with the words:* 'Temair toga ne tulach'.

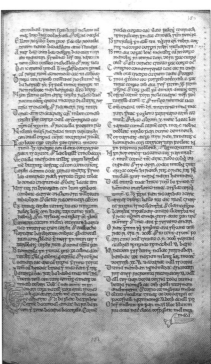

*'Round her house was built a rampart*
*by Tea daughter of Lugaid*
*she was buried beyond the wall without*
*so that from her is Temair named.'*[12]

magic words to his people: 'That they who are now tossing on the wide food-giving sea may reach now to the land. That they may find its plains, its hills and valleys, its forests that are filled full of nuts and fruits, its streams and rivers, its lakes and its waters. That we may have gatherings and our games on this land; that there may be a king of our own in Tara; that it may be the possession of our many kings.'[13]

Immediately the seas were calmed and the Milesians were able to land at Inver Sceine (Kenmare Bay in Co Kerry). There they fought a battle against the Dé Danann, led by Eriú, wife of the king, Mac Gréine. She was defeated and mortally wounded in battle, but before she died, Amorgen promised her that the island would bear her name forever – Eriú, Eire, Eireann.

The final confrontation between the Dé Danann and the Milesians was on the Plain of Teltown, north of Tara. There the Dé Danann were overcome but, in keeping with their god-like and spiritual nature, they did not leave Ireland. Instead they agreed that while the newcomers should rule on the earth, they would rule in the Otherworld, a supernatural realm which is placed in a number of locations – underground or across a stretch of water on a mythical island such as Tír na nÓg or the Land of Youth.

The Dé Danann legends are embedded in the very psyche of the Irish. This invisible Otherworld was a last refuge in times of trouble. Entry to it was to be gained through sacred places such as Tara, Newgrange on the Boyne and Loughcrew to the north-west. This realm was ruled over by the Daghdha, and other spiritual beings such as the love god Aonghus, Midhir the Proud and the sea god Manannán Mac Lír, who play important roles in the legends. In his book *Myths and Legends of the Celtic Race*, T. W. Rolleston concludes: 'There are two Irelands henceforward, the spiritual and the earthly. The Danann dwell in the spiritual Ireland, which is portioned out among them by their great overlord, Daghdha. Where the human eye can see but green mounds and ramparts, the relics of ruined fortresses or sepulchres, there rise the fairy palaces of the defeated divinities; there they hold their revels in eternal sunshine.'[14]

When the final battle between the Dé Danann and the Milesians was over, two of the sons of Míl were left alive – Eber and Eremón. They divided Ireland between them, with Eber ruling the southern half of the country from Cashel and Eremón, the northern half from Tara. But a rivalry broke out between the sons about the hills that were in each of their territories. It is said that Eber's wife felt that there was no hill in their half of the country to compare with Tara. The dispute led to a war and after a battle fought on the River Nore, Eremón became sole ruler of Ireland and Tara, the superior seat of kingship in Ireland. The *Annals of the Four Masters*, which attempted to write the history of Ireland, date this accession to power by the Milesians to 1498BC. But modern historians tell us that the coming of the Gael – or the Milesians – to Ireland dates to between 200BC and 50BC. That raises the question of just how much of the legends can be read as history. Very little, according to the most respected historians.

Up until recently the story of early Ireland, as set down in the *Book of the Taking of Ireland* and outlined in the earlier part of this chapter, was believed to be literally true. That was the accepted prehistory of Ireland, and historians down through the centuries have been slow to move away from those enjoyable legends.

Mid-way through this century, Irish medieval scholar Thomas F. O'Rahilly made an exhaustive attempt to construct an outline of when and how the various waves of people mentioned in the legends came into Ireland. In his work *Early Irish History and Mythology*, he used ancestor stories of people known as the Bolgi, the Laigin and the Goidel in an effort to create a reasonably believable succession of events. But his efforts have been deemed a failure precisely because they rely heavily on the invasion legends.

The latest academic studies have shown that neither the *Book of the Taking of Ireland* nor Tara's prominent place in its pages can be taken as factually correct. Undoubtedly, a thread of truth ran through the oral legends written down by the monastic authors of the seventh to the twelfth centuries. But the monks did not just copy the oral traditions down word for word. Rather they were authors who composed versions of the legends that suited them and the circumstances in which they lived – other agendas were being brought to bear.

First of all, as Celts, writing at the time of the hugely powerful Uí Néill dynasty and living in monasteries that came under their control, the scribes were anxious to give the greatest possible credibility to Uí Néill claims to high kinghip of Ireland. They did this by pushing the date of the Milesian arrival as far back in time as was possible. In this way the Uí Néill could claim a kingship that had been held by their ancestors for up to two thousand years.

*The monastery of Clonard, some 25 km west of Tara, was founded in the sixth century around the time of the abandonment of Tara. It was one of the centres of learning where ancient legends relating to Tara would first have found written expression. The monastery was suppressed in 1540, and all that remains is this font, preserved in the local Church of Ireland church.*

Secondly, as Christians, the scribes were trying to cope with a panoply of Celtic gods contained in the oral legends. Pagan belief, though still a reality among the Irish, was incompatible with Christian teaching. In reworking these ancient legends, the monastic writers were therefore also promulgating the story of Christianity's victory over the old religion of the Celts. Some historians contend that to this end they invented the Dé Danann invasion in order to simplify the vast list of gods in the legends on which they were depending for their material, by humanising the old gods into the Dé Danann.

Some recent works such as Kim McCone's *Pagan Past and Christian Present* state that the Dé Danann invasion was a fabrication and accept that their reign at Tara was a consciously constructed biblical allegory. McCone also sees this literary period in the monasteries of Ireland as producing texts that took Bible stories, couched them in the language and imagery of oral pre-Christian tales, and used them for what could be called the religious and political propaganda purpose of celebrating the dominance of Christianity over paganism in Ireland.

In McCone's scenario, the Fir Bolg of the invasion tales represented the pagans of biblical literature, the Dé Danann were *Tuatha Dé* – the 'People of God' or the Israelites of the Old Testament – while the sons of Míl and the Milesians were the triumphant Christians. Tara was the Babylon or Jerusalem in these scripture stories and the brilliantly crafted legends of the various invasions were just the introduction to the culminating moment when St Patrick confronted the pagan king, Lóegaire, on Tara.

So, where does this new interpretation of early Ireland, based on historical analysis of the *Book of the Taking of Ireland* leave Tara – the sacred hill, the royal hill, the Hill of Hostings that held such an important place in the writings of myth and wonder? Gone are the Dé Danann whose three kings were ruling at Tara when the Milesians came; gone too are the Milesians and the notion that for thousands of years they held the high kingship of Ireland at Tara long before the actual arrival of Celts.

Yet Tara still weaves its way into the fabric of the history that modern academics are compiling through their interpretations of the ancient legends. These historians are agreed that just about everything that happened in Ireland from prehistory up to the fifth century AD is all but hidden from our view. However, they do accept that a Celtic incursion into Ireland began around 200BC and they do not deny that a crucial battle in this migration may well have been that at Skryne near Tara.

The best approach to the controversy over fact and fiction, in my opinion, lies somewhere between two extremes – that of rejecting the legends completely and that of accepting them completely. F. J. Byrne in *Irish Kings and High King* has written: 'Throughout Irish history the glory of Tara has always lain in the past.'[15] In fact, when the medieval scribes were writing about Tara, it looked much as it looks today, with only its grassy mounds and trenches and wells to give any hint of what had happened there between one and seven thousand years previously.

In addition to the invasion legends, one of the most important eleventh-century texts about Tara is the *Dindshenchas Érenn*. It contains a prose account of every monument on the hill visible at that time – *'Dindgnai Temrach'* or 'Tara's Remarkable Places' and also a long poem called *'Temair Toga ne Tulach'* or 'Tara Noblest of Hills'. The poem is ascribed to Cuan Ua Lothcháin, poet to Mael-Sechnaill or Malachy II, the King of Tara, who was battling with Brian Boru for the high kingship of Ireland at the time. In the poem Ua Lothcháin makes every effort to restore the image of Tara's former glory and so he exaggerated of course, but the question still has to be asked – how much of what he wrote was based on the strong oral tradition that was still alive at the time?

My own view is that Tara served many functions during prehistory – it was a ritual holy place; a royal dwelling; a defensive site; and a burial place. The legends gave marvellously exaggerated accounts of what went on there, but there is a grain of truth in what they say. No archaeological investigation of the hill undertaken so far has contradicted this view. In fact, the investigations, which go back to 1953, have always turned up evidence to support Tara's claim to being important, royal and sacred.

This ancient site still remains one of the best windows we have on to Ireland's pagan past. As we will see in later chapters, when Ireland did emerge from the mists of mythical prehistory into something resembling true history, some thirteen hundred years ago, Tara was the most powerful royal name in the northern half of the country, and right up to the beginning of the eleventh century the kingship of Tara was the most sought-after title in all of Ireland.

Legendary chronology of the arrival of peoples to Ireland and their connections with Tara:

**Cessair**, *female leader of legendary first ever settlement in Ireland, arrived in 2956BC.*
**Parthalón** *and his people arrived from Asia Minor in 2678BC.*
The **Nemedians** *from Scythia arrived in 2098BC , 30 years after the Partholóns were wiped out by plague. They named Tara* Druim Liath, *or 'The Stone Ridge'.*
*From the* **Fir Bolg**, *hailing from Greece, came the first king of Tara, in 1972BC.*
The **Tuatha Dé Danann**, *a divine race from Greece whose kings reigned at Tara, arrived in 1896BC.*
The **Milesians**, *legendary ancestors of the Gael, arrived in 1498BC. It was predicted that many of their kings would reign at Tara.*

Brief chronology of Tara according to archaeology and early history:

**Mesolithic** *period, 7000-4000BC. No evidence as yet of the existence of Hunter-Gatherers at Tara.*
**Neolithic** *period, 3500-2000BC. During their latter years in the Boyne valley, Early Farming Folk built the Mound of the Hostages at Tara and left cremated burials there.*
**Bronze Age**, *1800BC onwards. Many burials and materials left by Food Vessel Folk and Cinerary Urn Folk at the Mound of the Hostages.*
**Iron Age**, *200BC onwards. During this time, the Celts were responsible for most of the earth works on Tara.*

*According to historians, everything prior to the fifth century AD is pre-historic and irrecoverable, apart from the Celtic incursion between 200-50BC. However, some major changes were firmly embedded in popular memory, and these endured in folklore. For example, the Laigin, or Leinstermen, had a royal seat at Tara before the Celts; and a crucial battle for control of the midlands was fought at Skryne near Tara.*

*When Tara emerged into the light of history in the sixth century AD, it had already been abandoned, but the most powerful kings in Ireland, the Uí Néill, reigned in its name as the Kings of Tara.*

1 Gwynn, Edward, *The Metrical Dindshenchas*, Todd Lecture Series, RIA, Dublin 1903, part I, Tara Poem I.
2 Macalister, R. A. S., *Lebor Gabála Érenn, The Book of the Taking of Ireland*, Irish Texts Society, Dublin, 1938-1956, part II, par 205; part III, par 222.
3 ibid., part III, poem XXXIX.
4 ibid., part II, par 204.
5 MS Trinity College Dublin, Class H. 1.15, f.58. Trans Mr. Petrie, *History and Antiquities of Tara Hill*, p. 283.
6 op. cit, *Lebor Gabála*, part IV, par 363.
7 ibid., part IV, par 296.
8 ibid., part IV, par 358.
9 ibid., part IV, par 305.
10 ibid., part V, par 440.
11 ibid., part V par 485.
12 op. cit., Gwynn, Tara Poem I.
13 ibid., part V, poem LXXII.
14 Rolleston, T.S., *Myths and Legends of the Celtic Race*, Bracken Books, London 1934. p. 136.
15 Byrne, F. J., *Irish Kings and High Kings*, p. 138.

# CHAPTER 2

# THE SACRED HILL

*'When Cormac was among the famous*
*bright shone the fame of his career;*
*no keep like Temair could be found;*
*she was the secret place on the road of life.'*

(Tenth-century poem)[1]

From the very beginning of man's association with Tara, the ancient hill must have been recognised as sacred – a 'secret place on the road of life'. The geology of the hill – its prominence above the central plain of Meath, its wells, its proximity to the great Boyne – all invested it with spiritual power in the minds of the early settlers whose way to the divine was from the visible features of the landscape to the invisible Otherworld of the gods.

In a study called *Sacred Geography in Éire*, a publication of the Irish American Cultural Institute of St Paul, Minnesota, the writer Paul Sheerin refers to the poem quoted above and theorises that the '"secret place" may refer to the special quality that Tara shares with other "Gateways", namely that of being an entry point to higher realms.'[2]

In *Celtic Gods and Goddesses,* R. J. Stewart writes: 'Celtic religion was primarily associated with the sanctity of the land and the power of certain key locations within the land. The entire landscape or environment was alive – the sacred groves or shrines were places of special power ... the land was usually represented by a goddess whose shape was clear to see in the rise of the hills and whose powers were apparent in the flow of rivers, the rising of springs and the growth of plants.'[3]

There is no evidence that the early settlers made images of their gods. Instead

Above: *Images thought to represent life, sun, moon and stars, on the stone inside the Mound of the Hostages.*

Below: *A depiction of the engravings on the stone. The heavenly bodies and other natural phenomena were held sacred by a very devout Stone Age people, who inhabited the area around Tara in the third millenium BC.*

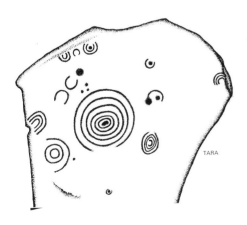

their sacred objects were the trees, the huge stones left behind by the glaciers, the wells, the groves, the ridges, the rivers and the hills. Their contact with the gods who governed their survival was through these features of the land. At Tara the landscape had them all and thus the place became a powerful spiritual force in their world – a force that was to diminish only with the arrival of Christianity in the fifth century.

The principal beliefs of pre-Christian religion at Tara centred on the earth-mother goddess and her relationship to the sovereignty of the king. She represented the fruitfulness of the earth, and her approval of his reign – acted out in a ritualised marriage at his inaugural feast – symbolised his right to be king, a right which was dependent on his ability to intercede with the gods for good harvests that would feed his people.

These fertility and sovereignty beliefs were celebrated at the four great annual festivals which divided the year and were fixed by the full moons of February (Oímelg or Imbolg), May (Bealtaine), August (Lughnasa) and November (Samhain). Each had its own magical rituals marking the seasonal progression from the first milk of early spring to pasturing in summer, harvesting at the onset of autumn and preparation for the scarcity of winter. Tara had close associations with all four of these sacred festivals, and the Mound of the Hostages gives us a key to this fact.

By 2000BC, when the mound was built, it may be that Tara was already part of a spiritual circle which included Newgrange and Knowth on the Boyne and the Hills of Loughcrew 24 kilometres to the north-west, near Oldcastle in Co Meath. The evidence to support this view is so far slight, but in the 1970s and early 1980s astronomer Martin Brennan conducted observations on the relationships between these three sites and their alignment to certain full moons and sunrises. His findings were published in his book *The Stars and the Stones*.

Brennan concluded that just as Newgrange is aligned to the winter solstice, the chamber under the Mound of the Hostages at Tara is constructed so that it is lit by the full moon of August – the date of the ancient Lughnasa celebration – and the rising sun of the festival periods of Samhain in November and Imbolg in February.

In her book, *Loughcrew, The Cairns*, Dr Jean McMann writes: 'The cairn architecture not only evokes a sun god such as Bal; it may also refer to an ancient earth goddess. As a few archaeologists have suggested, the dead could have been returned to the earth for rebirth. Some of the cairns appear to be oriented towards features of the landscape or monuments which were probably sited with reference to such features. Some face the Boyne Valley site, probably Newgrange; others seem to be directed towards Tara and the Hill of Skryne. A passage tomb at Sliabh Gullion in Co Armagh is aligned directly toward Loughcrew.'[4]

Images engraved on the large stone inside the entrance of the Mound of the Hostages at Tara are associated with the sun, moon and stars. They may represent some kind of calendar which helped identify the arrival of festival times.

## Imbolg and Bealtaine

Imbolg or Oímelg, which has been interpreted as 'budding time', 'parturition' or 'lactation', fell at the beginning of February when winter began to recede, new lambs were born and milk began to flow, and was presided over by the earth mother goddess. She appeared in the various religious centres under different guises and names – as Macha at Emain Macha in Co Armagh, as Tailtiu at Teltown in Co Meath. At Tara she was principally known as Maeve.

Clearly Rath Maeve is dedicated to her. This rampart of bank and ditch, 229 metres in diameter, lies just over one and a half kilometres south of the Mound of the Hostages in the townland of Belper. Some have called it a fortress, or 'the Palace of Queen Maeve', but it was probably a ceremonial site as well, associated with the rites of spring and also with the ritual union of the king of Tara with the goddess of the land and of sovereignty. An opening on the north side of its bank, which could have been the original entrance, is aligned directly with the Mound of the Hostages on Tara itself.

Maeve's name originally meant 'she who intoxicates' and was associated with the English 'mead' or honey drink. This image ties in with early Irish texts which symbolised Maeve's role as Goddess of Sovereignty as a goddess offering the prospective and successful king a drink. In the legends, she is described as 'the beautiful, pale

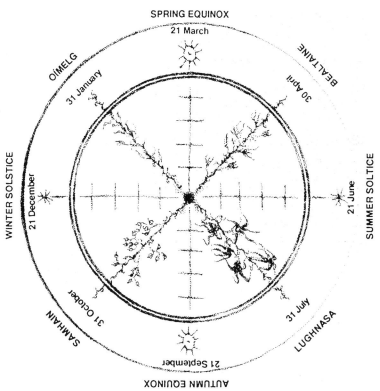

*Wheel of the Year, showing the major pagan festivals. (Illustration by Sinead McCarthy.)*

*Interior of Newgrange.*

woman, with long flowing hair'. But she also appears as Queen of Connacht, she is the battle goddess with flaming spear in hand, the instigator of the saga of the *Táin Bó Cuailgne* or *Cattle Raid of Cooley* against Ulster. She is also a sex goddess and could satisfy the appetite of a warrior whom it usually took seven women to sate. Maeve was said to be daughter of the Tara king, Eochaidh Fiedhleach, and wife of King Art Mac Cuin, who was father to the mythical priest king Cormac Mac Airt. And as if that is not enough, she is also credited with having been the only queen ever to reign at Tara – a connection which underlines her association with sovereignty *(see Chapters 3 and 6, Women of Tara* and *Priest Kings and Ancestors).*

Another persona of the earth-mother goddess was the fire goddess, Brighid, who in Christian lore evolved into St Brighid. It is interesting to note that just across the fields to the west of Rath Maeve in the townland of Odder are the remains of a medieval convent dedicated to St Brighid. The convent was a very powerful force in the area from the twelfth century until its dissolution by King Henry VIII in 1539.

In her pre-Christian form Brighid was very much part of the Imbolg festival. She was described in the *Glossary of King Cormac –*

transcribed from oral tradition in the tenth century – as a daughter of the father-god, Daghdha, and as having powers over the gift of poetry, of healing and the fires of the metalworkers.

Belper and Rath Maeve may well be the place of the early summer fires lit first by the King of Tara as a signal for the start of celebrations in surrounding districts. No wonder that in the traditional story about Christianity's first major confrontation with this pagan world, St Patrick is said to have mounted his challenge by lighting the paschal fire at Slane before King Lóegaire started the fires of Bealtaine on Tara. The time of this event has been pinpointed in the legends as the fire festival night, 25 March AD433.

Another persona of the mother goddess was Bóinn or the White Cow Goddess. Bóinn was wife to the Dé Danann king at Tara, Nuadhu. She also lived with the father-god Daghdha and bore him Aonghus, the love god, who played the magic harp of the Daghdha. Bóinn was symbolised by the cow, an animal associated with abundance. Thus it is not surprising to find other sites on Tara bearing mysterious bovine names like the 'Well of the White Cow', the 'Well of the Calf' and a now invisible earthworks named the 'Mound of the Cow'. The eleventh-century topographic guide, *Dindshenchas Érenn*, gives the location of this last mound as 'west of the Mound of the Hostages' and it was still very much in evidence when the historian George Petrie wrote about Tara in 1839. He described it as being of considerable size: '6ft. [1.83 metres] high and 40ft. [13.9 metres] in diameter at the base.' Another name for the mound was Glas Teamhrach, which could connect it to the enchanted cow, Glas, who belonged to the smith god Goibnui, and had a never-ending supply of milk. 'She walked all over Ireland in a day's grazing and gave milk to every one that came to her and there was no one hungry or sorrowful in Ireland in those days.'[5]

The Well of the Calf can still be seen on the western slope of the hill in a small triangular field called 'Fodeen'. Nearby in the same field, a monument called the 'Hill of the Cow' was also mentioned in the ancient documents. The Well of the White Cow, which is now known as 'St Patrick's Well', is directly opposite the Well of the Calf on the eastern slope. The *Dindshenchas* adds an extra bit of mystery to these two flows of water with the following proverb: '*Ní toet a loeg co a bóin find*'– 'the calf does not go to its white cow'. Water from the Well of the White Cow flows east to the Gowra

*The names of townlands tell us much about ancient Irish lore. Belper, in which Rath Maeve stands, for example, is thought to have been called after the fire god, Belenos. Thus it is associated with the sun festival of Bealtaine, which was celebrated with the lighting of fires at the time of the full moon, during the transition from spring to summer. This was the time when herds were returned to the rich pastures for fattening, and one of the rituals performed was that of driving cattle between two fires to purify them after the long months in confinement.*

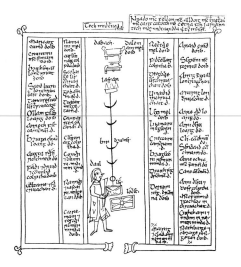

*From the* Book of Leinster, *this elaborate seating plan for the Banquet Hall at Tara designated the portions to be given to each category of guest.*

River; water from the Well of the Calf flows west to the River Skane. Both rivers join about one and a half kilometres from their rising and flow into the Boyne, which is named after the White Cow Goddess, Bóinn. It is probably not without significance that the Well of the White Cow and the Mound of the Cow are both situated in the townland that tops the hill, Castleboy. In his book, *The Three Sisters at the Well*, place-name expert Wiliam Battersby interprets the 'boy' of Castleboy to be the old Irish word *buidhe* ('yellow') and he notes that '[the meaning] extends itself beyond colour to the notion of cows, butter, milk and even generosity.'[6] In its own way, this cult celebrated health, fruitfulness and abundance of rich milk. These life-giving gifts were under the control of the earth-mother goddess in her many forms, and her fecundity and generosity were celebrated at the fertility festivals of Imbolg and Bealtaine.

## Lughnasa

The festival of Lughnasa has fewer associations with Tara than those of Bealtaine and Imbolg, since its celebration place is some sixteen kilometres to the north along the banks of the River Blackwater at Teltown near Kells. Yet the story of its origin centres around Tara and one of its great heroes, Lugh of the Long Hand. A ring fort just east of the hill in the valley of Gowra at Lismullen bears his name *(see Chapter 4, Home of Heroes)*. In memory of his foster mother, Tailtiu, Lugh created the festival of Lughnasa and the Tailten Games. Tailtiu is another symbol of the land and of sovereignty, just like Maeve, Brighid and Bóinn. Her festival took the form of a harvest feast encompassing games, dancing, matchmaking and horse-racing. It was also a testing ground for candidates to the royal seat. Even down into historic times there are stories of contenders to the high kingship creating a disturbance at the Tailten Games in order to draw greater attention to their cause.

It was the right of the King of Tara to preside over this festival and there he would receive gifts – 'the fish of the Boyne, the deer of Luibhnech, the mast of Mana, the bilberries of Brí Léith, the cress of the Brosnach, water from the well of Tlachtga, the hares of Naas', according to one ancient text.[7] All of these were brought to him and it was said that the year in which he consumed them did not count against him as life spent.

*Opposite: Decorated stone at Loughcrew Cairn, Oldcastle, Co Meath.*

## Samhain

This was when the doors of the Otherworld were thought to have been thrown open for contact between living mortals and those of the fairy realms. But the festival also had other important functions. More than the other three festivals, the feast of Samhain had a special association with Tara. This was when the god-king was united with the Goddess of Sovereignty in order to reaffirm his worthiness as representative of his people. In the ancient traditions no king of Tara could rule without the goddess's approval. Proof that he could ensure fertility of the land, fruitful harvests and absence of famine for his *tuatha* ('people') derived from joining with her during his inauguration Feis of Tara at Samhain time.

The twelfth-century texts make much of this festival. They give exact details regarding seating arrangements and the kind of food served to each category of guest. The Feis is said to have begun three days before Samhain, continuing for three days after, and it was attended by kings and chiefs from every corner of the country.

In the *Book of Clonmacnoise* and the *Annals of the Four Masters* it is claimed that Ollamh Fódla, son of Fiachu Finscothach, the twentieth of the kings of Ireland who ruled around 1000BC, first convened the assembly in pre-historic times. However, 'The Roll of Kings' in the *Book of Leinster* credits Túathal Techtmar with first instituting the Assembly of Tara in the early second century BC.

The festival appears to have been last called by King Diarmaid Mac Cerbaill, great-grandson of King Lóegaire, in AD560 before the 'abandonment of Tara', but vestiges of it remained down to the time of the last kings to rule in Tara's name during the twelfth century.

The stated purposes of the gathering included the giving of sureties to the high king, the review of genealogies for the chieftains, the making of laws, and the settling of successions and disputes.

R. A. S. Macalister gives a plausible explanation for why the Assembly was held every three years rather than annually. As he saw it, the original Celtic calendar was lunar and its year was thus some eleven days shorter than the solar year, which could have been initiated in Ireland around the time assigned to Túathal Techtmar in the second century AD. To bring the two calendars into harmony, a month of days was saved up and the adjustment made every three years. This almost magical playing with time may have taken place in some ceremonial way during the Assembly.

There were in fact three distinct festivals celebrated at the time of Samhain: the inaugural rite of a new king which happened only once during his reign; the triennial Feis; and the annual fertility feast which commemorated and in a way re-enacted the inauguration feast. At times all three would coincide, but it does appear that one way or another, Samhain was celebrated every year. Its aim was to strengthen the belief that the King of Tara was no ordinary mortal and that his life was in the hands of powers beyond this world. 'Irish kings were originally believed to be of divine descent,' says Francis Byrne in his book, *Irish Kings and High-Kings*. The festival was blatantly earthy and sexual in nature. It is little wonder then that the Lia Fáil, or coronation stone of Tara, is such a phallic symbol, or that the Feis lost prestige after the arrival of Christianity.

There may well be a close association between what occurred at such feasts at Tara and another monument on the north-west side of the hill, the Clóenfherta or Sloping Trenches. It is said that this was the site of a great slaughter of the women of Tara by Dunlaing, a king of Leinster, who sought revenge against the High King, Cormac Mac Airt. Mary Condren's book, *The Serpent and the*

*'The Feis of Temur each third year*
*To preserve laws and rules*
*Was then convened firmly*
*By the illustrious kings of Erin*
*Cathaoir of sons-in-law convened*
*The beautiful Feis of Temur;*
*There came with him (better for it)*
*The men of Erin to one place*
*Three days before Saman, always,*
*Three days after it – it was a goodly custom*
*The host of very high fashion spent*
*Constantly drinking during the week*
*Without theft, without wounding a man*
*Among them during all this time;*
*Without feats of arms, without deceit,*
*Without exercising horses.'[8]*

Above: *The tenth-century poet, Eochaidh O'Flynn, describing the Samhain festival.*

Below: *Kerbstone at Knowth in Co Meath.*

*'Squat on earth's floor, I scrawl.*
*It is memory that I am seeking*
*and will carve it on a rock. A standing stone.'*
*(from 'The Small God's Song', Seamus Cashman)*

*Goddess*, points to there having been a college of vestal virgins at Tara, which would indicate a highly organised cult surrounding the priest king in the centuries preceding the arrival of Patrick and the new Christian morality. However, the most recent archaeological studies of the site have not found any proof that this was ever a dwelling place.

Overseeing the cults of all these festivals at Tara, not as priests but rather as sages and diviners of magic, were the druids. Their power was in many ways greater and more feared than that of the king for they were in contact with the mysteries of the Otherworld. Some say that the reference to Ollamh Fódla's establishment of the Feis of Tara also includes evidence that there was a druidic college based there as well. 'And by him was the Assembly of Temair first convened; and by him was the Scholars' Rampart first made at Temair.'[9] However, this view is disputed.

Tara was, in any case, a centre of druidism, and it is of great significance that the legends and stories of St Patrick's confrontation with the existing religious powers of Ireland are staged on this hill. Whether Patrick did all the things he is supposed to have done is not the issue here. What is important is that the saint's early seventh-century biographers, Muirchú and Tíreachán, placed the intense battle between the old and new religions at Tara. In the view of these early Christian historians, writing some two hundred years after the time of Patrick, their sacred hero had to have confronted and defeated the powers of the old order in the place where it had its strongest centre – Tara.

Tara was a powerful pagan place. Thus:

> It is understandable then that St Patrick's declaration of intent as he moves towards the hill reads like that of a man taking on a huge and dangerous task. 'Before Tara, I arise today through a mighty strength.'[10] Patrick then calls on the might of Christ to protect him against: 'every cruel merciless power which may come against my body and my soul; against incantations of false prophets, against black laws of heathenry, against false laws of heretics, against craft of idolatry, against spells of women and smiths and wizards.'[11]

In Muirchú's account, Tara is described as the chief den of wizardry in Ireland, and of King Lóegaire, he says, 'a certain great fierce, pagan emperor of the barbarians reigned in Tara, which was the capital of the Irish.'[12]

The encounter at Tara between Patrick and King Lóegaire is couched in biblical language that appears to imitate the accounts of Christ's appearance to the apostles after his resurrection, of Elijah's battle with the prophets of Baal, and of Daniel's meeting with the mighty Nebuchadnezzar.

When Patrick enters the court at Tara, it is through a closed door he appears, 'as when Christ came into the dining-room'. Immediately he is credited with converting Dubthach, chief poet of Ireland, to the faith. Then he is summoned to the king's table and offered a poisoned cup of wine by the druid, Lucat-moel. Sensing the danger, Patrick blessed the cup, inverted it so that the poison fell out and then safely drank it. Word spread of what was taking place and 'then came the hosts till they were abiding without Tara in the plain'.

Encouraged by the audience, Lucat-moel then challenged Patrick to a contest in magic. 'I will bring snow onto the plain,' he said and snow fell until it reached men's girdles. But when Patrick asked him to remove it just as quickly, he could not do so. The saint blessed the plain and in an instant the snow vanished. Lucat-moel called down darkness on the plain but when he could not remove it Patrick called on the power of Christ and the sun shone.

Next came a test of fire whereby the sacred robe of Patrick was to be pitted against the druid's tunic as protection against the flames. Patrick's servant wore the tunic while the druid was draped in the sacred robe. The tunic burned but the servant survived. Patrick's robe did not burn but the druid perished. So too did twelve thousand 'impius' people on the plain perish in that instant.

Patrick then gave an ultimatum to King Lóegaire: unless he believed quickly, he too would die. Muirchú gives this ending to the story: 'So then Lóegaire knelt to Patrick and believed in God but he did not believe with a pure heart; and on that day many thousands believed.'[13]

Though Christianity's triumph is illustrated in the story of Patrick at Tara, the new religion did not rest all that easily on this centre of paganism. A chapel has existed on the hill since the Middle Ages but it was never to attract a monastic settlement like those that sprang up in the surrounding country.

To the north, there was the great settlement of Kells, where the *Book of Kells* was composed; to the east on the Hill of Skryne there

[1] TOMRIUᵹ [2] INDIU [3] NIURT [4] TREN [5] TO-
Ad    Temoriam    hodie    potentiam præpollentem   in-
ᵹAIRM [6] TRINOIT. [7]
voco     Trinitatis.
CRETIM [8]    TREODATAIO [9]    POISIN [10]
Credo        in Trinitatem       sub τη
OENDATAO [11] IN [12] DULEMAIN [13] DAIL. [14]
Unitate     του     numinis    elementorum.

Above: *A version of the beginning of 'St Patrick's Breastplate', or 'The Deer's Cry', a hymn attributed to the saint and first written by St Evin in the sixth century. The first line translates as 'Before Tara I arise today'.* (From Petrie's On the History and Antiquities of Tara Hill, *1839.)*

On his way to Tara, Patrick asked Christ to
be on his side:

*'Christ with me,*
*Christ before me, Christ behind me;*
*Christ in me, Christ below me, Christ above me,*
*Christ at my right, Christ at my left!'* [14]

*Old statue of St Patrick that stood at Tara for*
*up to one hundred years before it was removed*
*by the Office of Public Works in 1992. Created*
*by James Curry of Navan, its cement was*
*weathered in the river Boyne before being carted*
*to Tara. The saint's hand may at one time have*
*held a representation of the shamrock. According*
*to the legends, Patrick used a shamrock to*
*explain the mystery of the Trinity to the*
*assembled masses at pagan Tara. Shamrock has*
*come to symbolise Ireland.*

was a monastery established by St Columcille in the sixth century;
in the valley of Gowra between the two hills was the convent of
Lismullen; further to the east were the monasteries of
Monasterboice and Mellifont; to the south of the hill, the convent of
Odder; and to the west, Bective, and Newtown, Trim. Further west
was the great centre of Clonard, founded in the sixth century by St
Finian, where it is said some later abbots even bore the title 'King
of Tara'. But no monastic establishment appeared on Tara itself.

In fact, rather than overlaying the pagan centre at Tara with
Christian beliefs, as happened with many of the old institutions
and centres, the saints are said to have cursed the hill. The
abandonment of Tara in AD565 as the dwelling place of the most
powerful kings in Ireland will always be associated in folklore with
the curse of Ruadhán, who was half druid, half saint and a mighty
spiritual and political force in his time. 'May Tara be desolate to all
eternity,' said St Ruadhán according to legend (*see Chapter 7, The
Rise of the Uí Néill*).

The monk, Aonghus, writing his *Martyrology* around AD800 at
Mael-Ruain's monastery in Tallaght, did not disguise his delight at
Tara's gradual fall from glory when he wrote: 'The great settlement
of Tara has died with the loss of its princes; great Armagh lives on
with its choirs and scholars ... Thronged Glendalough is the
sanctuary of the Western World ... The great hills of evil have been
cut down with spear points while the glens have been made into hills.'

Tara may never have been inhabited to the extent indicated
here, so may not have been abandoned in such a dramatic fashion.
Nevertheless, the desire of the authors was obviously to symbolise
the victory of Christianity over paganism.

Some hundred years later, in the seventh century, another very
powerful holy man, Saint Adamnán, is reputed to have called a
synod at Tara to enact laws that gave greater rights to women. The
*Dindshenchas Érenn* names four monuments dedicated to his
memory in and around the Rath of the Synods: the Tent of
Adamnán, the Seat of Adamnán, the Mound of Adamnán and the
Cross of Adamnán. Their significance is obscure but they do stand
as symbols of Tara's spiritual past.

It is recorded that a small church was in existence at the top of
Tara in the early thirteenth century. Following the Reformation its
larger successor was dedicated as Church of Ireland but it appears
to have been allowed to go to ruin during the eighteenth century.

The church building now standing on Tara dates back to 1822-23. Kenneth MacGowan in his book, *The Hill of Tara*, writes: 'the construction of this church was severely criticised by the historian Russell who claimed that "Planting deal trees and erecting a modern church amid the hoariest monuments and on the most historic spot of European soil is little less than sacrilege".'

This church was refurbished early in the twentieth century and was used for services up until 1990. Then, having been sold to the Office of Public Works, it was deconsecrated in May 1991 and now houses the Tara Interpretive Centre. However, it reverts to its former use every St Patrick's Day when a service is held in memory of the legendary confrontation of beliefs in AD433.

That meeting of St Patrick with the druids, factually true or not, is symbolic of Tara's place in relation to the gods, be they old or new. There is no better way of explaining the spiritual importance of Tara than by viewing it as a timeless sacred place which cannot be claimed by any one religion, but is instead a sanctuary for all. Could it be that some day we will see a perpetual flame lit on Tara to represent for some Patrick's light of Christianity; for others a vestige of the old fires of the ancient priest kings; for others still a peaceful beacon for the future? For so long as Ireland lasts, Tara will always carry a spiritual message.

*Isaac Butt's report of his visit to Tara in 1740 says of it, 'The Church dedicated to St Patrick is unroofed, ye Chancell only being in use, ye steeple at ye West end is low & square & open, a worried bullock made a Shift to go up ye Stone Steps to ye first loft & fell into the waste part of the Church where he expired on the Spot.'*

Below: *1794 engraving by Grose of the ruins of the second church to be built at Tara. The present structure, sited on the foundation of this one, dates from 1822-23.*

Tenth-century poet Cinaeth Ua hArtacan
put the requiem for Tara into verse:
*'Perished is every law concerning high fortune*
*Crumbled to the clay is every ordinance;*
*Temair, though she be desolate today*
*Once on a time was the habitation of heroes.'[15]*

1 Gwynn, Edward, *The Metrical Dindshhenchas*, Todd Lecture Series, Royal Irish Academy, Dublin 1903, Temair IV, p. 31.
2 Sheerin, Paul, *Eire*, vol. XXIII, 3, p. 83.
3 Stewart, R.J., *Celtic Gods and Goddesses*, Blandford 1990, p. 15.
4 McCann, Dr Jean, *Loughcrew: The Cairns*, After Hour Books, Oldcastle 1993, p. 43.
5 Young, Ella, *Celtic Wonder Tales*, p. 55.
6 Battersby, William, *The Three Sisters at the Well*, Navan 1991, p. 14.
7 From tenth-century poem by Cuan Ua Lothcháin, translation by Francis Byrne, in *Irish Kings and High-Kings*, p. 23.
8 Poem attributed to Eochaidh O'Flynn as quoted in Haliday's Keating, p. 330, and in George Petrie's *History and Antiquities of Tara Hill*, p. 31.
9 'The Roll of Kings' in *Lebor Gabála Érenn* or the *Book of the Taking of Ireland*, translated by R. A. S. Macalister, part V, par 518.
10 Author's translation of 'Deer's Cry' from the Latin version, contained in *History and Antiquities of Tara Hill* by George Petrie, p. 58.
11 Stokes, Whitley, *The Tripartite Life of St Patrick*, Hodges Figgis, Dublin 1887, p. 51.
12 ibid., p. 41.
13 ibid., p. 51.
14 ibid., p. 53.
15 op. cit., Gwynn, Temair IV, p. 29.

# CHAPTER 3

# WOMEN OF TARA

*'Temair free from feebleness hides not*
*the glory due to women for its building;*
*the daughter of Lugaid obtained in her possession*
*an open plain that it were pity to pillage ...*
*The abode was a keep, was a fortress,*
*was a pride, a rampart free from ravage*
*whereon was to be the grave of Tea after death,*
*so that it should be an increase to her fame ...*
*Brega Tea, a teeming home,*
*is famed because Tea was a noble dame.'*

(Tenth-century poem)[1]

Tara was named for a woman. At least that is one of the interpretations of Temair or Teamur in ancient lore. And this is in keeping with Celtic traditions – sacred Emain Macha in Co Armagh was so called because of the horse goddess, Macha. Tailten of the royal games got its name from Tailtiu, foster mother of Lugh. Ireland itself takes its title from the goddess, Eriú. No greater honour could have been bestowed on Tara by the Celts than to have it associated with their Milesian ancestors: 'Rampart of Tea/wife of the son of Miled ... She was buried beyond the wall without/So that from her is Temair named.'[2]

As will become clear in the chapters that follow, the mythology and history of royal Tara is male-dominated: 142 men are listed in the *Book of Leinster's* 'Roll of Kings', while not one woman is included.

But the Tara legends abound with stories of women – the sovereignty goddess and

*The rampart of bank and ditch, 229 metres in diameter, on the southern slope of Tara – a ritual site named after Tara's Goddess of Sovereignty, Queen Maeve.*

warrior goddess, Maeve; the embodiment of beauty and femininity, Étaín; the assertive princess, Gráinne.

## Maeve at War

Maeve is a goddess in the Celtic tales and so can take on many forms – symbol of sovereignty, embodiment of voracious female sexuality, or power-hungry queen. It is in this latter guise that she appears in the epic saga of the *Táin Bó Cuailnge* or the *Cattle Raid of Cooley*. In wonder-tale form, this story recounts what may have been real provincial wars of pre-Christian times in which the kingship of Tara was extended into east Ulster. In its early oral form, the *Táin* probably depicted Maeve as a queen ruling at Tara. But as time went on various power struggles between north and south dictated that her seat of power be shifted from Tara to the royal centre of the west, Cruachain (Rathcroghan in Co Roscommon, 150 kilometres west of Tara). However, she is the same Maeve who appears as the Goddess of Sovereignty at Tara *(see Chapter 2, The Sacred Hill)*. But in this tale she takes on the role of Connacht's treacherous queen, waging a cruel war against Ulster.

The story begins with some teasing pillow talk between Maeve and her husband, Ailill Mac Mata, as to which of them has the greater possessions. When she found that Ailill had a great white bull which nothing she owned could match, Maeve sent her spies to find the best beast in Ireland. It was discovered in Ulster – the magnificent Brown Bull of Cooley 'on whose back a team could play a game of hurling'. This prize Maeve had to have by bribery or by war. In the end, the bull's owner, Daire of Cooley, chose war. And a great hosting was called of the Men of Erin, a band of warriors drawn from every corner of Ireland except the north.

The time was right for the attack, for the King of Ulster, Conor Mac Nessa, and his Red Branch Knights were in a deep winter sleep imposed on them by the horse goddess, Macha. They had angered Macha by mocking her decision to leave the royal palace and live with a farmer whom she loved. This slumber of the warriors was her revenge.

Intent on taking full advantage of Macha's spell, Maeve rode north in her chariot at the head of the Men of Erin. Only Cúchulainn, the Hound of Culann, who was expert in every art of magic and of war, was unaffected by Macha's spell. He stood single-handed in the path of Maeve's army. 'He was in the flower of his youth, smooth-skinned and blue eyed. His golden curls fell down upon his young strong shoulders and blew backwards on the wind with the speed of his approach.' In his hand was a tall bronze spear and on his left arm a great curved shield with a scalloped keen-edged rim. With him was his charioteer and druid, Laegh, who was keeper of the fearsome weapon, the spear called 'Ga Bolga'. Before him went his mighty horse, the Grey of Macha.

On their first encounter admiration and hate sparked between the warrior queen and the one man who stood between her and the prize she sought from Ulster. There could be no peace on the island of Ireland until one of them was vanquished. Maeve pushed forward with her troops. Cúchulainn took his stand in the Gap of Ulster at the Yellow Ford (near Slane in Co Meath). No matter how the Men of Erin strove they could not dislodge the brilliant warrior. He harried them, fought them in single combat, beat them in groups of a hundred, and, though severely wounded, he would not let them pass. At night his Otherworld father, Lugh, came and healed him so that he was fit for the next day of fighting. Belittling and infuriating Maeve even further, Cúchulainn came to the edge of her camp and with stones hurled from his sling knocked her pet squirrel and her favourite bird from her very shoulders, killing them.

Maeve then tricked Cúchulainn's own foster brother and greatest warrior friend, Ferdia, to stand and fight against him.

When he refused her every offer of riches and power, she lied to him and said that Cúchulainn had called him a coward. Only then did Ferdia take up weapons against the defender of Ulster. They fought an epic battle over three long days. Yet at night they rested together and bound each other's wounds. Finally, though severely injured by Ferdia's barbs, Cúchulainn called for the mighty Ga Bolga and, with deep sadness in his heart, slew his best friend.

While Cúchulainn and Ferdia fought, Maeve made a dash into Ulster and stole the great Brown Bull of Cooley. But it brought her no luck, for when the White Bull and the Brown Bull met on the borders of her kingdom of Connacht they fought as fiercely as Ferdia and Cúchulainn had fought. Ailill's bull was killed and Maeve's Brown Bull dashed his head against a hill as he rushed for home to Ulster.

Maeve now wanted only one thing – the death of Cúchulainn – and she plotted for years to bring it about. Enlisted in her plan were the bitter children of the druid, Celatin, whose father had died by the hand of Cúchulainn at the Yellow Ford. The years passed and the Ulster hero grew older and weaker. The children of Celatin saw their opportunity – they attacked and mortally wounded the old warrior.

Not wishing to die lying down, Cúchulainn crawled to a sacred stone pillar and tied himself to it. Only when a crow landed on his shoulder and drank his blood did the Men of Erin dare approach. They cut off his head and right hand and brought them to Tara for

*At the dramatic conclusion of the romantic tale of Étaín, she and her otherworld lover, Midhir the Proud, take the form of swans and rise through the roof of the royal dun at Tara in order to escape the wrath of Étaín's husband, King Eochaid. Joined by a golden chain, they fly away over the plains of Meath. The legend is captured in a beautiful mural by Belfast artist Desmond Kinney, which stands in the foyer of the Irish Dairy Board, Dublin.*

burial. The *Book of Glendalough* gives this account: 'The host then moved away from the place and carried with them the head and right hand of Cúchulainn until they reached Temur, where the burial place of his head and right hand is, and the full of the hollow of his shield of clay ... There is a monument for him on the ridge at the upper part of Temur ...'[3] This mound was said to have existed on the northern slope of the hill. Today, however, no sign of it remains.

Maeve herself met her death at the hands of Furbaidhe, son of the Ulster king, Conor Mac Nessa. According to one version of the tale, Maeve was responsible for the death of Furbaidhe's mother, who was also her sister. Furbaidhe spotted Maeve bathing one day in Lough Ree on the Shannon river. He took a piece of cheese. placed it in a sling and fired it with such force through Maeve's head that he killed her.

In another legend, *Bricriu's Feast*, Maeve appears once more with Cúchulainn, but this time instead of making war, she is enticing him to her bed. She arranges that he should win the champion's contest and 'had a desire for him'. But at Tara these two warriors remain enemies, lying apart in memorials dedicated to them in the legends – Maeve in her rath to the south of the hill, Cúchulainn in his at a spot on the northern slope that was called 'Cúchulainn's Shield'.

## Étaín in Love

What Maeve's story is to war, the legend of Étaín is to love. Credited with being 'the most beautiful woman in all of Erin', she shares her love with the Otherworld god, Midhir, while at the same time being wife to a king at Tara. In successive lives she flits between Tír na nÓg, the Land of Youth, and the physical world of Tara – never finding rest until she is finally wafted away over the plains of Meath by her Otherworld lover, Midhir the Proud.

The first part of Étaín's story is located on the banks of the Boyne at Newgrange in Co. Meath, one of the openings into the Otherworld. There she and Midhir met and sealed their love with a golden chain. She was daughter to the powerful Ulster king, Ailill Eochraid; Midhir was the handsome son of the father-god, Daghdha, and lived in his richly endowed dun at Brí Léith, west of Tara with his Otherworld wife, the powerful goddess, Fuamnach. Ailill Eochraid was reluctant to give his permission for Étaín to be with Midhir. In desperation Midhir enlisted the aid of his brother, Aonghus the love god, and of the Daghdha himself in clearing great plains and creating rivers to impress Ailill. The Blackwater, Mourne, Bann and many more rose from their springs at the Daghdha's command in order to please Ailill. But always more was demanded. He then wanted Étaín's weight in gold and silver, so that was given too.

After many idyllic nights together at Brugh na Bóinne in Newgrange trouble awaited the lovers when Midhir took Étaín to Brí Léith. His wife Fuamnach was furious about this and in revenge she had a spell cast on Étaín, transforming her into a butterfly which the winds blew up, down and around Ireland for what may have been a thousand years.

At the end of that time, Étaín took refuge from the wind in the great banquet hall of Etar, King of Leinster, at Inber Cichmaine (near Howth in Co Dublin). Perched on a beam high above the festive table she slumbered and her butterfly form wafted down into the wine glass of the queen. Without noticing, the queen swallowed the princess down and, nine months later, gave birth to Étaín who was now the princess of Leinster and even more beautiful than before.

The following fifteenth-century description of Étaín depicts the ideal of contemporary female beauty: 'Her two arms were as white as the snow of a single night and each of her cheeks was rosy as the foxglove. Even and small were the teeth in her head and they

Tara's counterpart in the north, the sacred royal site of Emain Macha near Armagh city. Emain Macha was central to the ancient legends of King Conor Mac Nessa and the Red Branch Knights, as Tara was to the stories of Cormac Mac Airt and the Fianna. Also known as Navan Fort, the monument was named for the horse goddess Macha, who represented sovereignty there as Maeve did at Tara. The fort is said to have been destroyed by the sons of the 114th king of Tara, Niall of the Nine Hostages. Emain Macha now has a brilliantly designed interpretive centre, which, through every form of visual aid, brings the visitor back 2,000 years and more into the legends of Ulster.

shone like pearls. Her eyes were as blue as a hyacinth, her lips delicate and crimson; very high, soft and white were her shoulders. Tender, polished and white were her wrists; her fingers long and of great whiteness; her nails were beautiful and pink. White as snow, or the foam of a wave was her neck; long was it, slender, and as soft as silk. Smooth and white were her thighs; her knees were round and firm and white; her ankles were as straight as the rule of a carpenter. Evenly set were her eyes; her eyebrows were a bluish black, such as you see on the shell of a beetle. Never a maid fairer than she, or more worthy of love, was till then seen by the eyes of men; and it seemed to them that she must be one of those that have come from the fairy mounds.'[4]

Étaín was a young woman when Eochaid Aireamh, the 82nd king of Tara, decided to hold the triennial Assembly at the feast of Samhain. But he had a problem: 'They could not convene the Festival of Tara for a king that had no queen: for Eochaid had no queen when he took the kingship. Thereupon Eochaid dispatched envoys to every Fifth throughout Ireland to seek out for him the fairest woman in Ireland. For he said that none should be his wife save a woman that none of the men of Ireland had known before him.'[5]

Étaín was found near Etar's dun in Leinster, and the Men of Erin knew she was the one they sought as wife for their king. So she came to Tara and was queen to Eochaid there. Although, in her

*About 25 km northeast of Tara is Newgrange, the largest and most dramatic of the prehistoric momuments in the Boyne valley complex. The heart-shaped mound is 36 ft high and 300 ft in diameter. Inside is a 36-ft passage of highly decorated stone, which leads to a vaulted chamber aligned so that it is illuminated but once a year by the rising sun of the winter solstice. In the legends, Newgrange, or Brugh na Bóinne, was home to the great father-god Daghdha and his son, the love god Aonghus. In historic times it and Lagore in Dunshaughlin were seats of east Meath kings of the people known as the Síl nÁedo Sláine, who were descended from the sixth-century Uí Néill king of Tara, Áed Sláine.*

*Ben Bulben, the distinctive prominence in Co Sligo, where Gráinne's lover Diarmaid is said to have met his death in a struggle with a wild boar.*

Midhir's love-words to Étaín:
*O Bé Find wilt thou come with me*
*to the wondrous land wherein harmony is,*
*hair is like the crown of the primrose there,*
*and the body smooth and white as snow.*
*There, is neither mine nor thine,*
*white are teeth there, dark the brows.*
*A delight of the eye the number of our hosts,*
*every cheek there is of the hue of the foxglove.*
*A gillyflower is each one's neck,*
*a delight of the eye are blackbirds' eggs.*
*Though fair the prospect of Mag Fáil,*
*'tis desolate after frequenting Mag Már.*
*Though choice you deem the ale of Inis Fáil,*
*more intoxicating is the ale of Tír Már.*
*A wondrous land is the land I tell of;*
*youth departs not there before old.*
*Warm sweet streams flow through the land,*
*the choice of mead and wine.*
*Stately folk without blemish,*
*conception of sin, without lust.'*[7]

new form, Étaín retained no memory of Midhir, he still pined for her and spent his time roaming the country, desperate for a trace of her.

Soon after Étaín's arrival at Tara Midhir happened to make his way there. 'And on a lovely summer day Eochaid Airem king of Tara arose and climbed the terrace of Tara to gaze over Mag Breg. It was radiant with bloom of every hue. As Eochaid looked around him he saw a strange warrior on the terrace before him. A purple tunic about him, and golden yellow hair on him to the edge of his shoulders. A shining blue eye in his head. A five-pointed spear in one hand, a white-bossed shield in the other, with golden gems thereon.'[6]

Midhir's heart soared when he saw Étaín, and he managed to speak to her alone, urging her to go away with him. She, for her part, was powerfully attracted to him, but still she had no memory of him. She replied that he would have to gain the permission of her husband. But Midhir persisted and, addressing her as Bé Find, promised her all the joys of the Otherworld if she would reconsider.

Midhir went once more onto the green at Tara and greeted King Eochaid. They sat and talked in the royal house for a time and then Midhir challenged the king to a game of chess. Midhir allowed Eochaid to win the first two games and he received rich stakes of gold. But the third time Midhir won and when asked his stake he replied, 'My stake is that I obtain one kiss from Étaín.'

Being a man of honour Eochaid did not refuse, but sensing that he might lose his beautiful wife forever to this handsome rival, he played for time. 'One month from now you may return and claim your stake.' And so it was agreed.

As the time drew near, Eochaid changed his mind: 'Midhir made a tryst for a month from that day. But Eochaid mustered the flower of the warriors of Ireland to Tara, and the best of the war-bands of Ireland, each encircling the other around Tara, in the midst, without and within, and the king and queen in the middle of the house, and the courts locked, for they knew that the man of great magic power would come.'[8]

When Midhir returned, nothing was said of this and he was granted his wish. He went to Étaín to claim a kiss. At the touch of his lips her memory flooded back and she held her Otherworld lover. Seeing this, Eochaid fell into a wild rage and called his guard. But they could do nothing: Midhir and Étaín rose together into the air and floated out through the roof of the royal house. When the king and his soldiers rushed outside all they saw were two white swans joined by a golden chain flying together across the plains of Meath.

## Gráinne's Flight to Freedom

Cormac Mac Airt married the beautiful Eithne, said to be a daughter of the 98th king of Tara, Cathaoir Mór, who according to the 'Roll of Kings', 'took the kingship of Ireland for a space of three years, till he fell by the Luaigne of Temair'.[9]

Gráinne was the daughter of Eithne and Cormac and it was said of her: 'She is the best make and shape and the best speech of the women of the whole world.' Not surprisingly then, this young princess had no shortage of suitors, but, as her father ruefully reported, 'There is not a son of a king or of a great prince, there is not a champion in Ireland my daughter has not given a refusal to.'

Thus when the most eligible of champions, Fionn Mac Cumhail, head of the royal warrior army, the Fianna, sent messengers to Tara requesting that Gráinne be his wife, Cormac said, 'Go to her yourselves for it is better for you to get her own answer.' Not knowing that Fionn was by this time an old man, Gráinne replied to the messengers in an unusually positive way: 'If he is a fitting son-in-law for my father, why would he not be a fitting husband for me?'

*When Waterford Crystal created a quality suite for the Asian market, they gave it the distinctive female name 'Tara'.*

A great betrothal feast was then held at Tara. But when Gráinne saw Fionn's greying hair and worn looks she wondered why they had brought her a man who was older than her own father. She gazed at Fionn's retinue. There she spotted Diarmaid, son of Duibhne, whom she described as 'a sweet-worded man with dark hair and cheeks like the rowan berry'. Daire, the poet at the royal court, told her that Diarmaid was the best lover of women in the world, and 'a great love for him came on her there and then'.

Gráinne formed a plan. She served a sweet drink laced with enchantments to all except Diarmaid and his closest companions. While the company slept, she went to him and declared her love, but he refused her, for he knew the consequences of their elopement. 'We will be hunted the length and breadth of Ireland and will have no place of refuge except travelling the bogs and hiding in the hills,' he said. If that were not reason enough, he went on, Fionn's guards were at all the gates of Tara and they would not be able to escape.

But Gráinne would not be refused. 'I will go out by the small gate near an Grianán, the women's sun house at Tara, and since under the rules of the Fianna every fighting man has leave to vault over any dun with the shafts of his spears, you will follow me like that.' Still Diarmaid hesitated, though a deep love and a longing to be with Gráinne was growing on him. But the bonds of loyalty to the Fianna and especially to his leader, Fionn, held him back. He sought counsel from Oisín, Fionn's son and Diarmaid's closest friend. 'I tell you to follow Gráinne and keep yourself out of the hands of Fionn,' he was told.

With that his mind was made up. Reaching for his spears, he ran to the palisade of Tara and leaped out onto the western slope. Gráinne's heart leapt high as she saw him race towards her. The soft wind of Tara blew over them as they embraced and fled west to freedom over the trackless wastes of Ireland, towards an uncertain future.

From that time on, over a period of seven severe years, Diarmaid grew in his love and dedication to Gráinne. A number of times he courageously defended their freedom in combat with Fionn and his warriors. The only ally the two wanderers had was Aonghus the love god, who many times brought Gráinne to safety while Diarmaid held the Fianna at bay. Eventually even Fionn grew somewhat tired of the hunt, and agreed to a truce which put an end to the fugitives' wanderings.

But Diarmaid knew that Fionn could never fully forgive him for breaking his trust. As a result he built a house as far away as possible from Fionn – at Keshcorran in the west of Kerry. There Diarmaid and Gráinne lived in great peace and well-being for the next seventeen years, during which Gráinne gave birth to a daughter and four sons.

Then Gráinne, in an uncharacteristic change of heart, began to long for the friendship of her father, Cormac, and his court at Tara. She wanted to visit again the maiden's sunny place and longed that Diarmaid should be able to meet his former comrades in the Fianna. Isolation had its price, but as she was to find out, re-union with those they had spurned also held deadly risks.

In a gesture of friendship Fionn and the Fianna paid a year-long visit to the couple at Keshcorran. But all the while jealousy gnawed at the warrior leader's heart. He could no longer hope to defeat Diarmaid in open combat, having agreed to a truce and accepted his hospitality. But learning of a prophecy that Gráinne's lover would eventually meet his death in hunting a wild boar, Fionn plotted to bring this circumstance about. One fateful morning he lured Diarmaid to the top of Ben Bulben in Co Sligo and left him to face a fierce boar alone.

After a fierce tussle Diarmaid managed to kill the beast but was mortally gored himself. Fionn returned and a further death struggle took place which brought to light the bitterness in the jilted lover's heart. Diarmaid lay dying, and pleaded with Fionn to use his healing powers to save his life by pouring water from a nearby well on his wounds. Twice Fionn went to the well, but twice the thought of Gráinne forced him to let the clear life-saving water flow from his cupped hands. With every lost second, the life ebbed away from Diarmaid's body. A third time Fionn went to the well and this time the warrior code and his earlier comradeship with Diarmaid overcame his jealousy. He returned to Diarmaid's side only to find him silent and dead.

Gráinne all but died of sorrow herself with the news of Diarmaid's death. What love was left in her, she now gave to her four sons. She knew that they would try to avenge their father's death on Fionn and the Fianna, so she chose the only path that would prevent their death – giving herself to Fionn for the rest of her life.

Despite taunts from the Fianna about her willingness to compromise, she and Fionn were finally united. War between her

*Lord Fingall's sword, reputedly used in the Battle of Tara, in which the heroine Molly Weston is thought to have died. (Courtesy of Laurence Steen.)*

sons and the Fianna was averted and she again knew the friendship of the maidens in the court of Tara. Though it must have been difficult to swallow her desire for revenge, Gráinne was at least content in the knowledge that she had tasted freedom and had known love.

## The Brave Molly Weston

It is impossible to end this chapter on the women of Tara without moving forward in time to include Molly Weston. Though she lived in the late eighteenth century, Molly Weston embodied all the qualities of Maeve, Étaín and Gráinne and clothed them with flesh and blood. Not unlike her mythical sisters, Molly was a mysterious figure and there is little known of her early life. She rode brilliantly and briefly into the 1798 Rebellion of the United Irishmen and then disappeared forever, leaving only the memory of her courageousness on the battlefield to mingle with the rest of Tara's legends.

Molly Weston was born into the landed gentry in the townland of Woganstown, near Oldtown in the Fingall area of north Co Dublin. An accomplished horsewoman, she may well have been part of the Anglo-Irish hunting fraternity which sprang up along the Meath/Dublin border during the 1790s. According to one version of her life, she was betrothed to a captain of the British forces against which she fought so bravely at the Battle of Tara.

Along with four of her brothers, she was deeply involved with the rebel United Irishmen movement that came into being at the beginning of the 1790s. Fuelled by the same philosophy that sparked both the French and American revolutions, this drive for independence – unique in that it united both Protestant and Catholic – culminated in the doomed 1798 Rebellion. For Molly and her brothers this meant a bloody confrontation with the British militia and local yeomanry at the Battle of Tara on 26 May 1798 *(see Chapter 12, Still a Hill of Hostings).*

Molly must have prepared with a great degree of patriotic fervour for the fight. In the book, *Fair Fingall*, author Patrick Archer notes that she devised her own riding costume of green, 'braided with gold in the manner of a uniform, and on her head she wore a green cocked hat bearing a white plume. Thus arrayed and armed with swords and pistols and mounted on her favourite white horse she rode out from Woganstown with her four brothers to meet whatever fate held in store.'[10]

That fate in the first place meant having her young idealism severely tried by the intemperance of her countrymen, who reportedly gave in to the enticements of their enemy, Lord Fingall, and became inebriated just prior to the battle. Next she saw the Irish force of 4000 cut down by a disciplined British attack, which included a troop of well-mounted cavalry, the Reagh Fencibles of the Highland Regiment. In despair, Molly took command of the depleted Irish ranks as they retreated to the vicinity of the churchyard on top of Tara hill. Archer says, 'This handsome young girl ... rode hither and thither upon the field with drawn sword in hand, rallying the pikemen and leading them in successive charges with the utmost fearlessness.'[11]

She captured one of the cannon and, turning it on the British cavalry, killed eleven of their number. A ballad commemorating the occasion records: 'Eleven petticoat rascals she killed on the spot.'

But the odds were against the rebels and defeat was inevitable. At least a quarter of them died, the rest were scattered. Molly Weston's white horse is mentioned in a British report on the battle's aftermath as being seen grazing quietly on the hill with its side-saddle still in place. But nothing is said of Molly Weston. Was she killed? Did she escape? Was she eventually re-united with her fiancé, the British captain? The truth of her story is like many other incidences at Tara, for which we must rely on legend and our own imaginations; but her death and burial with her brothers at Tara was the most probable outcome.

Like the stories of Maeve, Étaín and Gráinne, that of Molly Weston further imbues Tara with a feminine dimension. So too does the decision of parents the world over to call their daughters after this sacred and powerful place – Tara.

*Contemporary representation of Brighid, goddess of smithcraft, metalwork, therapy and poetic inspiration, in her triple aspect.*

One hundred years after her time, Molly Weston was commemorated thus in the nationalist newspaper, The United Irishman:

'And westwards as they marched away
Shanbaile joined the brave array
While Ballygara and Dunreagh
Sent forth their pikemen tall
And with them Molly Weston came
To Woganstown belongs the fame
Of her who fought in Freedom's name
With the brave sons, Fingall.'

1 Gwynn, Edward, The Metrical Dindshenchas, Todd Lecture Series, RIA, Dublin 1903, part I, Temair II, p. 7.

2 ibid., Temair III, p. 21; Temair I, p. 5.

3 From translation by George Petrie in History and Antiquities of Tara Hill, p. 226.

4 From fifteenth-century manuscript, translated in Heroic Romances of Ireland, Vol I, p. 12.

5 Tochmarc Étaíne from the twelfth-century Book of the Dun Cow, translation Eriú, Vol 12, 1937 by Dr R. I. Best and Dr Osborn Bergin, part II, par 2, p. 163.

6 ibid., part III, par I, p. 175.

7 ibid., part III, par 10, p. 181-182.

8 ibid., part III, par 13, p. 184.

9 Macalister, R. A. S., Lebor Gabála Érenn or The Book of the Taking of Ireland, Irish Texts Society, Dublin 1938-1956, Part V, par 596.

10 Archer, Patrick, Fair Fingall, An Taisce, Dublin 1975.

11 ibid., p. 90.

# CHAPTER 4

# HOME OF HEROES

*'Temair, though she be desolate today,*
*Once on a time was the habitation of heroes.'*

(Tenth-century poem)[1]

Invasion legends and royal legends make up the prehistory of Tara. Woven into these tales are not only the stories of kings and goddesses, but those of fabulous heroes – Sreng of the Fir Bolg, Lugh of the sagas of the magical Tuatha Dé Danann, Fionn Mac Cumhail of the Fianna warrior class. While these heroes cannot be taken as historic persons, their stories are the remnants of a lively and imaginative oral tradition. At royal banquets and around campfires, the heroic stories of these mythical figures were recounted as the entertainment of olden times, and they give us a flickering glimpse behind the curtain of prehistory. The regal setting of Tara was central to these tales. And it is from that vantage point that they are viewed here.

## Sreng the Explorer

When Eochaid of the Fir Bolg was king of Tara, the fearsome Tuatha Dé Danann invaded Ireland. Darkness fell on the land for three days at their coming and this struck terror into the Fir Bolg. The king decided to parley with the new invasion force and it was agreed to send their champion, Sreng, to see the strangers and to speak with them. This great fighting man then rose up and took his strong red-brown shield and his two thick-handled spears and his sword, and he set out from Temair and went to where the strangers had camped at Magh Rein.

There was great wondering among the Fir Bolg about this new people who appeared to be superior to them in their magic and their power over the elements.

**Description of colour pictures, pages I-VIII:**

I: Along with the Lia Fáil, the most ancient monuments at Tara are these two stones, one of which may correspond with the stone 'Blocc' or 'Bluicne' in the legends. In the royal inaugural rites, they were said to open wide and leave space for the rightful king's chariot to pass through, before closing up again.

II-III: **(Top):** Artist Jim Fitzpatrick captures the heroic dimensions of Brian Boru. **(Bottom):** Although it bears the title 'Brian Boru's Harp', this actually dates from the fifteenth century, much later than the tenth-to-eleventh century reign of the famous king of Munster and Tara. **(Main picture):** Edward McKeever, historian of Bective, suggests that its name derives from *beg-tí* or 'small house', as distinct from *teach mór* or 'big house', which was Tara. Cormac Mac Airt is said to have died here at Claddy on the Boyne. The Cistercian Bective Abbey dates from 1147 and is the burial place of Hugh de Lacy, Norman coloniser of Meath.

IV-V: **(Main picture):** The Lia Fáil. After it was Ireland named Inis Fáil. Some ancient texts refer to it as the 'penis stone'. In the tenth/eleventh century text, the *Dindshenchas* of Tara, such a stone was mentioned as being near the Mound of the Hostages. It was removed to its present position on the King's Seat to mark the graves of the fallen United Irishmen in the 1798 Battle of Tara. **(Top):** The larger of the two gold torcs of Tara. Dating from c.1200BC, they were found near the Rath of the Synods in 1830. They became part of the collection owned by Tara historian George Petrie, and were then purchased by the Royal Irish Academy in 1839 for £180. Together these priceless ornaments weigh over 40 ounces of pure gold. **(Bottom):** List of the Uí Néill kings of Tara from the *Book of Ballymote*.

VI-VII: **(Top):** The Petrie Crown. **(Bottom):** Bronze-coated iron handbell traditionally thought to have belonged to St. Patrick. **(Main picture):** Mound of the Hostages.

VIII: Many ancient wells at Tara helped designate it as a sacred place from the earliest times. This one on the eastern slope is now called St. Patrick's Well. In pagan Celtic times it bore names like 'Dark Eye' and 'The Healer'.

It was not known whether they came from the Otherworld or the earth or under the earth. Hence it was with dread that Sreng set out from Tara – venturing into the unknown. Sreng crossed the Shannon, his trepidation growing as he strode westward alone to his first encounter with a people that had hitherto unknown powers. What dire weapons of destruction would they possess? What spell could they use against him from a distance as he crossed onto the stony land of Connacht?

The moment of confrontation arrived when the handsome Dé Danann warrior, Breas, suddenly appeared before him. 'I have come to talk, not to make war,' Breas said. And Sreng was somewhat reassured when this new arrival spoke in his own tongue. But still wary, 'he put his shield before his body and struck it hard into the ground'. Sreng then observed the thin sharp-pointed spears in the hand of Breas and knew that he and the Fir Bolg had nothing that could match them. From that moment, he was intent on delaying as long as possible the moment when his people would have to face their cutting edge.

But Sreng did not betray his fears or his misgivings. Instead he boasted of the damage that his own heavy-handled sharp-sided spears could inflict. 'They will break through shields and crush flesh and bones so that their thrust is death or wounds that never heal,' he declared.

Breas then made this proposal – great slaughter to both sides could be avoided if the Fir Bolg agreed to share the beautiful island of Ireland equally with the Dé Danann. Sreng agreed to bring back that message to Tara and the two warriors parted friends. But it was with a feeling of heavy foreboding that Sreng returned to Eochaid. And even as he did so the Dé Danann sent threatening messengers to the Fir Bolg. Badb, Macha and the fearsome war goddess, Morrigu, went to Temair. By the power of their enchantments they brought mists and clouds and darkness over the whole place and they sent showers of fire and blood over the people.

But the druids of the Fir Bolg fought the enchantment off with their own magic and against the odds decided to go into battle. Despite his own misgivings, Sreng made his way a second time across the midlands to the west – this time at the head of eleven battalions drawn from the men of Tara.

Sreng bargained for time, hoping that the Dé Danann might still withdraw. When envoys arrived from the invaders' camp he told

Ancient stones at Tara.

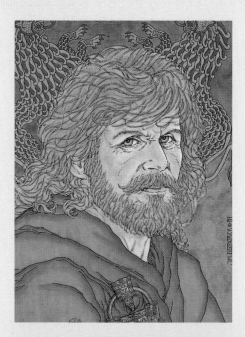

Brian Boru (top).

15th century Irish harp, known as 'Brian Boru's Harp' (bottom).

Bective Monastery (right).

Larger gold torc of Tara (top).

A list of the Uí Néill kings of Tara from the *Book of Ballymote* (bottom).

The Lia Fáil, Stone of Destiny or Stone of Sovereignty (left).

Petrie Crown (top).
St. Patrick's Bell (bottom).
Mound of the Hostages (right).

St. Patrick's Well.

withdraw. When envoys arrived from the invaders' camp he told them that his king Eochaid wished to postpone the battle.

Both sides agreed to wait ninety days before the fight would begin. After that Sreng still tried to gain advantage. He asked that just three times nine of the Dé Danann champions be sent against the same number of the Fir Bolg. This was agreed and on the first day of fighting all of the 27 Dé Danann fell. But it appears that King Eochaid may have cheated, for the next message from Nuadhu, king of the Dé Danann, demanded that only the same number from each side should be in the field at the same time.

Sreng and Eochaid agreed but then asked if the fight should go on every day or every second day. Breas and Nuadhu replied that it should be every day, and the fighting intensified. Gradually the sharp spears of the Dé Danann gained the advantage. The Fir Bolg were pushed back and King Eochaid himself was killed. It was left to Sreng, who had done mighty deeds during the four days of battle, to once more parley with Breas. But this time the Dé Danann offered the defeated Fir Bolg only one province of Ireland as settlement.

Just three hundred warriors remained of the hundred thousand men who had crossed the Shannon, and, to avoid further slaughter, Sreng agreed to take Connach and let the Dé Danann assume the kingship of Tara. Of Sreng's fortunes and those of his people after that little is told. But it is said that the warrior Ferdia, who fought Cúchulainn on the borders of Ulster, was descended from this remaining group of the Fir Bolg. It may well be that this part of the story holds a clue to the origin of the Uí Néill, who came out of Connacht, fought their way across the midlands and, having gained the kingship of Tara, went on to attack Ulster. It always suited Uí Néill propaganda to claim that their ancestors regained the kingship of Tara rather than took it for the first time.

## Lugh, the Son of Light

Lugh symbolises light. He was the sun god, a warrior, a king, but above all a hero in the legends of Tara. He bridged the gap between the godly race of Dé Danann and the evil force of the Fomorians. His father was the magical Dé Danann chieftain, Cian, while his mother was the very beautiful but mournful Ethlinn, daughter of the grotesque Fomorian leader, Balor of the Evil Eye.

Since it had been prophesied to Balor that he would be killed by his own grandson, he imprisoned his only daughter, Ethlinn, so

*Stone harp player, detail on the Castledermot High Cross, Co Kildare.*

*Artist Jim Fitzpatrick's representation of Sreng, the Fir Bolg hero, during the first battle of Moytura against the new invading force, the Dé Danann. His side defeated, Sreng negotiated a peace in which the Dé Danann allowed the Fir Bolg to stay in the west.*

Opposite: *Dating from the third century BC, this iron sword with bronze hilt mounts was found at Cashel, Co Sligo.*

that this executioner would never be born. But Cian, the Dé Danann chief, found a way around this obstacle. While on a search for the cow of plenty which the Fomorians had stolen, Cian put on a cloak of invisibility and made his way past the guards into Balor's lair. There he met the imprisoned princess and they shared an instant love. Of their union Lugh was born and he was so full of beauty that 'whatever place he was in seemed full of sunshine'. So Ethlinn named him 'Light' or 'Lugh' and Cian called him 'sun god'.

Lugh was kept hidden until he had grown into a bright young child. Then, although it brought her great pain and sadness, Ethlinn forced Cian to bring him away into the Otherworld to protect him from Balor.

'Say farewell to the mountains and rivers and trees and flowers of Ireland for you must go away with me,' Cian said. Lugh stretched out his hands and replied, 'Some day I will come back to the mountains and rivers and flowers that I love in this lovely land of mine.'

In the care of the sea god Manannán Mac Lír, Lugh grew to great wisdom, strength and beauty in Tír na nÓg. Befriended by the sea god's daughter, Niav, 'he raced the waves along the strand, he gathered apples sweeter than honey from trees of crimson blossoms and learned of all the wonders in the world.'

During this time Manannán kept watch on what was happening in Ireland and was saddened to see the Dé Danann losing control of the island to the Fomorians whose threats and intrigues gained them power. When Lugh was grown to manhood and had learned all the warrior arts, he was given the sad news about the happenings in Ireland.

'Though only the tops of the mountains in this land remain I must leave the happiness and peace of where I am and go back as I promised,' said Lugh. 'You have the hardiness that wins victory,' declared Manannán, and the Son of Light prepared for his return to Tara.

Lugh put on the helmet of Manannán and a shaft of light shot into the sky as if a new sun had risen. When he put on the breast plate, a great wave of music swelled and sounded through Tír na nÓg. Then, mounting Manannán's great white horse, he rose above the ground and over the waves and made his way back to Ireland.

Lugh wanted to be accepted in his mortal form by King Nuadhu of the Dé Danann. So, upon reaching Ireland, he dismounted, took off his shining armour and made his way across the plain of Brega in the guise of a workman. Around him as he walked he could see the devastation brought about by the Fomorian oppression. Duns lay smouldering and rubble lay along his path. No smile appeared on the faces of the once proud and happy Dé Danann as they wandered aimlessly through the wooded places, refugees in the land they had once ruled.

Lugh grew angry as he saw more and more signs of the terror being wrought on his people. How could Nuadhu of the Silver Arm have allowed this to happen? He hurried on for Tara to ask that question of the once great Dé Danann king.

When he reached the gate to Nuadhu's dun the doorman questioned him: 'Who are you, stranger?'

'I am Lugh, son of Cian of the Dé Danann, and of Ethlinn, daughter of Balor, King of the Formor. I am foster son of Tailtiu, daughter of the King of the Great Plain.'

'What can you do? For no one comes to Tara without an art.'

'I am a carpenter, a smith. I am a champion, I am a harper, I am a poet, a magician, a physician, a worker in brass,' he answered.

'We have people here already who can do these things and have no need of you,' came the surly reply.

'Go and ask Nuadhu if he has anyone who can do all these things and if he has I will not ask to enter Tara,' said Lugh.

Nuadhu admitted there was no such person at Tara, but that he would like to test this stranger himself to see what knowledge and magic he possessed. This he did and he was forced to declare, 'We have never had the like of this man before.'

Then Lugh told the true reason for his coming and demanded to know how it was that the Fomorians were allowed to impose their terror on the land.

'They hold our children and our women in ransom. If we resist they will fulfil their threat to kill and rape and pillage even more,' Nuadhu explained.

At that moment, an ugly mob of Fomorians made their way up the southern slope of Tara demanding the payment of further taxes. Nuadhu uttered not a word of objection and obediently reached for two golden goblets with which to pay.

'No!' cried Lugh, and the power of his voice shook the walls of the dun and then echoed out over the plain of Tara like the battle cry of ten thousand men at war. 'No, we will pay no taxes to the usurpers of the land we won with valour and which we are destined to live in forever.' With that he took up Nuadhu's sword

and cut down ten of the Fomorians with one fierce arc of his mighty arm. The remainder of Balor's tax men rushed outside to call their full troop but Lugh followed them and, regaining their courage, Nuadhu and his court picked up their weapons and hurried to join him. Together they fought the Fomorian band until just nine men remained standing.

Lugh then grasped their snarling leader by the neck. Holding him in one hand he gave this order: 'Go back to Balor of the Evil Eye, tell him the Dé Danann have taken control of their land again. Tell him to prepare for battle, for we are coming to rid this island of him and his robbers so that not one of them is left to darken this fair place. Go now and return only if you wish to be torn apart by Dé Danann power.' The nine Fomorians bowed in submission and slunk away toward the northern slope of Tara.

They made their way back to Lochlann where Balor was and told him of the young man with the fearsome light shining from his eyes who had destroyed their troop and sent them back as messengers. Balor's wife, Ceithlenn, was there and she said, 'I know who this warrior is. He is the son of your own daughter and as foretold he will bring an end to us.' So Balor got ready for war. He sought aid from Breas, who had been banished by the Dé Danann, and put together a mighty force with which to face the threat of Lugh.

Meanwhile, at Tara, Lugh also prepared for the final encounter which would rid Ireland of the Fomorians forever. But just at this time a great sorrow came on him because his father Cian was killed. He had come to Tara and offered help to his son in gathering the hosts of Ireland for the coming fight. Having been dispatched north to bring the Riders of the Sidhe, he encountered the three sons of Tuireann on the plain of Muirthemne and they had been enemy to him and his family for many years. They slew him and then made their way toward Tara to boast of their crime. When Lugh confronted them he demanded that they pay a fine by travelling the world and bringing back to him all the most magical things he had heard about when he was in the Otherworld and which he now needed for the battle with Balor. Included was the deadly spear of the King of Persia, and the chariot with two mighty steeds from Dobar, King of Siogair.

Now, at Tara there was a place called 'the Rampart of Whisperings'. Here Lugh met with Nuadhu and the Daghdha and the smith god, Goibniu, and the healer, Diancecht, to draw up a

*Detail from* The Marriage of Aoife and Strongbow *by Daniel Maclise (1806-70).*

battle plan that could not fail. They called together the druids, the smiths, the physicians, the chariot drivers and magicians, and asked that each give of his special power to the cause. Lugh asked of the magician Mathgen what he could do. 'I will throw down the mountains of Ireland on the Fomorians.' When he enquired from the cup-bearers what help they would give, they said, 'We will put a strong thirst on the Fomorians and bring the twelve great lochs of Ireland before them and however great their thirst will be, they will find no water in them.' Mamos the druid promised three showers of fire on the Fomorians; the two sorcerers, Bechulle and Dianan, promised enchantment on the trees and stones so that they became missiles against the Fomorians; even better, Goibniu the smith vowed, 'for every sword that is broken or every spear that has lost its shaft I will make a new one and the one I make will never miss its mark.' Luchta the carpenter promised shields that would not break. And from Diancecht the physician, healing for every one wounded, 'unless their head be cut off'.

The hosts of the Dé Danann then gathered at Tara to hear the battle plan. Lugh's voice echoed out over the hill and put strength in them so that each 'had the spirit of a king or a lord'. Then, mounted on the chariot of the king of Siogair, like a gleaming light he went before them from the plains of Meath north-west to the plain of Mag Tuired. There the Fomorians and their ally Breas were ready for the greatest battle yet fought in Ireland.

It was no easy fight for either side. And were it not for the magic of Goibniu in mending the Dé Danann spears and the healing powers of Diancecht, along with the great unquenchable thirst put on the Fomorians, Lugh's warriors might not have held their own. After four days of fierce battle, the issue was still undecided and then came the climax – a final swift and deadly duel between Lugh and Balor.

Balor first slew King Nuadhu and then, bellowing threats on every side, he advanced on Lugh. 'Hold up my eyelid so I can see this weakling who has come to torment me,' he demanded from his helpers. It took ten of them to raise the mountain of flesh covering his evil eye and when they did Lugh took his chance.

Lifting the deadly spear brought to him by the sons of Tuireann from the king of Persia, he drove it right through Balor's eye and out the back of his head.

That was the end of this tyrant and with his death the fighting spirit of the Fomorians also expired. They broke before the Dé Danann and ran in panic from the charging victors. On went the chase until the former oppressors were driven into the sea and away from Ireland forever. But before they disappeared beyond the nine waves, Lugh took from them the Cauldron of Plenty and the Harp of the Daghdha and bore them back in triumph to Tara.

Lugh became leader of the Dé Danann after that and held the kingship of Tara for many peaceful years. It is not known whether he ever died, for it is told that one Samhain eve he just disappeared. There is a fort named for him north of Tara. In legends that were to follow he became the Otherworld father of northern hero Cúchulainn and was counsellor to Conn of the Hundred Battles, to whom he foretold the names of all the kings of Ireland that would reign after him (see Chapter 6, Priest Kings and Ancestors).

After the battle of Mag Tuired Lugh searched for his mother,

Ethlinn, and brought her back to Tara. She was given in marriage to Tadg, son of Nuadhu, and her first child was a daughter, Muirne, who became mother to another of Tara's heroes ....

## The Giant, Fionn Mac Cumhail

Some say that Fionn was in fact Lugh living one more life, but that could never be proven. He was born the son of Cumhail, head of the high king's warrior band, the Fianna. But the day before his birth from Muirne, Cumhail was killed by a rebel group of Fianna led by Goll Mac Morna. In order to save her son from the same fate, Muirne gave him to a druidess who raised him in the Slieve Bloom mountains.

Named Demna then, the young man learned all the warrior lore, growing in strength and fleetness of foot. It was said of him that if he were in the same field with a hare or stag that neither would ever escape because he would always be before it.

Demna decided to go to Tara so that he could claim his rightful place in the Fianna and it was on his way there he earned the name Fionn. A group of boys were playing hurling and he joined in the game. So mighty and swift was he with the hurling stick that his opponents grew jealous and set upon him. They were soon all cut down and the chieftain who was watching the game asked, 'Who is that fair one who is better than all the rest at play and combat?' From that time on Demna became known as Fionn (the Irish for 'fair') son of Cumhail, or Fionn Mac Cumhail.

*Providing the material for modern heroic tales at Tara has been the Skryne GAA. From their ranks have come All Ireland finalists for the Meath county side, among them Pat 'Red' Donnelly and his brother Tony (men with caps in front and back rows). Their family have farmed the western slope of Tara for up to 300 years.*

Further along the way, by the banks of the Boyne, Fionn met Finnegas, a druid who sought to perfect his mental powers through finding and eating a fish known as the 'Salmon of Knowledge'. The source of this knowledge was said to be the hazel nuts which fell into the wells on the sacred hills. Every seven years they were swept down the streams into the Boyne. There they were eaten by the Salmon of Knowledge, and whoever ate of that fish would gain supreme wisdom.

Soon after Fionn's arrival on the banks of the Boyne Finnegas did indeed catch a salmon and set about cooking it. While it was on the grill Fionn saw a blister come up on its skin and pressed it down with his finger. It burned him, so without thinking he put the finger in his mouth and swallowed the morsel of salmon flesh that came away with it. Finnegas saw the light of wisdom suddenly shining in Fionn's eyes; and straight away he knew that the fish was the Salmon of Knowledge and that from then on the gift would be with Fionn.

Nor was it long before that gift of wisdom was tested to the full at one of its original sources on the sacred Hill of Tara. It was Samhain time and the High King, Conn of the Hundred Battles, was holding the Assembly which included the Fianna and their leader Goll Mac Morna. Fionn could see the ceremonial fires from where he was with Finnegas near the Boyne at Slane and quickly made his way west to Tara.

When he entered the Assembly House, the High King enquired as to who he was. 'I am Fionn, son of Cumhail, who was head over the Fianna and I have come to put myself in your service,' came the answer. Conn of the Hundred Battles welcomed Fionn and said, 'You are son of a great friend and a trustworthy hero. Come sit here beside my own son, Art.'

Now, for many years a troublesome goblin named Aillen of the Flaming Breath had each year caused chaos at the Assembly by burning Tara down. He came during the night and played such sweet music on his silver harp that everyone present fell into a deep slumber. Then flame shot from his mouth and it blew till every house was levelled.

Conn was deeply worried about this since none of his court had been able to stand in the way of Aillen. 'If one among the warriors of Ireland could keep Tara safe from fire this night until the morning then I would give him whatever inheritance is right for him to have.' None of the Fianna spoke, for they all knew they had no way of standing against the sweet music of the goblin.

The wisdom rose in Fionn then and he stood up to say that he would accept the challenge to keep Tara safe that night. His offer was accepted and he was promised that should he succeed, the inheritance of his asking would be his.

When night came dark over the hill Fionn went alone onto the rampart. As he pondered over what he would do when Aillen arrived he was joined by an aged warrior named Fiacha, who had been a former companion of his father in the Fianna. 'I have here an enchanted spear, wrought in the Otherworld by Len of Loch Lene, who beat into it the heat of the sun and the light of the moon and all the stars. You are a chosen one and if you place the head of this spear on your forehead no sleep will touch you.'

Fionn knew from his wisdom that Fiacha spoke the truth. He thanked him and then went back to patrolling the ramparts alone. For a very long time there was quiet across the frosty plain of Meath. But then as the night deepened, Fionn heard the faint sound of sweet harp music wafting in from the west. He became fully alert, uncovered the Spear of Len and pressed its cold blue metal against his forehead.

Aillen played his most enchanting tune, and Fionn wavered and wanted desperately to fall asleep. He pressed the spearhead tighter against his flesh until blood ran down in his eyes and only then did the drowsiness pass. He was ready to defend Tara when a tongue of flame shot from Aillen's mouth toward the thatch of Conn's dun. Fionn quickly threw his saffron cloak over the fire and the flames disappeared into the side of the hill. Seeing this happen, the goblin fled back toward Slieve Fuad. The warrior spirit rose in Fionn then and he followed Aillen down the glen of Nith. Wherever Aillen turned, Fionn was there before him. Then taking careful aim with the Spear of Len he pierced the creature's heart and pinned him to a tree.

When Conn rose from his sleep he was well pleased that Tara had been saved. 'What inheritance do you request?' he asked of Fionn. 'That I be given my rightful place as captain of the Fianna,' came the answer. He was brought before the Fianna and every one of them accepted him as their captain. Even Goll Mac Morna agreed and stepped down from the position he had held since the death of Fionn's father, Cumhail.

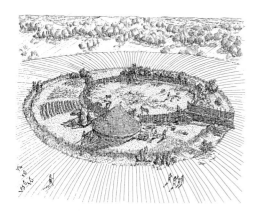

*Artist's reconstruction of Emain Macha or Navan Fort.*

The Fianna reached their full glory under Fionn's leadership which lasted the lifetime of three high kings. It is said that he ruled the warrior band both strongly and wisely. He devised a stringent selection test and only the bravest, swiftest, most knowledgeable and most resourceful candidates were chosen.

No man was enrolled into the Fianna until he had learned the twelve books of poetry. To test his valour he was placed in a hole up to his waist. With only his shield and a hazel rod to defend himself, he had to survive the spear casts of nine warriors. If he sustained even one small wound, he was deemed unfit to join. The next test demanded that he be set to run through the woods with only a branch length between him and his followers at the start. If he got any wound or if his spears trembled in his hand or if he cracked a twig under his foot, he was rejected. He had to take a leap over a rod held up to his own height and stoop under one the height of his knee. Finally he had to run his fastest and never lose pace while taking a thorn from his foot. When he had done all these things, he became a life member of the most élite and loyal band of warriors Ireland has ever known.

Fionn's way of life was one of chivalry. He and the Fianna were commissioned to fight for the High King whether the threat came from at home or abroad. From their base at the Hill of Allen, thirty-two kilometres south-west of Tara in Kildare, they kept peace in the land by standing against raiders and protecting the coast of Ireland from all invaders. Above all else they were men of the countryside – rejoicing in the beauties of nature, living by their hunting skills and making full use of the great resources of lake, river and forest.

The abiding image of Fionn is that of a warrior with spear and shield and hunting hound outlined against the background of a wild and open countryside. His own son, Oisín, said that the things he loved most were:

> 'The clamour of the hunt around the mountain steep
> The belling of stags in the rocky glen
> The screaming of gulls over the stormy sea
> And the sound of the torrent in valleys deep
> The song of the blackbird of Letterlee
> The strong wave pounding the rocky shore
> Tossing his boat on the plain of the sea
> The talk of the grouse on the heathery slope.'

The greatest among Fionn's warrior band was his son Oisín, who was also a poet, and whose mother came to the Hill of Allen in the form of a fawn but was transformed into a beautiful woman. Oisín's son, Oscar, was bravest of the Fianna. There was also the mighty Conan and Fionn's most faithful follower, Caoílte Mac Ronáin. There were also five druids who could foretell battles, five physicians, five poets and twelve musicians, who had among them Suanach – the best player of the harp that ever lived in Ireland. His huntsman was Comhrag of the five hundred hounds and the best of those was Bran.

There were 150 chief men among the Fianna and each of them had three times nine in his command, all of them bound to three things – to take no cattle by oppression; not to refuse anyone as to their needs in cattle or riches and never to fall back before nine opponents. And with Fionn at their head they were many times called upon to fulfil this promise. Oisín said of Fionn that he won 'nine times twenty battles in Ireland'.

In one of those battles, near the White Strand in Kerry, Fionn is said to have overcome the King of the World in single combat.

Fionn himself fought monsters and fierce wild animals. He performed mighty feats of strength that are associated with landmarks around Ireland. He is said to have built the Giant's Causeway in Co Antrim as stepping stones in his haste to reach a Scottish queen he loved. And he is credited with scooping out such a large clod of Ulster earth to throw at an enemy that it left behind the hole that became Lough Neagh. He is said to have married seven queens and, of course, after a long struggle he eventually became husband to Cormac Mac Airt's daughter, Gráinne (*see Chapter 3, Women of Tara*).

The legends record that this foremost leader of the Fianna eventually came into conflict with his own king, Cormac Mac Airt. On one occasion because of a dispute with the Fianna, the king imprisoned Fionn at Tara and when Caoílte came to rescue him he was told that the only way this could be done was by bringing to the royal seat two of all the creatures in Ireland. So Caoílte gathered together two of every animal, bird, fish and insect.

With all these creatures in his possession, the king of Tara released Fionn. But that did not heal the rift between them. As the years went by the disagreement between warrior and king grew more bitter. During a feast at his royal house, the King declared, 'I would sooner die fighting the Fianna, if I could bring them down

*Oisín, last of the Fianna, who, according to legend, put his lips to the soil of Tara and died.*

along with me, than live with Ireland under them the way it is now.' This message was sent to Fionn and the result was a mighty battle at Gowra, east of Tara. Many of the Fianna, including the great Oscar, died there, and when it was over Fionn cried for a day over his lost friends. It is said he never had peace or pleasure from that day.

The Fianna dwindled after that. Oisín was called from among them to go and live in Tír na nÓg. Of those few that were left, no one took notice of them. And when they saw that, they lay down on the side of the Hill of Tara and put their lips to the earth and died.

As for Fionn himself, there is a story of his dying at the hands of a fisherman. But some would hold that death never really caught up with this swift hero and that he has taken the form of Ireland's heroes down the ages – Eoghan Rua Uí Néill, Daniel O'Connell, Padraic Pearse. Who knows? He may be with us still.

1 Gwynn, Edward, *The Metrical Dindshenchas*, Todd Lecture Series, Royal Irish Academy, Dublin 1903, Vol VIII, part I, Temair II, 73; IV.

# CHAPTER 5

# TARA OF THE KINGS

*'The Seat of Kings was its name;*
*the kingly line of the Milesians reigned in it;*
*five names accordingly were given it*
*from the time it was Fordruim till it was Temair.*
*Though there be over imperial Banba*
*famous kings – high their mirth!*
*no kingly authority is binding on them*
*save from the king that possesses Temair.'*

(Tenth-century poem)[1]

More than anywhere else in the country, Tara represents Ireland's 'royal' past. Popular tradition, based on the 'Roll of Kings' included in the *Book of Leinster*, and later in the *Book of Ballymote*, holds that from the time of the Fir Bolg (roughly 1970BC) down to the 'cursing' of Tara by St Ruadhán and its abandonment in AD565 no fewer than 142 kings reigned there, and that another forty reigned in the name of Tara after that. It is called Tara na Rí – Tara of the Kings. On the crest of its hill stands the Lia Fáil, the Stone of Destiny, the coronation stone. To touch this ancient symbol is to touch perhaps two thousand years of Irish prehistory and a regal pagan past that will forever be embedded in the Celtic memory.

As mentioned in Chapter 1, the most recent historical studies of Ireland's high kings have cast doubts on the authenticity of what were previously accepted to be a true record. These doubts have gradually filtered down from the halls of academia to shake the traditional view of the Tara.

Just like many other matters in Irish life and lore, the list of 142 Tara kings should neither be taken too seriously nor be completely dismissed. For their own political and religious reasons, the medieval chroniclers adapted the 'Roll of Kings' which had been handed down by oral tradition. They added to it, adjusted it and ensured that the powerful ancestors claimed by the Uí Néill ruling dynasty were strategically placed within it. In the light of historical analyses, the Tara list can be interpreted but its authenticy can neither be proven nor denied.

In the same way, it cannot be categorically denied that the great mythical hero stories of Tara kings such as Lugh, Conaire Mór, Labhraidh Loingseach, Túathal Techtmar, Conn of the Hundred Battles, Cormac Mac Airt or Niall of the Nine Hostages do not in some exaggerated form represent historical figures who ruled in the distant past.

Francis Byrne, in his work *Irish Kings and High-Kings*, concludes: '... when the medieval tradition has been stripped of the accretions and misinterpretations resulting from the later political achievements of the Uí Néill, it is clear that the kingship of Tara was something out of the ordinary. In no other way can we explain the tenacity with which the Uí Néill high kings clung to the title even when they resided at Loch Ennell in Westmeath.'[2]

The fact still remains then that from very early times, right back to the first settlers, Tara was a most important place and it is safe to assume that from the time kingship of any sort arose among the early peoples a local king ruled here. Neither the social customs of those early peoples nor the physical features of Ireland easily lent themselves to the concept of high kingship of the whole island. In fact, until the ninth century AD, though unity was an aspiration, it was not a reality, and local kings of *tuaithe*, or 'peoples', were the norm. Some historians estimate that there were one hundred and fifty of these groupings in Ireland at the time of Christ, making up a total population of about five hundred thousand (three to four thousand to each *tuatha*).

These small units, bound together perhaps more by a shared belief in their local gods, their customs and their allegiance to a king, than by kinship, were the most important social and political reality in the land for hundreds of years – up until the rise of monasteries in the sixth century. The king of a *tuatha* ruled for his people, interceded for them to the gods – at times even appeared to be an incarnation of a god himself. The more powerful rulers became overlords of other *tuaithe*, and could then demand pledges

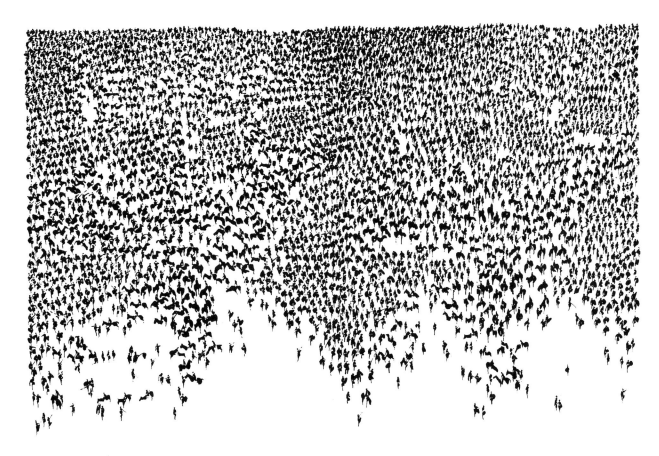

of allegiance 'by the sun, moon and the gods', backed up by the giving of hostages.

*Louis Le Brocquy's* Massing of the Armies.

Gradually, five provincial kingships evolved – the four provinces of Ireland which still remain today, and a fifth province incorporating Tara and the fertile central plain, called *Midhe* or middle. According to the legends, the king of Tara claimed to be king of Ireland from the earliest times. But the powerful dynasty of the Uí Néill began to claim high kingship of Ireland in or around the seventh century – though that claim did not become a reality until the middle of the eighth century. Significantly, when they did come to power, it was in Tara's name they ruled.

The kings of Tara, then, be they 142 or whatever number, were first simply kings of a *tuatha* or of a local people who lived on the fruitful edge of the central plain. But because the hill grew in fame as a sacred place, the power of the title 'King of Tara' also took on a greater meaning. Initially this king might not have been able to take the title 'King of Ireland' by force of arms; nevertheless he ruled over the most valuable grazing in the country. And one can

*Drawing by George Petrie of Irish kings.*

imagine him looking out from the rampart of Tara at the rich land stretching out endlessly before him and taking that honour to himself by reason of where he stood and what the place he stood on signified – the sacredness of that fertile land.

The ancient sacredness of the site and its commanding central position must explain why the legends constantly referred to the 'High King of Tara', or why the Uí Néill, when they took the title to themselves, did so in the name of Tara and no other place in Ireland – not Emain Macha or Ailech in Ulster, not Crúachain in Connacht, not Uisneach in Westmeath, not Cashel in Tipperary, but Tara.

The list of Tara's kings has to be taken as a type of fable, incorporating some truth which was transmitted orally over the centuries as legends and stories of the various peoples who came into Ireland during the last millennium BC. It is enough to highlight the interesting segments, knowing that the person mentioned could have lived on this holy ground. That, I think, is the best way to approach a pre-history that can never be pinned down definitively.

## From 'The Roll of Kings'

The nine Fir Bolg kings have already been mentioned *(see Chapter 1, Tara and the Invasion Legends)*. Among them was Sláine, 'by whom Tara was first raised', and Eochaid, the horse god, 'who sat in the beginning in Tara'.[3] God kings of the Dé Danann ruled there after these first kings – Nuadhu, Breas, Lugh, Daghdha the father-god and his son, Cernait or 'Honey Mouth'. It was the three sons of Cernait, Mac Cuill, Mac Ceacht and Mac Gréine – the hazel god, the smith god and the sun god – who were sharing the kingship of Tara when the sons of Míl arrived on the scene.

Then begins a new section of the list, concerning the Milesian kings of Tara. It stretches from Eremón 'in the time of David' down to the ancestor claimed by the Uí Néill, Conn Céadchathach or Conn of the Hundred Battles, who was said to have lived at the time of the Roman Emperor Marcus Antoninus in the second century BC. From Eremón to Conn, ninety-nine kings are listed and if the periods given for each of their reigns are added up they amount to a total of 1,300 years.

The Celts placed Eremón, a son of their ancestor Míl, at the head of their list and pushed the time of his reign back to about 1342BC. The fact that the Celts did not arrive until somewhere between

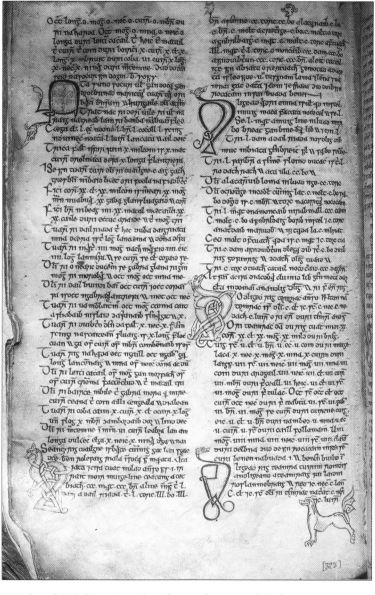

*A page from the* Book of Rights *as contained in the fourteenth-century* Book of Ballymote. *Among the rights stipulated for the king of Tara are: one hundred swords, one hundred shields, and one hundred horses along with coloured cloths and coats of mail. The king of Tara in turn was obliged to give his kings and the tribes of Meath such things as horns, hounds, cloaks and swords, and in some cases women and slaves.*

150BC and 50BC is a sign that those who compiled the genealogies and regnal lists for the Uí Néill in later centuries tampered with them in order to give the Uí Néill prominence. Chronology was not something the chroniclers felt had to be factual.

Thus in the 'Roll of Kings' attached to the *Book of Leinster*, Eremón is the first. His three sons, Muimne, Luigne and Laigne, are then said to have reigned together after him.

Many of these early kings are credited with various feats such as the clearing of great plains or the building of royal forts. It is

*The sacred hills of Loughcrew near Oldcastle are clearly visible from Tara, and the two places must have been closely linked in the ancient religions of the Boyne valley. This distinctive stone on Loughcrew has been variously named 'The Hag's Chair' and 'Ollamh Fódla's Seat' after the twentieth king of Tara. In the* Book of Clonmacnoise, *Fódla is credited with convening the first triennial Assembly or Feis at Tara.*

said about the fifth king, Ethriel, for example, 'that six plains were cleared by him, Tenmag in Connachta, Mag Lugair in Luigne, Mag Belaig in Uí Tuirtre, Mag Geisille in Uí Failge, Lochmag in Conaille, Mag Roth in Uí Echach Coba, till he fell in the battle of Rairiu at the hands of Conmael.'[3]

The seventh king, Tigernmas, 'broke thrice nine battles' and is said to be the first in Ireland to use drinking horns, the first to smelt gold and to put colours on garments. His successor Eochu Edgathach had reigned for only four years when he was slain by Cermna 'in the battle of Tara' – one of many battles, real and otherwise, to be fought around the Hill of Tara. Silver shields were brought into Ireland by the fifteenth king, Enna Airgdech, who reigned for twenty-seven years until he was killed and replaced by Rothechtaid. He in turn held the kingship for twenty-two years before he 'died thereafter of wounds in Tara'. It is said that Rothechtaid ruled at the time of Acrazapes, king of the Assyrians – an example of efforts by monastic scribes to synchronise the 'Roll of Kings' with biblical and world history.

Golden neck-torques were introduced at the time of the eighteenth king, Muinemon. 'Golden rings enclosed hands first in Ireland' during the time time of the next king, Faildergdoit. He fell at Tara by the sword of of the twentieth king, Ollamh Fódla, whose reign is dated by some at 1000BC.

The story of Ollamh Fódla is one that contains a hint of history and, according to the list, he is a most important monarch who ruled for forty years and first convened the Assembly of Tara. He is also said to have died alone at Tara, and six of his direct descendants reigned after him.

One of Fódla's sons and the twenty-second king, Slánoll, was treated as something of a pre-Christian saint by the monastic chroniclers: 'There was no disease during his reign [thirty years] ... he was found dead in his bed in the Midechuart House in Tara and his colour had changed not, nor did his body decay; and it was taken from the earth by his son Oilill at the end of a year and it was not decayed.'

During the time of Fiachu Findiolches, the twenty-fourth king, a tax was placed on the white-headed cattle of Ireland. The twenty-seventh king, Sirna Soegalach, separated the princedom of Ulster from Tara while his successor Rothechtaid first introduced four-horse chariots. It is claimed that the thirty-third king, Breas, ruled at the time of Nabuchodonosor, the king of Persia (600BC), for nine years. But poor Eochu Apthach who came after him lasted only for one, and there was a plague 'every month in his reign'. Fionn followed him and then came Setna Innarraid, 'the first who gave wage to hirelings in Ireland'. Another Eochu divided the island north and south and ruled for five years along with Conaing. But when we come to the reign of the fifty-sixth on the list, Ugoine Mór (possibly about 400BC), we find one of the best examples of how the regnal list was used to give royal Milesian ancestors to as many groups as possible. Ugoine is credited, anachronistically, with having had twenty-five children by a daughter of the king of the Franks. Even more fantastic than this, it is said of Ugoine Mór that while king of Tara he 'took the kingship of Europe' as well.

While statements like that stretch credibility to the very limit, it is still true that the *Annals of Tighearnach*, dating from about the eighth century AD, pinpoint the time of Ugoine and his foster-father Cimbaoth, around 400BC, as the earliest time from which any sort of authentic Irish history can be charted.

The next series of kings are supposed to have reigned from the fourth century BC until the time of Christ. This group bears a close relationship to the invasion stories of the Laigin or Leinstermen and to the later coming of the Gaels, Goedils or Celts between 200BC and 50BC. It is this period that T. F. O'Rahilly, in *Early Irish History and Mythology*, refers to as a 'dimly lit stage' on which are played out the strivings of these two peoples for the royal seat at Tara.

The Laigin invasion is unfolded in a saga called the 'Destruction of Dinn Rig' about fierce family treachery, cunning and revenge between the descendants of Ugoine Mór. One of Ugoine's many sons, Cobthach the Meagre, was king of the plain around Tara while another son, Lóegaire Lorc, was king of Tara itself. Out of jealousy the ailing Cobthach killed Lóegaire when the latter came to visit him on his sick bed. He then poisoned Lóegaire's son and heir, Ailill Ane, who was king of Leinster, and proceeded to take over both the Tara and Leinster crowns.

But Ailill had a son, Labhraidh Loingseach, who becomes the hero of the piece. He goes into exile and then returns with a force to wreak vengeance at the 'Destruction of Dinn Rig' and take over as the fifty-ninth king of Tara. However, after a thirty-year reign, Labhraidh was killed by a son of Cobthach, Melge, who regained the kingship for his side of the family, who appear to have been forebears of the Uí Néill.

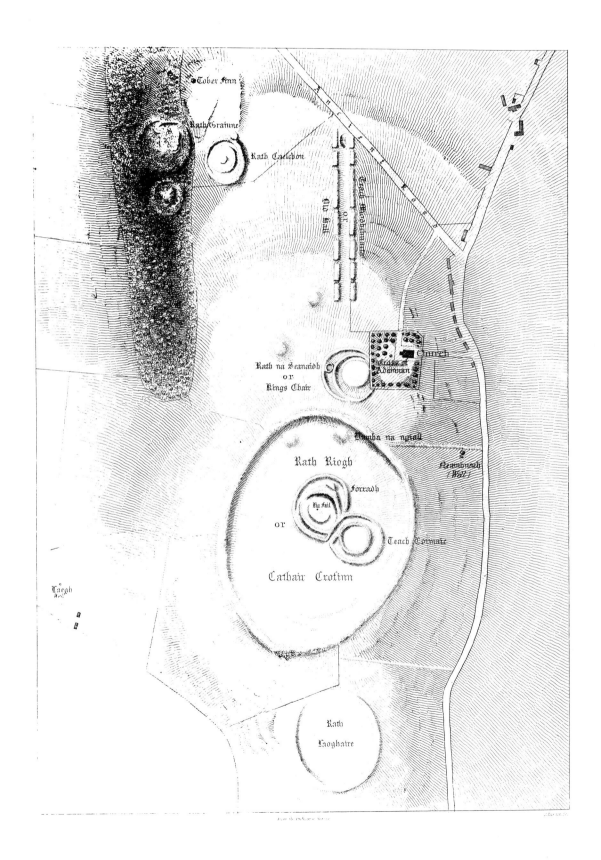

After some one hundred years, in which the Tara kingship alternated between the descendants of Lóegaire and Cobthach, another important name appears – Aonghus Tuiremech of Tara. He was of the Cobthach line and therefore an Uí Néill ancestor, and, seventieth king on the list, he reigned for sixty years in the fourth century BC. It is at this time the chroniclers begin setting the stage for the emergence of the Uí Néill. They tell us that 'his children took the kingship of Ireland and of Alba, namely Eterscél Maccu Iair, Conaire Mór'. Aonghus Tuirmech Tamrach came to power when he slew Fergus Fortamail at a battle near Tara, possibly about 383BC. The *Annals of Clonmacnoise* say of him: 'He was a very good king who left issue two goodly and noble sons, Enna Aighneach and Fiacha Ferwara.' His first son, Enna the seventy-third king of Tara, is ancestor to Conn Céadchathach or Conn of the Hundred Battles, who in turn was ancestor to the Uí Néill kings. The second son, Fiacha, was born of incest between Aonghus and his own daughter. He survived being abandoned at sea, and among his descendants – perhaps two hundred years later – is one of the great legendary priest-kings of Tara, Conaire Mór. It is said that during Conaire's reign, 'The Virgin Mary was born and Cúchulainn died and the hosting of the Táin Bó Cuailgne took place.'

Between the time of Aonghus and that of Conaire Mór, fifteen kings of Tara are listed. Along with Enna Aignech, there was Rudraige, from whom the 'true people of Ulster descended'; Bresal Bo-Dibad, who was so named because during his reign a pestilence came upon the cattle of Ireland; Dui Dallta Degaid, of whom it is said, 'he was ten years in the kingship and in his time was fought the Civil War between Pompeius Magnus and Julius Caesar.' The chroniclers were then nearing the time of Christ's birth in their narratives, and new layers of Otherworld magic enter into the stories of this last century BC. The lives of Eochu Feidlech, the eighty-second king, that of his brother Eochaid Aireamh, who ruled after him, and of Eterscéle are all interwoven into the beautiful Tara-based saga called the 'Wooing of Étaín' *(see Chapter 3, Women of Tara)*. This in turn leads to the legends of the great priest kings of Tara – Conaire Mór, Túathal Techtmhar, Cormac Mac Airt and Conn of the Hundred Battles. In their colourful sagas Tara shines through brightly as a sacred royal site. They are the subject of the next chapter.

Opposite: *Aerial drawing of Tara by George Petrie.*

78 • THE BOOK OF TARA

Chronological list of invasion legend kings and the length of their reigns. (Names in bold are mentioned in the text.)

First king at Tara:
**Eochaid of the Fir Bolg**

Dé Danann Kings:
*Nuadhu*
**Breas 7 years**
**Nuadhu 20 years**
**Lugh 40 years**
**Daghdha 80 years**
*Delbaeth 10 years*
*Fiachna 10 years*
*Mac Cuill, Mac Cecht, Mac Gréine, joint kings*

Milesian Kings:
**Eremón 15 years**
*Muine, Luigne, Laigne jointly 3 years*
*Er, Orba Feron, Fergna jointly 2 years*
*Iriel Fáid 10 years*
**Ethriel 20 years**
*Conmáel 30 years*
**Tigernmas 77 years**
**Eochu Edgathach 4 years**
*Sobairce and Cermna 40 years*
*Eochu Faebarglas 20 years*
*Fíachu Labrainne 24 years*
*Eochu Mumu 21 years*
*Óengus Olmucaid 14 years*
**Énna Airgdech 27 years**
**Rothechtaid 22 years**
*Sétna 5 years*
*Fíachu Finscothach 20 years*
**Muinemón 5 years**
**Faildergdóit 30 years**
**Ollamh Fódla 40 years**
*Fínnachta 20 years*
*Slánoil 30 years*
*Géde Ollgothach 8 years*

**Fíachu Findoilches 30 years**
*Berngal 21 years*
*Ailill 15 years*
**Sírna Soegalach 50 years**
**Rothechtaid 7 years**
*Elim 1 year*
*Gíallchad 9 years*
*Art Imlech 12 years*
*Nuadu Finn Fail 60 years*
**Breas 9 years**
**Eochu Apthach 1 year**
**Fionn 20 years**
**Sétna Innarraid 20 years**
*Siomón Brecc 6 years*
*Dui Finn 10 years*
*Muidedach Bolgrach 1 year*
*Énna Derg 12 years*
*Lugaid Íardonn 9 years*
*Sírlám 13 years*
*Eochu Uirches 12 years*
**Eochu and Conaing 5 years**
*Lugaid Lámderg 7 years*
*Conaing 10 years*
*Art 6 years*
*Ailill Finn 9 years*
*Eochu 7 years*
*Airgetmar 30 years*
*Dui Ladrach 10 years*
*Lugaid Laigdec 7 years*
*Cimbáeth 38 years*
*Macha 7 years*

*Rechtaid Rígderg 20 years*
**Ugoine Mór 50 years**
*Lóegaire Lorc 2 years*
*Cobthach Cóel Breg 50 years*
**Labhraidh Loingsech 19 years**
**Melge 17 years**
*Mug Corb 6 years*
**Aonghus Ollom 18 years**
*Irereo 7 years*
*Fer Corb 11 years*
*Connla 4 years*
*Ailill Caisfiaclach 25 years*
*Amadir 5 years*
*Eochu Ailtlethan 11 years*
*Fergus Fprtamail 12 years*
**Aonghus Tuiremech Temrach 60 years**
*Conall Collamrach 5 years*
*Nia Segamain 7 years*
**Énna Aighneach 28 years**
*Crimthann Coscrach 4 years*
**Rudraige 70 years**
*Finnat Már 3 years*
**Bresal Bó-Díbad 11 years**
*Lugaid Luaigne 15 years*
*Congal Cláirengnech 16 years*
**Dui Dallta Degaid 10 years**
*Fachtna Fathach 25 years*
**Eochu Feidlech 12 years**
**Eochaid Aireamh 15 years**
**Eterscéle 5 years**
*Nuadhu Necht*

1 Gwynn, Edward, *The Metrical Dindshenchas*, Todd Lecture Series, Royal Irish Academy, Dublin, Temair, I , p. 5 and Temair V, p. 45.
2 Byrne, Francis J., *Irish Kings and High Kings*, Dublin 1973, p. 57.
3 'The Roll of Kings', translated by R.A.S. Macalister from the Irish Texts Society Series, Vol XLIV, Education Company of Ireland, 1956, par 502. Following quotes on the kings in this chapter are all taken from this source.

# CHAPTER 6

# PRIEST KINGS AND ANCESTORS

*'Temair, noblest of hills,*
*under which is Erin of the forays,*
*the lofty city of Cormac son of Art,*
*son of mighty Conn of the hundred fights.*

*Cormac, constant was his prosperity,*
*he was sage, he was poet, he was prince*
*he was a true judge of the men of Fene.*
*He was a friend, he was a comrade.'*

(Tenth-century poem)[1]

The priest kings of Tara were no ordinary mortals. Although never so called in the Irish sagas, Conaire Mór, Túathal Techtmar, Conn of the Hundred Battles and Cormac Mac Airt are referred to by writers and historians as the 'priest kings'. Genealogical tables, lists of kings, along with the sagas and legends contained in ancient texts such as the *Book of Leinster*, the *Book of Ballymote*, and the *Yellow Book of Lecan* all give them a sacred dimension – spiritual happenings surround their conception and birth, supernatural signs accompany their coming to power as kings, and certain *geasa* or taboos govern their destinies. Thus their personalities are more richly portrayed than the figures in earlier legends and the stories of their lives at Tara are embellished with descriptions of ornate halls, great banquets and huge gatherings of nobles from every part of Ireland. They act as mediators between otherworldly powers and human destiny, and their reigns bridge the distance between pure mythology and the faint beginnings of true Irish

*The word geis (plural geasa) appears to mean 'destined occurrence'. In the ancient sagas, a number of geasa were placed on sacred and important persons. For the king of Tara these were certain, very specific, actions which had to be performed, or which had to be avoided by him. The penalty for infringing this code of behaviour was usually death. But the fact that they were applied to the king of Tara confirmed the holder of the title as a sacred person. A tenth-century poem lists some: 'The king of Tara might not let the sun rise on him at Tara; he should not break a journey on Mag Breg (plain of Meath) on Wednesday; travel over Mag Cuilinn after sunset; strike his horses in Fan Commair; enter north Tethba (Longford) on a Tuesday; have a scout at Bethra on the Monday after Bealtaine nor the track of his army at Ath Maigne (in Westmeath) on the Tuesday after Samhain.'[2]*

history. And lastly, they reigned in the sacred place of Tara, hence their title of 'priest king'.

**The period assigned to the exploits of Conaire Mór, Túathal Techtmar, Conn of the Hundred Battles and Cormac Mac Airt begins in the century before Christ and continues through a shadowy five hundred years of prehistory to the time of King Lóegaire, who was on the throne at Tara when the pagan cults of the Celts had their dramatic confrontation with the newly arrived Christianity at the start of the fifth century AD.**

Both Conaire Mór and Cormac Mac Airt were part of the origin legends of the Laigin or Leinstermen, who are said to have held the kingship of Tara prior to its takeover by the Uí Néill dynasty. However, because they appeared as such glorious figures in the sagas, embellished no doubt by the Uí Néill chroniclers, these early Laigin kings were adopted into the Uí Néill genealogy. There they enhanced both the Uí Néill ancestry and their claim that their right to the kingship of Tara stretched back to the beginning of time.

The story of Túathal Techtmar appears to be largely an Uí Néill fiction to create a clear link through to important names, like Ugoine Mór in the fifth century BC, whom the Uí Néill also wished to claim for their ancestry *(see Chapter 5, Tara of the Kings)*. Túathal also provides a link forward as grandfather of Conn of the Hundred Battles.

## Conaire Mór

The first of these colourful kings is Conaire Mór, or Conaire the Great. Conaire's mother, Meas Buachalla, was grand-daughter to the mythological fairy queen, Étaín *(see Chapter 3, Women of Tara)*. On the night before she married Eterscéle, the eighty-fourth king of Tara, she conceived Conaire through union with a beautiful Otherworld being from Tír na nÓg. 'This child will be a warrior lord,' she was told, and he would be surrounded by many sacred *geasa* which he must obey if he was to avoid death.

Meas Buachalla then married Eterscéle, and so the Otherworld-conceived Conaire was born into the royal house – and into the 'Roll of Kings' where he is listed as 'son of Eterscéle'.

While very young, Conaire was fostered out according to custom to a lord named Desa at the Curragh of Kildare. Also in fosterage there were three of his future enemies, Ferlee, Fergar and Ferrogan. Still unaware that he was destined to be king, Conaire grew into a strong, brave, handsome warrior.

Since in ancient Ireland the son of a king did not inherit the throne by right, when Eterscéle died a 'bull feast' had to be held at Tara to determine who the next king should be. Conaire was invited to attend and set out in a chariot from the Curragh. Destiny then began to take a hand, for on his way he was met by Nemglan, a representative of his Otherworld father, who told him of the *geasa* that he must obey if he was to avoid death. Among them he was told that rapine should not be wrought during his reign; that he must not go right-handwise around Tara; nor left-handwise around Bregia; he must not follow three red-haired people to a house of red; he must not sleep in a house from which firelight showed after sunset, or in which light could be seen from without; after sunset, no one woman alone or man alone should enter the house in which he was; and he must not interfere in a quarrel between two of his subjects.

*Early stone carving of Irish king.*

Then Nemglan said to Conaire, 'Go to Tara tonight, the bull feast is there and through it you will be made king.' He was told by Nemglan that the vision seen by the seer at the bull feast was that of a 'naked young man coming along the road to Tara at dawn bearing a stone in a sling'. So it was in this manner, 'naked and carrying a sling' that Conaire travelled on to Tara so that he would be recognised as king.[3]

But when he got to the royal enclosure further tests awaited before the druids would accept him – the royal mantle had to fit him; he had to drive a chariot through the narrow space between the sacred stones of Blocc and Bluicne; and the Lia Fáil, or coronation stone, had to roar its approval of him as the true successor.

Conaire was accepted and as the eighty-sixth king of Tara is said to have reigned during the time of the Emperor Augustus Caesar Octavian (63BC-AD14) for the space of seventy years which enjoyed 'fair seasons and bounteous harvests and during which foreign ships came to the ports; oak-hast for the swine was up to the knees every autumn and the rivers swarmed with fish.'[4] It is also noted of his reign that during it 'no one slew another and to every one in Erin his fellow's voice seemed as sweet as the strings of lutes. From mid-spring to mid-autumn no wind disturbed a cow's tail.'[5]

*Dedicated to Queen Maeve, the Tara Goddess of Sovereignty, Rath Maeve lies just 1.5 km south of the Mound of the Hostages. It is in the townland of Belper, which is thought to be named for the Celtic fire-god Belenos. A gap on the northern rim of its 750-ft-diameter bank opens directly toward the summit of Tara itself. These ridges in Lord Dunsany's field appear to point the way.*

But that idyllic peace was eventually disturbed by his three foster brothers who had become notorious robbers and bandits. They were brought before Conaire for judgement. Out of respect for his kinship with them, instead of putting them to death as the people asked, he banished them from Ireland, thus breaking one of the *geasa* laid on him – 'rapine shall not be wrought in thy reign'. By not applying the death penalty, he failed the *geis.*

Inevitable doom followed for the good Conaire. He broke another taboo when travelling to Munster to settle a quarrel between two kings. On his return he saw fire on the plains of Meath and 'went right-handwise around Tara' to avoid it. Then lured to 'the red man's house', Da Dearga's Hostel (believed to be in south Co Dublin), he met his death at the hands of his foster brothers, who had secretly returned from exile.

Following Conaire's death, we are told, the Dé Danann king, Mac Céacht, god of the plough, bore his body back to Tara for burial.

## Túathal Techtmar

'Ruler of the People', 'Voyager from Afar' is the meaning of the ninety-second king's name. He is portrayed as a saviour warrior who returns from exile to reclaim the kingship of Tara and become a just ruler over his people. Instead of being the embodiment of a mythological ideal of a true king, like Conaire, Túathal Techtmar is more flesh and blood and it is thought that his story may be the embroidered history of a takeover by Celtic warriors in the Irish midlands of peoples like the Laigin and the Luaigne.

The period following the death of Conaire Mór is depicted as one of conflict for control of Tara and the east midlands. Túathal's ancestor group, the Erainn, are said to have won out in the first century AD when Fiachu Finnoilches became king of Tara, during the time that Nero was Emperor of Rome – AD54-68. Fiachu was slain by Éilim Mac Conrach in what is described as a massacre of the Erainn by the descendants of the Fir Bolg, who are called 'the provincials'. After this slaughter the male descendants of the important ancestor line of Ugoine Mór were wiped out, except for three who were in their mothers' wombs at the time. One of them was Túathal Techtmar, son of king Fiachu Finnoilches, and Eithne, who was daughter of the king of Scotland.

The chroniclers then say that Túathal's mother Eithne brought him over the sea to Scotland where she nurtured him until he was twenty and then accompanied him 'to guide him to Tara'. Túathal landed near Malahide, and with a warrior band of eight hundred, marched on Tara. He defeated Éilim at the Battle of Achall at Skryne near Tara and was then crowned king. During his thirty-year reign he established the Assembly at Tara; designated the four great meeting places as Tailtiu at Teltown in Co Meath, Tlachtga near Athboy in Co Meath, Uisneach in Co Westmeath and Tara; won 110 battles against vassal tribes of all four provinces; created a fifth province called *Midhe* on the central plain and imposed a cattle tax, the *bóraimhe*, on the people of Leinster.

In other versions of his origins, it has been said that Túathal was in fact a Roman legionary who joined a contingent of Celts seeking new lands in Ireland. There is no proof of this but his imposition of the *bóraimhe* could indicate Roman training. The finding of ancient Roman artifacts at the Rath of the Synods on Tara also points in that direction but could also be due to trade with the Continent.

> The *bóraimhe*, or 'cattle-computation' was largely paid in cattle. The *Annals of Clonmacnoise* record that such a tax involved up to 150 cows a year along with hogs, sheep, cloaks and cauldrons. A more fantastic version, given in both the *Book of Leinster* and the *Book of Lecan* states that Túathal's levy on the Leinstermen was: 'thrice fifty hundred kine, thrice fifty hundred boars, thrice fifty hundred wethers, and twelve cauldrons along with a brazen cauldron into which would go twelve beeves.'[6]

The tax was to be the cause of intermittent war between the kings of Tara and those of Leinster up until the eighth century. But it was re-imposed as retribution on the Leinsterman, Dunlaing, after his slaughter of the thirty princesses and their maidens at the Clóenfherta in Tara during the reign of Cormac Mac Airt. King Lóegaire, who was high king at the time of St Patrick, died trying to impose the tax in AD439. In the eleventh century the levy was imposed again by Brian Boru, who takes his surname from it.

In addition to the *bóraimhe*, one other long-lasting tradition begun by Túathal Techtmar was the triennial Assembly or Feis at Tara at which, among other rituals, allegiance was sworn to the king by the lesser kings or 'provincials' who also agreed that 'though the Provincials of Ireland should be equal in power, they should not be equal in right of the kingship of Ireland and that the

The ninth-century poet Maelmura Othna gave this dramatic account of the allegiance demanded by Túathal from lesser kings.

'These are the sureties which Túathal took,
Mighty at exacting,
Heaven, earth, sun, pure moon, sea, fruitful land,
Feet, hands, mouths with tongues, ears, eyes,
Horses, javelins, shields, valiant swords with
their hardness,
Countenances of men, dew with colours, strand
with flood;
Corn, milk, fruit, each good likewise which man
doth.
These sureties all are given according to the law,
To Túathal's children, to his race, and to his tribe
While the sea exists around Erin, isolated
solitary,
That the lordly Temur would be defended against
Túathal's children.'[7]

*The concept of* cuige *or 'fifth' for the Irish provinces is a very old one going right back to the legends of the Fir Bolg's arrival in Ireland. According to the* Lebor Gabála, *the country was divided into five areas, with Meath as the central province and Tara as its capital.*

progeny of Túathal should have the kingship for ever'. Chief among Túathal's anointed descendants was his grandson, Conn of the Hundred Battles.

## Conn Céadchathach, or Conn of the Hundred Battles

Túathal Techtmar's exploits portray the invasion of Ireland's midlands (real or otherwise) by the ancestors of the Uí Néill. The wars attributed to Conn of the Hundred Battles relate to the Uí Néill claim to have consolidated power right across this rich heartland over the following hundred years. Conn means 'head' or 'chief' and under his leadership one hundred battles or *chathaig* were won as the territory controlled by his people, the Gaels, was extended into Leinster, Munster and Ulster.

Just as with Conaire Mór, the stories of Conn's birth are embellished with portents and prophesies. The time of his reign is synchronised with that of the gentle Roman Emperor Antoninus, c. AD142. His father, Feidhlimidh Rechtmar, the son of Túathal Techtmar, died at Tara and was succeeded by Cathaoir Mór, an important ancestor king of the Leinstermen. He expelled the young prince, Conn, from the royal enclosure and thus he was raised as an exile by Conall, ruler of the west of Ireland. This area west of the Shannon, Connacht, is named after Conn, and the sept from which the Uí Néill derived, the Connachta, means 'the descendants of Conn'.

When Conn was of age, Conall provided him with men and weapons for the fight to claim his birthright, the kingship of Tara. According to the *Annals of Clonmacnoise*, at a battle near the hill 'King Cathaoir's army was overthrown. He himself was slain and buried near the river of Boyne.' The ancient name for the Hill of Skryne, Ochil, is said to be derived from the traditional keening word *ochón*, uttered by the local tribeswomen mourning their king's death.

According to one ninth-century poem, Conn thereafter 'won one hundred battles against Munster ... one hundred against Ulster and sixty against the Leinstermen.' 'The Roll of Kings' says that on one occasion he was driven back toward Tara and pursued by the Laigin warriors, Eachlann and Nuadhu, who wounded him. But on his home ground he turned on them and beheaded both. Nonetheless Conn was for a time driven out of Tara, for the account goes on to say that 'the king of Laigin remained in Tara till the end of seven years. Then the strength of Conn increased again and he put him out of Tara and exacted the *bóraimhe* from him.'[8]

But the achievements with which the chroniclers would most like to credit Conn are those in relation to Munster. He and Eoghan Mór or Mugh Nuadhat, after whom the southern Goidels, the Eoganacht, were named, fought many battles. At one point they divided Ireland between them along the line of a glacier ridge known as the Eiscir Riada ('Gravel Hills of the Kings') that runs from Dublin to Galway. The northern half was *Leath Choinn* or Conn's half, with Tara as its capital, while the southern half was Mugh Nuadhat's half, *Leath Mhogha*, and was to have a rotating capital, the principal one being Cashel in Co Tipperary.

A thirteenth-century text, *The Battle of Moylena* or *Cath Maighe Lena*, gives a more definite end to the conflict between these two great Gaelic ancestors. Just north of Tullamore, the text says, Conn made an attack on Munster's forces, defeated them and slew Eoghan, thus himself becoming the 'unchallenged king of Ireland' – a title which the Uí Néill wanted applied to their forefather but which cannot be verified.

But there is much more to the story of Conn than battles. The chronicles not only depict him as a mighty warrior but also as a divine figure – a sacral-king to whom virtually any wonder could be attributed.

His birth and death are both said to have happened at the time of Tara's most sacred and magical feast, Samhain *(see Chapter 2, The Sacred Hill)*. The time and details of his birth were foretold by an Otherworld woman to the druid, Fínghein Mac Luchta: 'a son will be born to King Feidhlimidh who will unite the five provinces and be the progenitor of fifty-three kings of Ireland.' It was also prophesied that on the night he was born, a great river, to be called the Boyne, would break forth from the earth; the five roads to Tara would instantly spring into being and among a host of other magical happenings, 'nine bright birds would sing beautiful music over the rampart of Tara.'[9]

That same rampart of Tara was to be scene for the fulfilment of another prophesy when Conn was walking the hill in the company of the Tara druids. First, the Lia Fáil screeched as he stepped on it. Then he was met by the god king Lugh, who told him the names of the twenty-eight high kings of Ireland who would succeed him.

Conn is said to have reigned for some thirty-five years and was slain at Tara by a group of Ulstermen disguised as women who

Chronological list of legendary kings who reigned at Tara from c.150BC to AD400, and the length of their respective reigns. (Names in bold are mentioned in the text.)

*Conaire Mór 70 years*
*Lugaid Riab Nderg 25 years*
*Conchibor Abrat-Ruad 1 year*
*Crimthan Nia Náir 1 year*
*Cairpre Cinn-Chait 5 years*
*Feradach Finn Fechtnach 20 years*
*Fíatach Finn 3 years*
*Fiachu Finnoilches 17 years*
*Elim 20 years*
**Tuathal Techtmar 30 years**
*Mál 4 years*
*Feidlimid Rechtmar 9 years*
**Cathair Mór 3 years**
**Con Ceadchathach (Conn of the Hundred Battles) 20 years**
*Cónaire Coem 7 years*
*Art Óenfer 20 years*
**Lugaid Mac Con 30 years**
*Fergus Dubdétach 1 year*
**Cormac Mac Airt 40 years**
*Eochu Gunnat 1 year*
*Cairbre Lifechair 26 years*
*Fothaid 1 year*
*Fiachu Sroiptine 36 years*
*Colla Uais 4 years*
*Muiredach Tírech 30 years*
*Cáelbad 1 year*
**Eochaid Mugmedon 8 years**
**Crimthan Mac Fidaig 13 years**

It was said that during the kingship of Conn:
*'One ploughing in spring yielded three crops*
*the cuckoo cry was heard on the cow's horns*
*a hundred clusters grew on each stem*
*and a hundred nuts in each cluster.'*[10]

*'When Cormac was in Temair,*
*beyond all high prowess for his great might,*
*a kingly equal of the son of Art Oenfer*
*was not to be found among the men of the world.'*[11]

Below: *Detail from the* Book of Kells.

pretended to be attending the feast of Samhain.

Third on the list of kings Lugh foretold would succeed Conn was Cormac, his grandson.

## Cormac Mac Airt

Of all the kings said to have ruled at Tara, none embodied the mystery and glory of Tara so fully as Cormac Mac Airt.

Some historians accept that Cormac may well have been a real person. He most probably ruled at Tara as a Leinster king and, having achieved great fame as a man of wisdom and valour, was appropriated by the Uí Néill chroniclers. These medieval writers absorbed him into the Uí Néill genealogy and surrounded him with a host of wonderful feats which helped glorify that ancestry. Like Conaire Mór, Cormac offers an archetype of ideal kingship.

According to the *Annals of the Four Masters*, Cormac reigned from AD227 to AD266. The *Annals of Inisfallen* have him take the throne in AD219, while the *Annals of Ulster* would have us believe he belonged to the fourth rather than the third century. According to the *Annals of Tigearnach*, he ruled for forty-two years, save during two occasions when he was driven out of Tara by the Ulstermen. On one of these exiles he is said to have taken up kingship in Scotland.

In the chronology given to his reign by the Uí Néill, three kings held Tara between Conn of the Hundred Battles and Cormac Mac Airt. After the death of Conn, his kinsman, Conaire Coem, took the kingship for seven years. Art Oenfer, son of Conn and husband to Queen Maeve, held it for twenty years after that until he fell in the battle of Mucrama at the hands of Lugaid, son of Conn's great enemy, Eoghan Mór. Lugaid then took the kingship of Tara until Cormac claimed it in AD227.

Just as with Conaire Mór, Cormac's conception and birth carry Otherworld overtones. The night before going into battle with Lugaid at Mucrama, Cormac's father Art was staying at the house of a druid and foresaw his own death in the coming fight. In order to ensure his progeny succeeded him in the kingship he was advised to lie with the druid's daughter, Étaín. Art told her she would bear a son who would be king of Ireland, and in order that this son's rightful parentage would be known, he left with her two identifying objects – his own royal ring and the Sword of Light which had belonged to Cúchulainn and with which the Ulstermen has slain his own father, Conn.

As foretold, Art was indeed killed in battle and when Étaín was near to her time she decided to travel to the foster home chosen by Art – that of the druid, Lugna Fer Tri. But along the way she felt the first birth pangs and her child was born in open country. After the birth she and her maid both fell asleep and Cormac was abducted by a she-wolf who reared him until he was finally found as a beautiful and fair child by his foster father.

Cormac grew up learning both the wisdom of the Otherworld and the warrior arts of Ireland's greatest heroes. When he was of age, Lugna told him who he really was. 'There will be no prosperity in Tara until you reign there,' he said. 'Let us go then,' said Cormac, 'and seek recognition in my father's house in Tara.'[12]

Soon after his arrival at the royal hill, this recognition came through a test of wisdom. A judgement had to be made by the reigning king, Lugaid Mac Con, regarding compensation due to the queen for the grazing of her field at Tara by some trespassing sheep. Lugaid decided the sheep should be given to the queen as forfeit for the grazing. But Cormac declared this a wrong and unjust ruling. 'The shearing of the sheep for the shearing of the field is a more just judgement, since both the grass and the wool will grow again,' he said.

Cormac's judgement was recognised as the true one while that of Lugaid was condemned as false. 'At that, one side of the house in which the false judgement was given, fell down the slope. It will remain thus for ever, the Clóenfherta, that is the Crooked Mound of Tara.'[13] True or false, the Crooked Mound can be seen to this day sloping down into the glen at the western side of the hill.

Following his false judgement, Lugaid's power as a ruler was considerably weakened and after a time he gave up the kingship peacefully in favour of Cormac. However, it is noted in the legends that Cormac had to live at Kells until the sovereignty goddess, Maeve, who is portrayed as the jealous wife of his father, Art, gave her consent for him to reign in Tara.

Of that reign the *Dindshenchas* states: 'It was well with Ireland in his time. The rivers teamed with fish, the woods with mast, the plains with honey on account of the justice of his rule. Deer were so plentiful that there was no need to hunt them. And Cormac built the noblest building that ever was raised at Tara.'[14]

In addition to the 'Psalter of Tara', which is no longer in existence, the *Annals of the Four Masters* credits Cormac Mac Airt with compiling the Brehon laws of Ireland and with authorship of

*Design for the seal of Meath County Council.*

*Cormac is also associated with what is now called St Patrick's Well. The* Dindshenchas *says it was first known as 'Caprac Cormac', while on the western slope of the hill of Tara, over beside the Well of the Calf in the little field known as 'Fodeen', there was a mound named Cormac's Kitchen which, sadly, is no longer visible.*

a very early tract called 'Teagasc na Ríogh' or the 'Instruction of the Kings', contained in the *Book of Ballymote*, which has been compared to the 'Proverbs of Solomon'. It is also said that he restored Tara so that it was grander than ever before in terms of houses, fences and buildings. Many of the earthworks visible at Tara today are vestiges of buildings attributed to him. Archaeologists agree that mounds such as the King's Seat or Cormac's House do indeed date from the early centuries after Christ, roughly the period when Cormac Mac Airt is said to have reigned.

As king Cormac Mac Airt was famed for the prosperity of the land and the justness of his judgements; as warrior he protected the kingdom against attacks from both the west and the north. Twice driven out of Tara by the Ulaid or Ulstermen, he fought back both times to regain the seat of power. He is also credited with having in his service an heroic warrior band called the Fianna, whose exploits under Fionn Mac Cumhail make some of the best reading from ancient Irish literature *(see Chapter 4, Home of Heroes)*.

Ruler, warrior, sage then, but Cormac was also a practised lover – he stole the heart not only of his wife Eithne, who was daughter of Cathaoir Mór, the king of Leinster, but also of the bondsmaid, Cernait. For her he built the first mill in Ireland on the stream of

*The Claddy Bridge. Near Bective Abbey on the Boyne, about six km west of Tara, Claddy is thought to correspond with the sacred spot Cleiteach, where Cormac Mac Airt died when a salmon bone stuck in his throat. The two-arch Claddy Bridge is just five feet wide and is reputed to be one of the oldest bridges in Ireland.*

Nith which still flows down the eastern slope of Tara into the river Gowra from the well, Neamnach.

During an attack on his palace at Tara, one of Cormac's eyes was knocked out. As the king had to be without blemish, Cormac had to give up the throne. He withdrew into retirement at the Hill of Skryne. His final days are said to have been spent in quiet contemplation, and it is during this time that he is supposed to have composed 'Teagasc na Ríogh'.

There is a touch of Otherworld mystery surrounding Cormac's death. This is said to have happened on the River Boyne near Bective, when a salmon bone stuck in his throat. An attempt to float his body to Newgrange for burial failed. According to the Christian chroniclers, this was due to the fact that he had secretly become a believer in their god before his death and wished to be buried in Ros na Ríogh near Slane.

One of the most beautiful epitaphs concerning Cormac states: 'The great sigh which a cow gives when she lies down on the grass of Meath is for the happy days when Cormac the great king reigned at Tara.'

*Stone head discovered at Corravilla, Co Cavan. Dating from the second or third century BC, it was most likely the head of a pagan god king.*

1 Gwynn, Edward, *The Metrical Dindshenchas*, Todd Lecture Series, Royal Irish Academy, Dublin, Temair III, p. 15.

2 Byrne, Francis, *Irish Kings and High-Kings*, p. 23.

3 ibid., p. 60.

4 Rolleston, T W, *Celtic Myths and Legends*, p. 169.

5 ibid.

6 Macalister, R.A.S., 'The Roll of Kings', Irish Texts Society, Vol. XLIV, part V, p. 327.

7 Petrie, George, *On the History and Antiquities of Tara Hill*, p. 34.

8 'Roll of Kings', *Lebor Gabála*, trans. R.A.S. Macalister, part v, par 597.

9 O hOgain, Dr Daithí, *Myth, Legend and Romance, An Encyclopedia of the Irish Folk Tradition*, BCA, London 1991, p. 116.

10 ibid.

11 op. cit., Gwynn, Temair IV, p. 25.

12 Dillon, Myles, *Cycles of the Kings*, p. 25.

13 ibid.

14 ibid.

*Rath Lóegaire – see page 93 below*

# CHAPTER 7

# RISE OF THE UÍ NÉILL

*'The progeny of the smooth king of a forest of javelins*
*Of Oengus Tuirmech of Temair*
*Temair and Ireland of knowledge*
*A troop of generations divided it*
*Men with the clear descendance of the Gaedil*
*The seed of Eremón son of Míl.'*

( 'Roll of Kings')[1]

Claiming descent from Eremón, son of Míl, and taking their name from Niall
Naoi-Ghiallach or Niall of the Nine Hostages, the Uí Néill above all others are wedded
to the royal Hill of Tara. While little is known of their origins, what can be called the
history of Tara's kingship – as distinct from its mythology – begins and ends with this
powerful sept who dominated Ireland from approximately AD400 to 1022.

The best explanation for the Uí Néill rise to power is that given by Gearóid Mac
Niocaill in his book, *Ireland before the Vikings*, when he says: 'It is eminently possible
that the establishment of the Uí Néill in Tara was in some sense a thrust eastward by
the Connachta – an attempt by a younger member of the ruling dynasty to acquire
sword land for himself.'[2] The sept's origins in Connacht pre-date true history. There is
even doubt as to whether Niall of the Nine Hostages himself ever really existed.

But if he did, the time assigned to him is the first half of the fifth century. Real or
imaginary, Niall has been credited with the origin of almost every branch of the
Uí Néill dynasty.

There is no way of knowing when the Uí Néill ancestors first took the title 'King of Tara'. As for Niall of the Nine Hostages himself, some historians say his reign began at the end of the fourth century and lasted until he was killed abroad in AD427. This date works in nicely with the traditional story that his son Lóegaire was king of Tara when St Patrick arrived in AD432. In relation to Tara, it is sufficient to say that he is credited with the origin of the Uí Néill dynasty. This meant the chroniclers had to bestow on him enormous fertility. He had fourteen sons and among them were Eoghan, after whom Tyrone (Tír Eoghan, or the land of Eoghan) is named, Conaill Gulban, who gave his name to Tír Conaill (again, the land of Conaill) or Donegal. These two joined forces with a third son, Enda, to destroy the sacred site of the Ulaid or Ulstermen, Emain Macha in Co Armagh. Along with a fourth son, Aonghus, they were also founding fathers of the northern Uí Néill. The southern Uí Néill claimed descent principally from two more sons of Niall – Conall Err Breg, from whom came the Clann Cholmáin of Uisneach in Co Westmeath, and Lóegaire, mentioned above. Over the next six hundred years these two groups of the Uí Néill provided almost an equal number of kings of Tara.

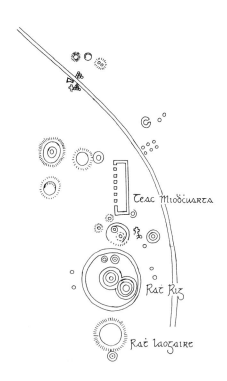

*A plan of the main earthworks on the Hill of Tara by map surveyor John O'Donovan, who worked for the Ordinance Survey in the 1830s. It is now thought that this is a correct placing of the sites, particularly in relation to Cormac's House and the Forradh or King's Seat.*

Niall is listed as the 114th King of Tara in the 'Roll of Kings' and is the fifteenth king after Conn of the Hundred Battles. He was son to Eochaid Mugmedon, who made raids into Britain and brought back hostages. Among them was Cairenn, whom Eochaid took as his second wife and who was to be Niall's mother. This created problems regarding succession to the throne since his father already had four sons with his wife Mongfind. It also made for unhappy relations between Mongfind and Cairenn. Mongfind forced her to draw water right up to the full term of her pregnancy.

Cairenn's birth pangs began one day as she went to the well and thus Niall was born on the green at Tara. For fear of Mongfind no one would take up the baby until the poet Torna came along, foresaw that this child would be king and took it away to a safe place.

Not until Niall was of age did he return to Tara. And when he did, he found that his father had died, his mother was still being treated as a slave and Mongfind's brother, Crimthann, had become king. Niall then had to prove his claim to royalty in a series of tests initiated by the druids to determine which one of Eochaid's five sons should be next in line for the throne. In the first challenge, a forge was set on fire with all five contenders inside. Each emerged with an implement, but because Niall brought out the anvil, he was proclaimed the winner.

The second test had to do with the Celtic idea of sovereignty. All five would-be kings were sent to the woods for water. Each in turn went to a well guarded by a horrible-looking hag who demanded a kiss in return for water. None of the other four would oblige and thus came back to Tara empty-handed.

Niall, however, recognising her as a goddess in disguise, kissed her, lay with her and then saw her transform into a beautiful young woman who told him she was Sovereignty and prophesied that he and his race would be kings of Ireland forever. When he returned to Tara with water he demanded seniority over his four brothers. This was done and Niall was declared the rightful heir. However, Mongfind still wanted one of her sons to be king and tried to poison Niall. She did not succeed and when Crimthann died, Niall took the title. The 'Roll of Kings' notes, 'Niall Naoi-giallach took the kingship of Ireland and of the Western World for the space of twenty-seven years.'[3]

Niall is credited with an attack on Roman Britain and may even have ventured on to the Continent. One tradition has it that he met his death along the banks of the River Loire near Boulogne at the hands of one of his own men. It is from these raids at home and abroad that part of his name derives. He took hostages from each conquered area; the nine represented one from the five provinces of Ireland and four from Britain – one of which was said to have been St Patrick, who was sold into slavery on Slieve Mish in Co Antrim.

When Niall died, he was buried by his sons on a hill some sixteen kilometres north-west of Tara beyond Navan at Faughan. From that time until the surrender of Malachy II to Brian Boru at the foot of Tara in 1002, some six hundred years later, over forty descendants of Niall are said to have held the title 'King of Tara'.

Naill's son Lóegaire became the 116th king of Tara at some time between AD430 and AD470. And it is he who legend claims was the powerful pagan king at Tara when St Patrick appeared to do battle (see Chapter 2, The Sacred Hill).

*See page 90 above: the Rath of Lóegaire on the southern slope of Tara. Much of its bank and ditch is now ploughed into the field, but the remains can still be detected from the air. In the main Lóegaire's story concerns the battles of his fifth-century reign against the Leinstermen, the Laigin. Lóegaire died trying to impose the bóraimhe or Tara tax on the Laigin, and is said to be buried in this rath according to his wish – standing sword in hand facing the sacred burial place of the Leinstermen at Mullaghmast, Co Kildare.*

Above: *Contemporary representation of Gaelic warriors. (Illustration by Ann Fallon.)*

Below: *This page from the fourteenth-century Yellow Book of Lecan contains a version of the conflict between Diarmaid Mac Fergus Cerbaill and St Ruadán. The argument led to the saint's cursing of the hill which, according to legend, resulted in its abandonment as a royal seat in the sixth century.*

However, Lóegaire's reign involved not only spiritual combat with Christianity but also renewed warfare with the Laigin or Leinstermen over the *bóraimhe* tribute. Having inflicted a resounding defeat on the Laigin in AD453, Lóegaire was then defeated and captured in the battle of Athdara. In return for his release he is supposed to have sworn 'by the sun and moon, water and air, day and night, sea and land' never again to demand the *bóraimhe*. He reneged on that promise and after many more battles lost his life in one final effort to impose it.

Lóegaire was buried at Tara in his own rath, standing with sword in hand facing the sacred burial place of the Leinstermen in Mullaghmast, Co Kildare. His mound is still plainly visible on the south slope of Tara – a memorial to the fierce hatred that burned between the descendants of Niall and the kings of Leinster.

During a hundred-year period from the death of Lóegaire, six kings of the Uí Néill continued the battle to consolidate their power over Leinster and Ulster. The stories of these kings also include many references to a growing conflict between them and the Christian church. It is the outcome of this conflict which is blamed for the abandonment of Tara as a dwelling place of kings. One has the suspicion that much of what is said about this group of kings was fabricated by the Uí Néill themselves for a very definite reason – to explain to people of the ninth and tenth centuries why this sacred home of god kings like Lugh or priest kings like Cormac Mac Airt, which they had so graphically portrayed in their version of the legends, was then but a deserted, grassed-over hill – just as it is today.

For example, when Lóegaire's son Lugaidh came to power he is said to have been promised great blessings if he would become Christian. He refused and, according to the fourteenth-century *Book of Lecan*, was cursed along with 'all the kings and queens that might live at Tara from that time on'.[4]

Lughaidh held the title for twenty-six years. Following his death in a battle against the Laigin in AD510, a decade of in-fighting among the Uí Néill prevented any one of them taking firm hold on the kingship. Finally Muircheartach Mac Earca, a great-grandson of Niall and one of the northern Uí Néill, dominated around AD520 and consolidated his position with defeats of the Laigin at Kineagh in north Kildare and Asigh on the Boyne in AD528 (close to where Cormac Mac Airt was supposed to have died some 260 years earlier).

Muircheartach also found it difficult to accept the new religion. Having been baptised by Erc, the Bishop of Slane, he still held to the pagan belief that he could take a concubine. Sheen or Sín had lost her family at the hands of the Uí Néill and is said to have brought about Muircheartach's death in revenge. She threw herself in the king's path to gain his attention. Once established as his concubine at Cletty on the Boyne Sín had Muircheartach's wife thrown out. In a final act of vengeance she burned the house over his head; he jumped into a vat of wine to escape the flames and drowned.

Sheen is represented as half-pagan, half-Christian, and Muircheartach's union with her appears to be symbolic of a new phase in the kingship of Tara: one in which the usurping Uí Néill had to battle resentment from the old tribes around Tara – of which Sin was a member – and in which they were caught in a middle ground between the Otherworld powers of the old religion and the heavenly powers of the new.

As Ireland entered the sixth century a new relationship between temporal and spiritual power must have been taking hold. The traditional priest kings of Tara – from whom the Uí Néill claimed descent – had combined in their one person both Otherworld and earthly power. These kings ruled, but they also mediated with the gods on behalf of their people and were closely linked with the druids in the exercise of religious power. Now, in an ever more Christianised Ireland, a new group composed of bishops, abbots and saints claimed exclusive control over matters spiritual. From this time onwards the kingship became increasingly confined to temporal affairs.

According to historian George Petrie, Muircheartach may have been the first king of Tara to become a Christian. Other commentators say, however, that he may have been the invention of a didactic monk intent on illustrating the new spiritual battle that was underway. Whatever the reality, that battle came to a head some thirty years after the time assigned to Muircheartach during the reign of one Diarmaid Mac Fergus Cerbaill.

Diarmaid was a great-grandson of Niall of the Nine Hostages and of the midland southern Uí Néill. He is the first king of Tara to be generally accepted by historians as historical. His kingship began in AD554 after he brought about the death of Muircheartach's successor, Túathal Maolgharbh, who was also a great-grandson to Niall. During a period of hiding in the midlands,

The *Lebor Gabála's* account of Sín's killing of the king:

*'I am fearful of the woman,*
*round whom many storms shall move,*
*for the man who shall be burned in fire*
*on the side of Cletty wine shall drown.*
*Sín is the woman who kills thee,*
*O, son of Erca, as I see;*
*many shall be her names here,*
*she will put one astray.*
*Not loving the woman*
*whose name is Sín,*
*for whose sake fire shall burn the king;*
*in the house of Cletty wine shall drown him.'*[5]

*Grianán of Aileach. The stone fort overlooking Lough Foyle and Lough Swilly on the Donegal/Derry border dates back to the early Christian era. It served as a royal seat for the northern Uí Néill, who provided many kings of Tara between the fifth and twelfth centuries.*

Historic kings of Tara, c.AD400 to 565. (Names in bold are mentioned in the text.)

**Niall Naoi-Ghiallach (Niall of the Nine Hostages)** *27 years*
Nathi *30 years*
**Lóegaire Mac Néill (died c.463)**
Ailill Molt *(died c.482)*
**Lugaidh (died c.507)**
**Muircheartach Mac Earca (died c.536)**
**Tuathal Maolgharbh (died c.544)**
**Diarmaid Mac Fergus Cerbaill (died c. 565)**

forced on him by Túathal, Diarmaid is supposed to have helped St Ciaran in the building of his monastery at Clonmacnoise. The saint then prophesied that Diarmaid would soon be king of Tara. Wishing to hurry matters along, Diarmaid arranged to have Túathal assassinated.

Diarmaid held his inaugural feast at Tara in AD558 – even though this pagan practice was frowned on by the bishops – four years after he had begun what was to be a disastrous reign. Born a pagan, Diarmaid was apparently converted to Christianity but did not fully give up the old religion. In addition to seeking advice from clerics he is also said to have consulted with his own druid. He even had a phalanx of druids at the head of his troops in battle. But this did not prevent him suffering a crushing defeat in AD560 at the hands of two northern Uí Néill sons of Muircheartach Mac Earca at the battle of Cuil Dreimne near Ben Bulben in Co Sligo. Prior to this battle, Diarmaid antagonised the powerful northern Uí Néill churchman, St Columcille, by awarding judgment against him in a dispute with St Finian, founder of Clonard monastery. In deciding who should own the copy of a book that belonged to St Finian and which had been made without permission, he decided 'to every cow her calf and to every book its copy'.

Relations between the king and Columcille were further aggravated when Diarmaid failed to respect the claim to immunity from prosecution by a criminal who had killed a guest at the Feast of Tara and then taken refuge with the saint. Whether in revenge for this or not, Columcille, who was himself part of the royal line of the northern Uí Néill, became deeply involved in organising the forces of the north-west which were to defeat Diarmaid at Ben Bulben.

Another dispute over clerical immunity lies at the heart of the story about the cursing of Tara. In this instance one of Diarmaid's tax collectors demanded that the new oak doorway of a man's house be broken down. The owner, Aedh Guaire, killed the officious tax man and the king sought to punish what he saw as the murder of his representative. Aedh Guaire sought sanctuary at the house of another saint, Ruadhán. Again Diarmaid ignored this, exercised his temporal authority and arrested the culprit.

Diarmaid brought Aedh Guaire to Tara for execution, and was followed there by the saint, who with his holy friends camped by the side of the hill and went on hunger strike against the king. The king, protesting the justice of his stand, fasted against the priests and the stand-off lasted for a year. When Diarmaid would not give in, Ruadhán rang his sacred bells and pronounced the fateful words 'Desolate be Tara for ever and ever'. As Elizabeth Hickey says in her *Legend of Tara*, 'One's sympathies ... go out to the obstinate and bewildered king in the unequal contest that ended so unhappily.'[6]

*The Hill of Slane was named after Sláine, one of the legendary kings of the Fir Bolg. It is a prominence of 500 ft (just 15 ft lower than Tara) overlooking the Boyne. St Patrick is said to have lit the first pascal fire in Ireland upon this site, which brought him into conflict with King Lóegaire of Tara. St Erc founded the first monastery here early in the Christian period. The present ruins date back to the sixteenth century, to Sir Christoper Flemying's foundation of a small Franciscan friary.*

### THE ABANDONMENT OF TARA:

**'When the morning came the king, nobles, and prelates arose, and after the clergymen had don with their prayers, they besaught the king againe to enlarge unto them Hugh Gwairye, which he did as absolutely refuse as hee did before; and then Roadanus and a bushop that was with him tooke their bells that they had, which they rung hardly and cursed the king and place, and prayed God that noe king or queen ever after would or could dwell in Tarach, and that it should be wast for ever, without court or pallace, as it fell out accordingly. King Dermot himself nor his sucessors kings of Ireland could never dwell in Tarach, since the time of that curse, but every one of the kings chose himselfe such a place as in his one discression he thought fittest, and most convenient for him to dwell.'[7]**

The abandonment of Tara may not have been quite so sudden as is indicated in the story of Diarmaid and Ruadhán. In fact this process may have taken place over a period of many years as a result of practical considerations such as defence and the distance

An ancient poem had this succinct requiem for royal Tara:

*'From the reign of Diarmait,
Son of Fergus, son of Conall
From the judgement of Ruadhán on his house
There was no king at Tara.'[8]*

*Psalter attributed to Cormac Mac Airt.*

of Tara from the home base of the northern Uí Néill and from the lake country of the midlands. But it is a fact that from the end of the sixth century to 1022, through the reigns of some thirty-five more kings of the Uí Néill, Tara was no longer the residence of the king of Ireland, though for many years during this time they ruled in its name.

As for Diarmaid himself, he met his end in AD565 while trying to extend his power north-east into Co Antrim. In the 'Roll of Kings' it is said that his head was carried back to the monastery of Clonmacnoise. Oddly enough, despite his problems with the Church, all must have been forgiven, for some 150 years after his death St Adamnán, biographer of St Columcille, wrote that Diarmaid was 'ordained by God ruler of all Ireland'. That title was still an exaggeration but in the next chapter we look at those who tried to make it a reality during the following centuries.

1 *Lebor Gabála Érenn* or *The Book of the Taking of Ireland*, translation Macalister, part IV, p. 259.

2 Mac Niocaill, Gearoid, *Ireland Before the Vikings*, Gill and Macmillan, Dublin 1972, p. 10.

3 op. cit., *Lebor Gabála*, part V, par 612.

4 *Book of Lecan*, translation, *Mr Petrie on the History and Antiquities of the Hill of Tara*, p. 121-122.

5 Petrie, George, *History and Antiquities of Tara Hill*, p. 120.

6 Hickey, Elizabeth, *The Legend of Tara*, Dundalgan Press, Dundalk 1970, p. 36.

7 *Book of Clonmacnoise*, translation Connell MacGeoghegan, in 1627 and printed in *Mr Petrie on the History and Antiquities of the Hill of Tara*, op. cit., p. 127.

8 Ancient poem from ms in Trinity College Dublin, MS, Trin. Col. H1 17 fol 97 p. 2. Translation, *Mr Petrie on the History and Antiquities of the Hill of Tara*, ibid., p. 125.

# CHAPTER 8

# QUEST FOR HIGH KINGSHIP

*'Though there be over imperial Banba*
*famous kings – high their mirth*
*no kingly authority is binding on them*
*save from the king that possesses Temair.'*

(Tenth-century poem)[1]

From the time that the Uí Néill took over Tara (about AD400), they worked to extend their control over the entire country. They wanted the title 'King of Tara' to be synonymous with that of 'High King of Ireland' and claimed it to be so from AD600. As Francis Byrne has written in *Irish Kings and High-Kings*: 'Whatever the mystique that lay behind the title of king of Tara, and however vague the dominion exercised by its holder, it remains true that from their first appearance in the fifth century the Uí Néill had introduced a dynamism which disrupted the archaic hierarchy of the Five Fifths. Although tribal kingship never entirely disappeared, the new dynastic polity evolved by the Uí Néill relegated it to the position of a primitive survival. And as early as the seventh century the Uí Néill claimed to be kings of all Ireland.'[2]

Despite these claims, between AD628 and the coming to Tara of Brian Boru to take the crown in 1002, only seven of the Uí Néill kings of Tara could be called high kings of Ireland. The authoritative twelfth-century *Annals of Ulster* accord this honour to Domnall Mac Áedo (AD628-642); Loingsech Mac Oengusso (AD695-704); Maelsechnaill Mac Maele Ruanaid (Malachy I) (AD846-862); Niall Glundub Mac Aeda (AD916-919); Congalach Cnogba Mac Maelmithig (AD944-956); Domnall Ua Néill (AD956-980); Maelsechnaill Mac Domhnaill (Malachy II) (AD980-1002, when he surrendered to Brian Boru, and 1014-1022, when he took up the kingship again after Boru's death).

Above: *13-cm brooch dated from the crannóg at Lagore near Dunshaughlin, some six km south of Tara. Lagore was a royal seat of the Síl nÁedo Sláine of the southern Uí Néill, who came from the area around the Hill and provided four kings of Tara.*

Below: *Lough Owel, the lake in Co Westmeath around which the southern Uí Néill lived. Malachy I, King of Tara, drowned the Viking leader Turges here in AD846.*

After the abandonment of Tara, the area appears to have gradually come under the control of a son of Diarmaid's, Áed Sláine, while Diarmaid's other son, Colman, became dominant in the midlands.

Áed Sláine concentrated on the area stretching from Tara to the ancient site at Newgrange. From that time on the land around Tara fell under the control of a people known as Síl nÁedo Sláine. They were to provide only four kings of Tara, including Áed himself, and there are indications that for a long time this tribe resisted Christianity and clung to the old ways. For instance in an eighth-century poem Áed is referred to as 'Áed Sláine of the Sid' or Otherworld. His descendants are said to have lived at the *crannóg* near Dunshaughlin just eight kilometres south of Tara.

The Síl nÁedo Sláine effectively turned their back on the title. In contrast to the northern Uí Néill and indeed to their closer cousins in the southern Uí Néill, the Clann Cholmáin of Uisneach, the sons of Áed Sláine and their sons after them seemed more intent on carving up the rich plains of Meath and establishing small kingdoms for their own branches of the clan, than on seeking to wield the power that the title 'King of Tara' and 'High King of Ireland' could bring. Only one of the Síl nÁedo Sláine – Congalach Cnogba – ever had the title 'High King of Ireland' applied to him.

After Diarmaid's death in AD565, perhaps due to the influence of St Columcille who was from the northern Uí Néill, the title 'King of Tara' was held by members of the Cenel nEoghain of Tyrone and Cenel Conaill of Donegal for the next thirty-three years. Seven from those north-west clans controlled the kingship during that time. Not until AD598 had Áed Sláine, Diarmaid's son, gained sufficient power in his own kingdom of Meath to vie for the title. He entered joint kingship with Colman Rimid of Tyrone (an Uí Néill) for a period of five years until both met violent deaths in the year AD604.

The title then passed to the northern Uí Néill for some fourteen years during which Baetan quietly held it while a young relative, Áed, son of Ainmire, built up his strength and reputation. It was he who represented the high kingship at an important meeting of church and political leaders called at Druim Ceit, Derry, in AD575 to decide on the future role of the *file*, or poets, in relation to the emerging high kingship and also to decide on Tara's control over the peoples of east Ulster and their colonies in Scotland. Áed took over the kingship of Tara in AD586 and had a rather peaceful reign

*Irish chieftain feasting.*

until one of his sons brought him into conflict with the king of
Laigin, Bran Dub. During a visit to Leinster, this wayward son had
demanded the right to sleep with Bran Dub's wife and as a result
was slain by the king. In revenge, Áed advanced south with a
powerful force but after initial success his way was blocked in the
Wicklow hills and he was killed in a battle at Donard in Co
Wicklow in AD598.

It was Áed's son, Domhnall, who was the first king of Tara to be
called 'High King of Ireland' by the *Annals of Ulster*. During his
reign, which lasted from AD628 to AD642, he not only realised his
father's desire to defeat the Laigin but also Diarmaid Mac
Cerbaill's ambition of extending the high king's power into Co
Antrim. This achievement came about in AD637 at the battle of
Moire, Co Down.

The Abbot of Iona, St Adamnán, records in his biography of
Columcille how at the time of Domhnall's birth the saint blessed
him and prophesied that he would outlive all his brothers, be a
famous king and die peacefully in his bed. Domhnall appears to
have done all of these things.

It was fifty years after Domhnall's death before the Ulster
annals give the title 'King of Ireland' to another of Tara's kings –
Loingsech Mac Oengusso, also from the northern Uí Néill of
Donegal. He was a contemporary of, and related to, St Adamnán.
While Adamnán's writings were mostly concerned with the great
Irish monastic settlement in Scotland and with the achievements of
Columcille, he also made references to secular politics. Thus, for
the first time in the long story of Tara, a king bearing its name was
being written about during the years of his reign. Adamnán
referred to Loingsech Mac Oengusso as 'High King of Ireland' in

*High-altitude picture showing Tara (centre of photo c.40mm up from bottom). The River Boyne is at the top left corner, just off this image. Fish from the Boyne were a right of the king of Tara.*

his *Life of Columcille*. Loingsech died trying to assert that right against the men of Connacht at the battle of Corann in south Sligo on 12 July AD704.

Yet again a member of the Donegal Uí Néill, Congal, took the Tara kingship after Loingsech and held it until AD710. Loingsech's own son Flatbertach later reigned from AD728 to AD734 before entering a monastery. He was the last of the Donegal-based Uí Néill to be called 'King of Tara'. From that time on all the Tara kings from the northern Uí Néill came from the Cenel nEoghain of Derry and Tyrone.

Although not accorded the title 'High King of Ireland', Áed Allen acted as though he was. This powerful member of the northern Uí Néill ruled for ten years from AD734 until AD743. He had such a strong reputation as a warrior among his own people, the Cenel nEoghain, that there was no opposition to his taking over the kingship. He immediately set about demonstrating his strength in east Ulster by defeating the Ulaid in AD735 at the legendary battleground of Muirtheimne in Co Down.

Áed Allen also focused his attention further south in Munster. He met and parlayed in AD737 with the king of Cashel, Cathal Finnguine, at the monastery of Terryglass, north Tipperary (where the *Book of Leinster* and the *Dindshenchas Érenn* were later written down). There is no record of what was decided but it is significant that Cathal supported neither Áed Allen nor the Leinstermen in the battle of Ata Senaig in Kildare later that year. Though wounded himself, Áed Allen killed the Leinster king at this battle in single combat.

Áed defeated the Leinstermen. However, he must not have been giving sufficient attention to enemies in his own dynasty, for in AD743 the Clann Cholmáin king of Meath, Domhnall, went on the attack. His forces met those of the High King and defeated them at Kells where Áed died in the battle.

One indication of the degree to which religion and politics were still united at this time is the fact that Domhnall held both the high kingship of Tara and the Abbacy of the Meath monastery at Clonard until his death in AD763. His son Donnchadh, king of Uisneach, was soon the dominant figure within the southern Uí Néill dynasty. Even before he became king of Tara, Donnchadh was acting like high king. In an effort to draw attention to his claim to kingship, he caused a disturbance at the royal fair of Tailten near Kells, then he attacked Leinster, Munster and Tyrone in turn.

Donnchadh's reign officially began in AD770 and he maintained a strong grip on the title for the next twenty-five years. However, as time went by his enemies grew stronger. While Donnchadh led a thrust into Munster, Áed Oirdnide (meaning 'ordained') of the northern Uí Néill took the opportunity to bring an army down into Meath territory, and by AD797 he was strong enough to strike at Donnchadh, six kilometres south-west of Tara at Drumree and to kill him. The northern Uí Néill were back in power for the next twenty-three years.

Oirdnide, the suffix to Áed's name, would suggest that he was

Chronological list of historic kings of Tara, AD566 to 819. (Names in bold are mentioned in the text.)

*Domhall and Fergus (died 566)*
*Báetan and Eochaid (died 572)*
*Ainmire (died 569)*
*Báetán (died 586)*
*Áed Mac Ainmirech (died 598)*
*Colman Rimid and Áed Sláine (died 604)*
*Áed Allan Uairidnach (died 612)*
*Máel-Coba (died 614)*
*Suibne Mend (died 628)*
***Domhnall Mac Áeda (died 642)***
*Cellach (died 658) and Conall Cael (died 654)*
*Bláthmac and Diarmaid (died 665)*
*Sechnasach (died 671)*
*Cenn Fáelad (died 674)*
*Finnachta Fledach (died 710)*
***Loingsech Mac Oengusso (died 704)***
***Congal Cind Magair (died 710)***
*Fergal (died 772)*
***Fogartach (died 770)***
*Cinaed (died 728)*
*Flaitbertach (died 734)*
***Áed Allan (died 743)***
***Domhnall Mac Murchada (died 763)***
*Níall Fossach (died 770)*
***Donnchadh Mac Domhnall (died 797)***
***Áed Oirnide (died 819)***

**Description of colour pictures, pages I-VIII:**

I: Ancient carved stone, formerly known as Adamnán's Cross. The figure is thought to be the Celtic god Cernunnos, the horned one, seated in a Buddha position.

II-III: (Main picture): Mounds from the ground. (Inset): Oisín and Diorraing on their way to royal Tara. In the legends, a great warrior band known as the Fianna were sworn to the service of the king of Tara. Most of their stories centre on the time of King Cormac Mac Airt and the heroic deeds of Oisín's father, Fionn Mac Cumhail. This evocative scene from the hand of Jim Fitzpatrick shows Oisín and his companion with a snowcapped Tara in the background. They were the emissaries sent to Tara seeking permission to have King Cormac's daughter Gráinne marry their leader, Fionn. In the end the wilful Gráinne changed her mind and eloped from Tara with another member of the Fianna, Oisín's closest friend, Diarmaid.

IV-V: (Top): This window in St. Patrick's Church depicts the descent of the Holy Ghost, and was created by artist Evie Hone in 1936. Evie was a great lover of Tara and often drove there from Leixlip, in a pony and trap, with her sister Mrs. Nancy Connell, who was Master of the Meath Hunt from 1931 to 1952. (Centre): The Patent of Lord Tara, kept by the Briscoe family at Assigh on the Boyne. (Bottom): Cover of Macalister's book; New York, 1931. (Main picture): One of Ireland's most priceless treasures, the eight-century silver-gilt 'Tara Brooch', found 50 km away at Bettystown in 1850.

VI-VII: (Main picture): Aerial view of the ring fort, Dun Áilinne. (Top): 25-foot modern monument in corten steel and architectural bronze, created by Ronan Halpin. (Bottom): To enhance their appeal with Tara's romantic associations, many modern-day commercial products are named after the famous hill. When a company was formed to create quality Irish bone china in 1953 it was given the name 'Royal Tara', even though it was based on the other side of Ireland. Their display of distinctive Celtic designs can be seen at Tara Hall in Galway.

VIII: St. Patrick's Church at Tara.

one of the few high kings 'ordained' to his royal position by the bishops, who during his time stood on an almost equal footing with the Irish kings. But there is no other documentary proof of the fact. This blessing on his reign, if such it was, did not keep Áed Oirdnide from conflict with the Church, however. During one of his raids into Leinster he violated the sanctuary of the monastery at Tallaght by following one of his enemies there and slaying him. In punishment the community is said to have boycotted his feast at the Fair of Tailten so effectively that 'neither horse not chariot arrived there'.

At this time Tailten had been approved by the Church as a replacement for Tara as the site of royal inaugurations of the Uí Néill. A curse on any event there would have been a severe blow to Áed's prestige. However, he did keep Leinster and Munster at bay and was strong enough not to allow the Vikings, who first arrived in Ireland during his reign, more than a small foothold on the east coast. His death in AD819 is recorded on the margin of an Irish manuscript of Bede's history as '*Aed rex Hiberniae moritur*'. So, although the *Annals of Ulster* never recognised him as such, Áed Oirdnide did earn the exalted title 'King of Ireland' from at least one scribe.

But we now near the time when that term 'High King of Ireland' became more of a reality. During the first half of the ninth century a new era for the high kingship of Tara opened – a two-hundred year-period in which the threats to its very existence from both at home and abroad increased enormously.

1 Gwynn, Edward, *The Metrical Dindshenchas*, Todd Lecture Series, RIA, Dublin 1903, Temair, V, p. 45.
2 Byrne, Francis J., *Irish Kings and High Kings*, p. 254.

Ancient carved stone, formerly known as Adamnán's Cross.

**The banks and ditches of the royal seat (main picture).**

**Oisín and Diorraing on their way to Tara (inset).**

TARA: A PAGAN SANCTUARY
OF ANCIENT IRELAND

The Tara Brooch (main picture).

Evie Hone window at St. Patrick's Church (top).

Lord Tara's Patent (centre).

Jacket to R.A.S. McAlister's book
on Tara, 1931 (bottom).

Sculpture on the banks of the Boyne (above).

Royal Tara tea service (below).

Dún Ailinne, Kildare – the royal seat in Leinster (left).

St. Patrick's Church, now
the Tara Interpretive Centre.

# CHAPTER 9

# THE MUNSTER AND VIKING CHALLENGE

*'Thirteen years in all*
*was submission paid to Niall Caille;*
*from the vigorous Callann which drowned him*
*he found loss of a life of lofty battle*
*Mael-Sechlainn, sixteen years,*
*son of Mael-Ruanaid of the royal roads,*
*the king of prosperity died in noble Mide*
*prince of truth and of the white hosts.'*

('Roll of Kings')[1]

During the reign of Áed Oirdnide the Vikings had begun making their first tentative raids into Ireland along the east coast. Almost simultaneously, the Munster kings of Cashel began seeking greater recognition north of the line that traditionally divided Ireland north and south, the Eiscir Riada. These two threats came to a head after Áed Oirdnide's son Niall Caille became King of Tara in AD833. During the next thirteen years – until his death in AD846 – Niall faced challenges to his kingship from the Viking leader Turges, and the King of Cashel, Feidhlimidh Mac Criomhthain, who were each seeking to proclaim themselves High King of Ireland. Tara may no longer have been the official home of Ireland's kings, but it and the surrounding country were still the setting for a good deal of the drama in those turbulent years of change.

At about the time that Niall Caille became the Uí Néill king of Tara, Feidhlimidh Mac Criomhthain fought his way to power as king of Cashel. Next, although he was not a priest, he became Abbot of Cashel. Not satisfied with that, Feidhlimidh went on to seek the title of 'Primate of All Ireland'. His ultimate target was the high kingship, and the Munster annals – in whose compilation he had a hand – actually declare for the year AD838: 'A great Assembly of the men of Ireland in Clonfert and Niall son of Áed, King of Tara, submitted to Feidelmid son of Crimthann, so that Feidlimid became full king of Ireland that day.'[2]

This was a bold boast. To fulfil it the pretender raided north into Meath in AD840 and camped on the Hill of Tara. Then in another daring act aimed at symbolising his union with the Goddess of Sovereignty, Feidhlimidh abducted Niall Caille's wife, Gormlaith, and brought her back to Cashel. The following year, when he was making his way to a feast where he was to proclaim his overlordship of Leinster, Feidhlimidh and his army were met by Niall Caille and routed. Of this victory it was said in satire: 'The crozier of vigil-keeping Feidlimid was left behind in the thorn bushes.'[3] So ended the threat from Munster to the Tara kingship. Feidhlimidh's hostings after this were mostly against monasteries such as Clonmacnoise, which he burned. His death in AD847 came from a mysterious ailment said to have been wished on him by a saint.

In AD845, four years after he defeated Feidhlimidh so soundly, Niall Caille had to meet another brazen challenge to his kingship – this time from Turges of the Vikings. Up to AD830 Viking activity in Ireland had been confined to seasonal raids. But when in that year Turges, brother to the Danish king Hardicanute, sailed up the Boyne he was intent on conquering a new land of which he intended to be king. He is credited with having built a substantial fort near Tara. His plundering focused on monasteries and passage-grave sites, wherever treasure was still to be found and much of Leinster was subdued by the most violent acts imaginable. It was at the mouth of the Liffey that Turges established his permanent base. This creation of a town, where before there were only temporary quarters, signalled the start of a process through which the idea of Tara as the capital of Ireland would slip away to the new coastal centre of Dublin.

Niall Caille had been king of Tara for twelve years before he confronted Turges. The Viking leader had pushed inland to conquer territory in Westmeath, Roscommon and Sligo. When their forces finally met on the Sligo border in the year AD845, three hundred men were killed. Niall was victorious but Turges managed to slip through his fingers. Before Niall Caille could corner Turges once more, he himself drowned while saving a friend from a swollen river in Callann in Co Sligo. It was then that Turges proclaimed himself 'High King of Ireland'.

That proved to be a fatal mistake because in AD846 Niall Caille's successor in the Tara kingship, Maelsechlainn Mac Mael Ruanaid or Malachy I of the southern Uí Néill, captured Turges at his camp on Lough Lene near Castlepollard in Co Westmeath, brought him in chains to his own base at Lough Owel, fifty kilometres west of Tara, and drowned him there.

Apparently intent on paying more attention to the symbol of Irish kingship, Malachy then turned toward Tara and in AD848 won a battle there against the Vikings. Afterwards he settled matters with the local Síl nÁedo Sláine, who were siding with the Vikings, by drowning their king Cinaed Mac Conaing of Knowth in 'a filthy stream' at Drumree as an example to others. The king of Lagore, Tigernach, dealt another blow to the Vikings just south of Tara. They were similarly beaten in Kildare and also near the seat of Munster kingship at Cashel. It appears that after that the Vikings concentrated on settling at Limerick while the Norse were to take over their base-building efforts at Dublin.

Following his victory over the Vikings Malachy I turned his attention south to Munster. Up to this point in Irish history, Ireland had existed as a divided island along the natural border drawn by

*Irish chieftain in full dress.*

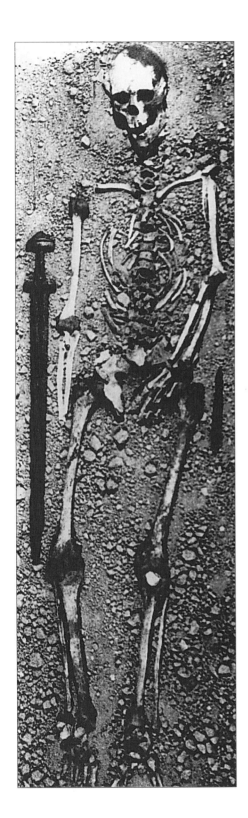

the glaciers across the midlands – the Eiscir Riada. In a very real sense, there were two countries, *Leath Choinn* or Conn's half, named after Conn of the Hundred Battles, and *Leath Mhogha*, Mug Nuadhat's half *(see Chapter 6, Priest Kings and Ancestors)*. For centuries the Uí Néill dominated the northern half, the Eoganacht or descendants of Eoghan Mór the southern half. And except for the occasional raid, mostly by the Uí Néill, the division was respected.

This state of affairs changed quickly under Malachy I. During the 850s, having made an ally of a powerful and ambitious Leinster king, Cerball Mac Donngaile, Malachy sent him on an expedition to take hostages from the royal seat of Munster at Cashel while he marched south in AD858 to defeat the powerful kings of the east and west of the province. The following year at a royal assembly in his home territory of Meath it was accepted that Malachy had extended the high kingship of Tara over the whole of Munster.

What had long been dreamt of by the Uí Néill could now be declared a reality – the island of Ireland was united under one king who reigned under the banner of Tara.

It was a short-lived unity. The northern Uí Néill, realising the power Malachy I had achieved by gaining the submission of the Munster kings, began to fear that his branch of the family – the southern Clann Cholmáin – would take permanent control of the high kingship to the exclusion of the northern sept. Thus, no sooner had Malachy achieved what had hitherto been impossible than he had to defend it against his own relatives. He marched to Armagh in AD860 with forces drawn not only from Meath but from the rest of Leinster, from Connacht and even from Munster. There Malachy put down an insurrection led by Áed Mac Néill of Ailech – a victory that confirmed him in his position as High King of Ireland.

Having come closer than any other historic Irish king in achieving what the storytellers had long claimed in mythology, Malachy died quietly at his home on the shores of Lough Ennell, some thirty-two kilometres west of Tara, on 27 November 862. Áed Mac Néill of Ailech, whom Malachy had faced down just two years before, took over immediately. But it must be said that neither he nor those who followed him inherited the title 'High King of Ireland'.

In AD879, Malachy's able son, Flann Sinna, began a forty-seven-year reign which provided stability until AD916.

During that time he re-established his father's claim on Munster by raiding all the way from Kilkenny to Limerick. But he was powerfully opposed by Cormac, king of Cashel, who drove north into Meath in AD907 to defeat Flann at Moylena. When the two forces met in a final test of strength at the battle of Belach Mugna near Carlow the following year, however, the High King prevailed.

In one of the first recorded incidents of Irish mounted combat it is noted that Cormac fell from his horse and was killed during the battle. The defeat that followed brought Eoganacht control in Munster to an end. But it also paved the way for a rise to power of the hitherto subservient Dal Cais from which the greatest threat yet to the Uí Néill dynasty would emerge in the person of Brian Boru.

Before that would happen however, a third element in the power struggle that dominated the tenth century appeared in AD912. Reginald, first of the Norse kings of Dublin, landed unhindered and with a strong following in Waterford. Over the next two seasons he moved north to the growing town of Dublin.

Flann Sinna died in AD916 before he could mount any effective response to the new challenge, and it fell to a strong and much respected representative of the northern Uí Néill, Niall Glundub Mac Aeda, to marshall the Irish defence.

He met the Norse in an indecisive encounter in AD918 and moved on toward Dublin. The Norse stood to fight at Islandbridge and, though the Irish seemed to gain the early advantage, Niall was killed and his forces withdrew.

Like his grandfather Niall Caille before him, this King of Tara lost his life before being able to put down what had now become a full-fledged invasion. Many were to pay the price of this loss of leadership in the years ahead.

It was a son of Flann Sinna, Donnchadh Donn, who succeeded Niall Glundub. Unfortunately he was a weak ruler who afforded the Norse time to consolidate their power base. He did achieve one thing, however, which shows how the power of the high king had been enhanced during previous reigns. He appointed the deft and brave son of Niall Glundub, Muircheartach as *Tánaiste* or second-in-command and assigned him the task of making a circuit of the whole island to ensure the subservience of each kingdom. This Muircheartach did in AD940 with such effectiveness that before the year was out he was able to send Donnchadh Donn important hostages from all the most important ruling families. As is reported in the annals 'it was [Donnchadh] that was at Tara and

Lament for Niall Glundub:
*'Fierce and hard was the Wednesday*
*On which the hosts were strewn under the feet of shields*
*It shall be called till Judgement Day*
*The destructive morning of Ata Cliath*
*On which fell Niall, the noble hero.'*

Opposite: *Viking skeleton and sword discovered in Kilmainham in Dublin.*

Below: *Decorated Viking combs, unearthed in Dublin.*

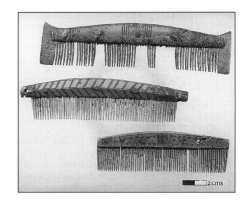

Chronological list of Tara kings from AD819 to 980. (Names in bold are mentioned in the text.)

*Concobor (died 833)*
**Níall Caille (died 846)**
*Máelsechlainn Mac Mael Ruanaid (Malachy I) (died 862)*
**Áed Mac Néill of Ailech (died 879)**
**Flann Sinna (died 916)**
**Níall Glundub Mac Áeda (died 919)**
**Donnchadh Donn (died 944)**
**Congalach Cnogba Mac Maelmithig (died 956)**
**Domhnall Ua Néill (died 980)**

the sovereignty had come to him'. Here 'Tara' is synonymous with the dwelling of the High King, even though he was headquartered at the time at Dun na Sciath on Lough Ennell in Co Westmeath.

Muircheartach was killed in a battle with the Norse leader Blacar in AD943 near Ardee in Co Louth. Donnchad Donn survived him by just one year and Congalach Cnogba Mac Maelmithig of the Tara tribes gave twelve years of good leadership after him.

Just four years elapsed before Congalach avenged Muircheartach by slaying Blacar. But eight years later he was to pay the price when he was ambushed by a combined force of Norse and Leinster men on the banks of the Liffey near Dublin.

His successor Domhnall Ua Néill, although accorded the title 'High King of Ireland' in the Ulster annals, was one of the least warrior-like of the Uí Néill kings. Although he was from the same stock as Muircheartach and Niall Glundub, he seemed more suited to the monastery than the high kingship. During his twelve years as King of Tara, Domhnall made but one attempt to stem the Norse spread inland and that was to attack them near his own midland base at Lough Ennell.

But the time was near when the issue of the high kingship was to be decided during one of the most dramatic periods in Ireland's history. Between AD980 and the first decade of the new millennium two powerful and determined young men, Maelsechnaill Mac Domnaill or Malachy II, king of Tara, and Brian Boru, king of Munster, sought to outwit each other for the greatest prize in Ireland – the Tara kingship and control of the whole island. It was a confrontation that would bring the ancient Hill of Tara once more into the limelight.

1 'Roll of Kings', poem CXXXVI, p. 551.
2 from *Brian Boru: King of Ireland*, Roger Chatterton Newman, Anvil Books, Dublin 1983.
3 ibid.

# CHAPTER 10

# TWO KINGS IN CONFLICT
## Malachy II and Brian Boru

*'Maelsechlainn of spears*
*Tree of Banba, Summit of the Gaedil,*
*the Noble of Rules was wounded*
*before twenty-three years.*

*A boiling of sea, a nimble flood,*
*Brian, a flame over Banba of varied fame,*
*without sadness, without wrong, without judgement,*
*twelve years his good favour.*

*The Danes of Ath Cliath of the Families*
*the warlike pirates of Lochlann,*
*long after they assumed deeds of valour,*
*they slew Brian Boroma.*

*Mael-Sechlainn was dead westward in his house,*
*the proud raper of Uisneach;*
*nine rough years after tuneful Brian*
*he was chief noble over Ireland.'*

('Roll of Kings')[1]

In the accounts of Brian Boru's taking of the high kingship of Ireland on the slopes of Tara in the year 1002, the partisan Munster annals place these words in the mouth of the aristocratic Uí Néill king, Malachy II: 'I surrender you this sceptre and this crown which my ancestors for so many generations bore and which I have now worn for twenty years.'[2] It is a dramatic moment in the genealogies of a kingship which the Uí Néill annalists could trace back for three thousand years.

The title 'King of Tara', which they claimed was symbolically and spiritually synonymous with that of 'King of Ireland', had also, according to the chroniclers, been the special preserve of the Uí Néill from the very dawn of Irish history. But it was only in the ninth century that fact and fiction came together when an Uí Néill king, Malachy I, finally extended his rule over the whole of the island – from Armagh and Ailech in the north to Cashel and Limerick in the south.

But in the very act of extending the kingship beyond their own traditional territory of the midlands, the west and the north, the Uí Néill opened up the possibility of other dynasties claiming the right to the kingship of Tara and of all Ireland. It was only a matter of time before some powerful king from Munster, Connacht, Leinster or indeed from among the newly arrived Vikings would move in that direction.

As Ireland entered the last twenty years of the first millennium of the Christian era, two mighty men saw themselves as the

*The Rock of Cashel, legendary and historic seat of the Munster kings, who reigned in Leith Mhogha (Mugh Nuadhat's half) as distinct from Leith Choinn (Conn's half). These corresponded to the northern and southern parts of ancient Ireland, and were divided by the Gravel Hills of Kings, the Eiscir Riada glacier ridge that runs from Dublin to Galway. Brian Boru was crowned King of Munster at Cashel in AD 976.*

rightful owners of the title: the reigning king, Malachy II, and the newly crowned king of Munster, Brian Boru.

Malachy was of the southern Uí Néill and had been king of Meath prior to succeeding the rather weak King Domhnaill Uí Néill in AD980. The Uí Néill high kingship was in need of strong leadership and Malachy was perfectly suited to provide it. Within months his first challenge came when the Viking king, Olaf, sent his sons, Sitric and Reginald, into Meath with auxiliaries from the Norse-ruled Scottish Isles and the Isle of Man to test the strength of the new king.

They found their answer when Malachy took a stand at the Hill of Tara and defeated them there. Reginald was killed. In the aftermath, the elderly Olaf abdicated and his son Sitric became King of Dublin. He was the child of Olaf's marriage to the extraordinary Kildare princess, Gormfhlaith, who was soon to become wife to both main protagonists of the next thirty years, Malachy and Boru. Thus in the battles that lay ahead Sitric was to be in conflict with his two step-fathers. A unique situation indeed.

Just two years prior to Malachy becoming king of Tara, Brian Boru had been hailed king of Cashel – only the second of his rather obscure people, the Dal Cais, to do so. His elder brother Mathgamain had claimed the Munster crown in AD970 soon after he and Boru took Limerick dramatically from the Danes. Unlike Malachy, who had been groomed for the high kingship of Tara from birth, these two Dalcassian brothers fought their way to Munster power – first in a guerilla campaign, then in direct attack that routed the foreign opposition in their native territory, and finally in a show-down with the ruling Eoghanacht dynasty.

Mathgamain's reign in Cashel was short-lived, however, for the old ruling class, jealous of their four-hundred year tradition, had him assassinated and put one of their own Eoghanacht in the Munster kingship. But their troubles were just beginning because Boru immediately vowed, 'My heart will burst within my breast until I avenge this great king.'[3] Within two years he demolished both Eoghanacht and Viking power in Munster and in AD978 he was the undisputed king of Ireland's southern half, Leit Mogha. It was said of him that, 'he was a hero in place of a hero and he was valour after valour.'[4]

A man acutely conscious of both the importance of symbols and ceremony, Brian Boru was inaugurated king of Munster in Cormac's Chapel on the Rock of Cashel. A crown was placed on

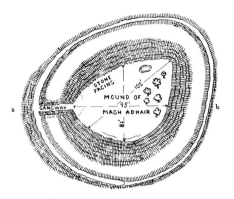

Above: *Plan of the main mound at Magh Adair.*

Opposite: *As the traditional inaugural site of the kings of Thomond, Maigh Adair in Co. Clare was Brian Boru's symbolic home base. For this reason it was raided by king of Tara Maelsechlainn, Malachy II, as he attempted to assert his right to the title High King of Ireland.*

his head, a white staff in his hand and all the nobles from the south of Ireland came and placed their hands between his to signify their obedience. Then words from an ancient Irish text, the *Collectio Canonum Hiberniensis*, were read: 'The justice of the king is the peace of the peoples, care for the weak, the joy of the people, mildness of the abundance of corn, fruitfulness of the trees.'

The High King Malachy, who had been similarly inaugurated himself at Tailten (now Teltown in Co Meath) with the words 'for he whom the living do not glorify with blessing is not a true ruler', was very aware of Brian Boru's growing fame and did not delay in matching and even exceeding it. His initial success on the sacred ground of Tara against the Vikings was immediately followed up by a three-day siege that brought Dublin's surrender. With regal authority he entered the city and declared, 'As many of the Irish nation as lived in servitude and bondage in the territory of the foreigners should pass out without ransom and live freely in their wonted manner in peace and happiness.'[5]

But his own peace and happiness now hinged on his facing up to the new threat to Uí Néill high kingship from what he must have seen as a rebel upstart from the south. Having returned to Meath and strengthened his forces, Malachy marched south in AD983 intent on proving that there was but one king of Ireland.

First he went into Leinster to put down a new alliance between Sitric and the Laigin king, Domhnall, whom he had released from bondage in Dublin just three years previously. Then, without warning, Malachy shifted direction and swept across Munster into the heartland of Brian Boru's power base at Thomond in Co Clare. Half-way between Tulla and Quin in Clare he found and uprooted the royal inauguration tree of Maigh Adhair, which for generations had been to the Dalcassians what the Lia Fáil at Tara was to the Uí Néill. No other act, not even victory in battle could have more clearly declared his message: 'I am king of Ireland.'

It did not take long for Brian to react. Using some of the warfare learned from his contacts with the Limerick Danes he sailed up the Shannon in longboats and, according to the annalists, 'laid Meath waste'. However this appeared to be more a raid than a true invasion. The king of Munster could wait for the right time and place for final confrontation and the realisation of his undoubted plan to become sole ruler of all Ireland.

In 988 he again sailed up the Shannon – this time to defeat and kill the king of Connacht at Lough Ree and thus come one step

closer to that goal. According to the *Annals of Clonmacnoise*, any claimant to the High Kingship from the southern half of Ireland had to control not only his own half, but the provinces of Connacht and Ulster plus Tara.

Meantime Malachy had married Sitric's mother Gormfhlaith, who in some way appears to have become a symbol of Sovereignty. He again moved on Dublin in 989 and having once more subdued the troublesome Vikings, carried away their two most prized heirlooms, the Ring of Tomar and the Sword of Carlus. Malachy was indeed a man who understood symbolism.

In both 992 and 994 the High King's troops met and defeated those of Brian at locations in Meath and Tipperary. But then there were several years of relative calm during which the most obvious threat to either man seemed to come from the Dublin Vikings and their Leinster allies. Under Sitric they broke out into open country and attacked Kildare in 998 – an act which brought about a momentary alliance between Brian and Malachy.

The two kings joined forces for the battle of Gleann Mama, half way between Dublin and Naas. Despite making use of his newly developed mounted cavalry, Sitric was routed and sent back to Dublin with Brian's army in pursuit.

Brian was to benefit most by the victory, for it brought his power right into Malachy's hinterland. No sooner had the battle been won and Dublin sacked than he began acting more like High King than just King of Munster. First of all he married Malachy's

*The death of Brian Boru.*

wife Gormfhlaith, who was taking her third royal husband. Next he made his first direct attack on Malachy himself. In the very first year of the new millenium, according to the *Four Masters*, he sent 'a great hosting with the chiefs and forces of south Connacht, with the men of Leinster and the foreigners of Dublin towards Tara'.[6]

Brian was at all times learning new methods of warfare and this may have been a test of his latest addition – a large contingent of cavalry. It failed; for the annals record that the mounted soldiers, pushed forward ahead of his other troops, were cut down by the Meath battleaxes. Brian withdrew following this first tentative feint toward his final goal. His next move was toward neutralising Malachy's own northern kinsman and in this he was eminently successful. He controlled Munster, there was no doubt about that. He had laid claim to Connacht at Lough Ree what he needed now was Ulster before he could have a true show-down for the High Kingship at Tara itself.

Skirting around to the east of Malachy's home territory Brian brought his increasingly mighty army up along the coast to what we now call Dundalk. There he was met by Aodh son of Domhnall at the head of the Northern Uí Néill. No battle ensued but there must have been plenty of negotiating. The result appears to have been a promise by the men of Ulster not to back Malachy in the final confrontation. It was a daring diplomatic move and it worked.

Early in 1002 the climax came – the new order against the old. Despite the best oratorical eloquence of one Giolla Comhgaill O'Sleibhin, chief bard of Ulster, on behalf of the High King, the Northern Uí Néill steadfastly withheld support from their kinsman. Malachy had to defend the right his people had claimed since the dawn of history with whatever force he could muster on his own from among the southern branch of his family. Fires flickered again on the ancient seat of Ireland's high kings as Malachy and his troops camped at Tara. Brian, having fully regrouped at Dublin after his Dundalk foray, moved north to within a mile of the hill.

There he paused; stopped not, I feel, by the strength of Malachy's army but rather out of respect for the very hill itself and for the man who at that moment still laid claim to its sacred kingship. Instead of sending his invincible force charging up the gentle southern slope, Brian dispatched messengers to ask for the High King's peaceful surrender. Outflanked and outnumbered and bereft of vital support from his northern kinsmen, Malachy had but two choices – fight to certain death for all his followers or abdicate in favour of another great Irishman. With good sense and dignity he chose the latter course.

At that moment, in my opinion, the royal history of Tara came to an end. When Malachy rode out to face Brian at the Dalcassian camp south of the hill, the crown he wore represented all that had gone on before, be it legend of times long past or the reality of the previous six centuries. And when he handed it to a great king who would bear it back to his own southern Christian centre at Cashel before having it placed on his own head, the curtain closed for ever around the pagan royal seat of Tara. It had been stage to the final act in its own legendary kingship. Looking then much as it looks today, its future role in Ireland's history was set – as symbol of a past that will always stir the Irish soul and which has ever since then brought to its ramparts new hostings of people drawn there by the desire to have some part of a long lost Ireland live again.

Malachy, for his own good reasons, did not take part in the Irish victory over the Danes at Clontarf. But upon Brian Boru's death there in 1014 he re-assumed the High Kingship for another twelve years. In a sense he put the finishing touches to the Danish defeat by attacking and burning Dublin in January 1015. Then putting his own Uí Néill stamp on the war, he imposed the age-old Borama tax on the Leinster men. He fulfilled the role of king right up to his quiet death in 1022, and the Tara kingship well a truly died with him. The O'Neills did not elect anyone in his place and the only one who even laid claim to the title was Brian Boru's son Donnchadh. In what was even more of a symbolic gesture than he may have realised, this Munster king willed that at his death the crown and sceptre his father had taken from Malachy should be bequeathed to Pope Alexander II. He died an exile in Rome sometime in 1064 and there is no reason to doubt that his will was fulfilled.

1 'Roll of Kings', edited and translated with notes by R.A.S. Macalister; Irish Text Society Dublin, Educational Company of Ireland, 1938-1956. Vol XLIV, part V, p. 553.
2 *Brian Boru: King of Ireland,* Roger Chatterton Newman, Anvil Books, p. 124.
3 ibid., p. 94.
4 ibid., p. 94.
5 ibid., p. 105.
6 ibid., p. 120.

# CHAPTER 11

# TARA AND THE NORMAN KNIGHTS

*'After fortunate Mael-Sechlainn*
*son of Domnall son of Donnchad*
*the free hill Temair was sundered from all the families*
*till Henry took Ireland.'*

('Roll of Kings')[1]

Tara was no longer a residence of kings, and could no longer boast a king as ruler in its name. It would have been no surprise if Tara had faded from the pages of history after the death of Malachy II. But that has not been the case. For nearly a thousand years – from the time when Donnchadh, the last High King of Ireland, bequeathed that symbol of power, the sceptre, to Pope Alexander II up to today – Tara has continually emerged from the shadows to be the backdrop for significant moments in Ireland's life story.

During the last century before the arrival of the Normans, the glory of Tara was eclipsed. Following Donnchadh's death in Rome in 1064, the Uí Bhriain of Munster, with little or no reference to Tara, held the title of 'High King' for fifty years through the reigns of a grandson and great-grandson of Brian Boru – Tairrdelbach (1064-1086) and Muircheartach the Great (1086-1119). In what is almost a contradiction in terms, the latter shared the title of 'High King with opposition' with Domhnall Mac Lochlainn, one of the northern Uí Néill who had also laid claim to the kingship of Meath.

The Ó Conchubhair or O'Connors of Connacht, who claimed descent from Conn of the Hundred Battles through a brother of Niall of the Nine Hostages, made a valiant effort during the second half of the twelfth century to revive some of the traditions dropped by Tairrdelbach and Muircheartach Ó Bhriain. In 1121 Turlough O'Connor

*Representation of Norman knight Hugh de Lacy in the twelfth-century historical tract* Expugnatio Hibernica *by Welsh priest Giraldus Cambrensis. Hugh de Lacy was given all the lands of Meath by Britain's King Henry II in 1172. Included in that grant was the Hill of Tara, which he in turn gave to Adam de Feypo, who built his castle on the Hill of Skryne. From those early times the actual hectares on Tara itself appear to have come under the ownership of the Pentony family, who held them until the time of Elizabeth I.*

took over from Domhnall Mac Lochlainn. He restored the inaugural feast of Tara and celebrated it sixteen kilometres west of the Hill at Athboy, and it was Turlough who, in 1123, commissioned the magnificent processional Cross of Cong which is to this day preserved in the National Museum.

At the time of Turlough's death in 1156 a dispute broke out between his son, Ruairí and the Mac Lochlainn as to who had a right to the kingship of Tara. Ruairí shared it with Muircheartach Mac Lochlainn for ten years, but the dispute eventually led to war between the two. In 1066 the Mac Lochlainn was slain and thus until his own death in 1198, the title 'King of Tara' rested with the last recorded High King of Ireland – Ruairí O'Connor of Connacht. At his inaugural feast, the prediction for his reign was couched in the old marriage-to-sovereignty themes of his Uí Néill ancestors:

'A good mast this year as well as wealth and abundance of all things good has been given by God in this year of the reign of

Ruairí O'Connor.' 'Prosperous was his reign,' says the *Book of Ballymote*.

But Ruairí was not without a rival for the title. An ally of Muircheartach Mac Lochlainn, the powerful and ambitious king of Leinster, Diarmuid Mac Murrough had long coveted the kingship. And it is a series of events initiated by this inscrutable man that first brought the Normans into Ireland.

In 1152, Diarmuid Mac Murrough had foolishly made an enemy of Tighernán O'Rourke, King of Breffni, by abducting his wife Dervorgilla. The story is the antithesis of everything that sacred sovereignty in Ireland stood for, yet it supplies the final lines in the last chapter of Tara's kingship. Dervorgilla, who was related to the family of Malachy II, is said to have plotted her own abduction by Mac Murrough while her husband was away on spiritual retreat in Lough Derg. When O'Rourke returned he wasted little time enlisting the aid of the O'Connors of Connacht, not only to retrieve

*The Norman military construction, Trim Castle on the Boyne. Built c.1200, the castle was later extended and added to. It became the de Lacy stronghold in Meath, and the last king of Meath was hanged there. The fortification was attacked by the last king of Ireland, Ruairí O'Connor of Connacht, but to no avail. Its last private owner was Lord Dunsany, whose family had been heirs to lands of the original Norman settlers south of Tara, the de Cusacks. The castle is now owned by the Office of Public Works, who intend restoring it for tourist purposes. It featured in the Hollywood film* Braveheart.

his wife but to inflict war on Mac Murrough's Leinster territories over the next fourteen years.

When, in 1166, Ruairí O'Connor had defeated Mac Murrough's ally Muircheartach Mac Lochlainn, he and O'Rourke joined forces to administer a humiliating defeat to Mac Murrough and drive him out of Leinster altogether. Mac Murrough, in need of new allies, found them across the Irish sea. Thus his next desperate move was to affect Ireland right down to the present day. He went to Wales, where he sought help from the ambitious Norman-Welsh Earl of Pembroke, Strongbow. Mac Murrough offered him the title to his former Leinster kingdom and marriage to his beautiful daughter Aoife in return for an army of knights.

Strongbow gave Mac Murrough an expeditionary group of thirty knights in full armour, sixty horsemen in half armour and three hundred archers. Combined with five hundred of his own followers, this force allowed Mac Murrough to win back some territory in south Leinster during May of 1169.

Eventually he was confronted by the High King himself, Ruairí O'Connor, who had initially taken scant notice of this new threat. During a parley, Ruairí O'Connor offered to return Mac Murrough his kingdoms in Leinster on condition that he send his allies back to Wales. Mac Murrough pretended to agree to these terms but then broke his word and instead sought more reinforcements from Strongbow. Thus, when the High King marshalled his troops at the Hill of Tara the following year in September 1170, it was to face the formidable cavalry and cross-bowmen of a major invasion force led by Strongbow himself. The Norman earl, having conquered Waterford and

*Modern day warriors, the Tuatha na nGael.*

Dublin, was then making his way north to the central plain.

There can be no doubt at all that no matter how bravely they fought, the Irish under O'Connor were no match for the better equipped Normans. From the very beginning they were on the defensive and were gradually forced back toward the west, leaving the rich plains of Meath to the newcomers. At times over the next three years O'Connor pushed east once more in an attempt to wrest the ancient royal lands from Strongbow and his agents. But for him, just as for wave after wave of insurgents down through the next 750 years of Irish history, it proved to be an unequal task.

In those three years, 1169 to 1172, Ireland was to undergo the most dramatic changes to occur since the arrival of the Celts some 1300 years earlier. Despite the fighting and internecine quarrels that had gone on during that long period the island had remained a relatively peaceful place. The rules of play under Brehon law were clearly defined and even a conquered king still remained in charge of his homeland until his own people or *tuatha* decided otherwise.

But the Normans brought with them a new concept of conquest. Their king, Henry II, did not *marry* the land; he *owned* the land and, as monarch, he had the right to do with it what he willed. Thus, whatever ground the knights gained in his name or their own name they gained for keeps. This was very different to the Irish system of tenure under the Brehon laws, by which the king held lands only for his lifetime, after which the land reverted back to his *tuatha*.

Amidst this change the Hill of Tara, which had never been owned but by the gods, became just another parcel of land to be shared out. Through pre-Christian times and well into the Christian era, Tara had been the earthly embodiment of the Goddess of Sovereignty. Now it became the possession of a new and very powerful sovereign, Henry II, who came to claim his lands in 1171. The following year Henry II gave all of Meath to one of Strongbow's knights, Hugh de Lacy: 'Henry, by the Grace of God, King of England. Know ye that I have given and granted and by this my charter confirmed unto Hugh de Lacy, in consideration of his services, the land of Meath, with the appurtenances; to have and to hold for me and my heirs, to him and his heirs, by the service of fifty knights in as full and ample manner as Murchard Hy-Melaghlin held it, or any other person before him or after him ...'[2]

*Mounted warfare was part of Brian Boru's attack on Malachy II at Tara. His cavalry was initially repulsed, but when Brian returned again with a larger force, Malachy surrendered his crown. This beautiful Bronze Age horse bit was found in the valley between Tara and Skryne.*

De Lacy in turn carved Meath up among his most favoured knights and the sacred Hill of Tara became a few more fields of land within the Barony of Skryne. Its overlord, Adam de Feypo, built his castle across the valley on the sister hill from which his barony took its name.

In 1175 Geoffrey de Cusack arrived from France to help in the colonisation of Meath and was given the lands three kilometres south of Tara where Killeen Castle still stands today. De Cusack's heirs, the Plunketts, became the Earls Fingall and the Lords Dunsany, who for generations controlled huge tracts of land in south Meath. These families were later joined by the Barnwalls, the Pentonys, the Prestons and the Dillons who were to own land on and around Tara itself. Their descendants have all played parts in its history since then.

In 1175 Ruairí O'Connor had concluded the Treaty of Windsor with Henry II, in which he submitted to the king in return for retaining control over the territory not yet conquered. Thus began what was an English/Irish division of the country. Over the next three to four centuries, Tara and the surrounding area were consolidated into what was known as 'The Pale' – that segment of the east which could be easily controlled by the English king and his representatives against the hostile 'rest of Ireland'.

At times the borders of the Pale would be extended further west; at other times the Pale would shrink inside the elbow of the Boyne. But at all times Tara was within the area fully controlled by England and in possession of the Anglo-Irish. During those dark centuries in Irish history little is known of what happened on Ireland's former royal seat.

1 'Roll of Kings', poem CXXXVI, p. 555.
2 Historical Manuscripts Commission, Report 1906, p. 208.

# CHAPTER 12

# STILL A HILL OF HOSTINGS

*'There is in Meath an hill, called the Hill of Taragh*
*Wherein is a playne twelve score long,*
*Which was named the Kemp-his-hall.*
*There the countrey had their meetings and falckmoates,*
*as a place that was accounted the high Pallace of the Monarch.*
*The Irish historians hammer many fables*
*in this forge of Finne Mocke Coyle & his Champions,*
*[just] as a Frenche historie doth*
*of King Arthur and the Knights of the rounde table.*
*But doubtleise the place soemeth to beare the shoe of*
*an ancient and famous monument.'*

(as written by Raphael Holinshed in
*Irish Chronicle*, 1577)[1]

In a plan for Ireland's 'reformation' submitted to Henry VIII in 1515, it was proposed that the Deputy and Captain of the King's army in Co Meath should 'ordain that all the common folk of Eastmeath from the Barony of Delvin exclusive to the sea, shall muster in their best array before them every Saint George's day, on the Hill of Tara.'[2] The purpose of this muster was to train a force which would put down any rebellion against the king's rule and protect the Pale against what were called 'the wild Irish'. By the seventeenth century both the Irish and the largely Catholic Norman-Irish were feeling threatened by the waves of English and Scottish settlers. Their lands were no longer secure. Thus, in 1641 the Norman-Irish, or Old English as they were known,

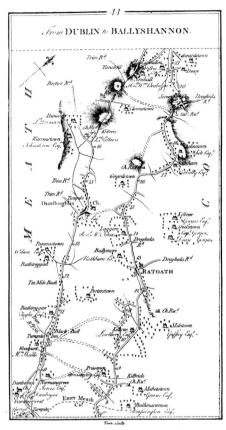

*As indicated on this 1777 Taylor and Skinner map, the road north from Dublin to Navan and beyond cut through Lord Fingall's Killeen estate, and then over the Hill of Tara (centred at top of map). It was along this route that Fingall sent his lethal cartload of spirits during the 1798 Battle of Tara. The present Dublin-Navan road, 1km east in the valley, although planned as a toll road at the time, apparently was not opened until a later date.*

found themselves banding together in support of Catholic liberty along with Gaelic chieftains such as Sir Phelim and Eoghan Rua Ó Néill. It was to be an uneasy marriage.

Hence on 7 December 1641 there was a hosting at the Hill of Tara to protest against the 'intolerant government at Dublin Castle'. It included Christopher Plunkett, 2nd Earl Fingall of Killeen Castle; his father-in-law Nicholas Barnwall, Viscount Gormanston who was a Preston and nephew to the commander of the Confederate rebel forces in Leinster, Colonel Thomas Preston.

Also at the meeting were members of the Dillon family, including Sir James Dillon, who was to command Irish troops in the coming rebellion. Many of these people later had their lands confiscated by Cromwell and given to his adventurers in payment. However, when Charles II brought the House of Stuart back to power in 1660 most of the lands were restored.

Local tradition holds that the Irish earl, Red Hugh Ó Domhnaill, used Tara as a rallying ground during the crucial Nine Years War of the late sixteenth century – a war which resulted in 'the flight of the earls' as the defeated Irish chieftains left for the Continent, effectively putting an end to Gaelic culture and customs in Ireland. It is not known whether his nephew, Eoghan Rua Ó Néill, ever used this ancient seat of his ancestors in his campaign against the English during the summer of 1643. But this brilliant general was the first chieftain to use the symbol of the golden harp of Tara on a green field in his flag.

> **A report to Rome of Eoghan Rua's return to Ireland from the Continent, dated July 1642, states, 'O'Néill's frigate bears the Irish harp in a field of green, in a flag on the maintop'.[3] That same harp on a field of green is now the Irish naval ensign, while the golden harp on a field of blue is the official flag of the President of Ireland.**

The only other historic mention of Tara in the war that raged from 1641 to 1649 is that of British Colonel Michael Jones drawing up his Parliamentary army of 7,000 foot soldiers and 2,000 mounted cavalry on the hill prior to attacking and roundly defeating General Thomas Preston's Confederate Irish force near Summerhill on 8 August 1647.

Oddly enough, after a truce was signed between Cromwell and the Catholic Confederacy in 1649, Colonel Preston was created

*Graveyard at Tara. The Hill of Tara has been a place of burial from the earliest times. Headstones in this atmospheric picture by Peter Gallagher are a mixture of old and new, the earliest dating back to the 1600s.*

Viscount Tara in 1650. The title died with him and was not resurrected until John Preston of Bellinter took it for his term of life in 1800. On that occasion, however, it was after Preston had fought on behalf of the Crown along with Lord Fingall and had been largely responsible for the defeat of the Irish rebels, the United Irishmen, at the Battle of Tara on 26 May 1798.

## The Battle of Tara, 1798

For almost 150 years after the time of Cromwell, rebel fervour in Ireland lay dormant. Then, inspired by the French Revolution and the drive toward independence in America, the United Irishmen movement was born in Dublin and Belfast during 1791. In the years that followed there was heightened political tension in almost every county, and none more so than in Meath.

The main aim of the United Irishmen was to achieve widespread parliamentary reform and Catholic emancipation. Initially, the United Irishmen were virtually unique among Irish revolutionary movements in being led (and initiated) by Protestants and Catholics in an attempt to form the United Ireland of their name across traditionally hostile religious divides. However, inevitably conflict arose between the insurgents and the Protestant landed gentry who were responsible for civil authority in communities like Meath.

A very active contingent of the United Irishmen operated in and around Tara under the name of the 'Defenders'. In 1793, the same year as the Boston Tea Party and the American Declaration of Independence, Killeen Castle, home of the 8th Earl of Fingall Arthur James Plunkett, was plundered by the new revolutionaries in search of arms. Three years later, in October 1796, King George's Lord Lieutenant for Ireland commissioned Lord Fingall as Captain of the Skryne Cavalry. Ralph Dillon of Lismullen became his First Lieutenant while John Preston of Bellinter was named Captain for Navan. Thus, in contrast to 1641 when they fought on the Irish side, less than two hundred years later these rebel familes were fighting the King's cause as the local yeomanry.

The 1798 Rebellion began on Wednesday 23 May. Meath units of the United Irishmen were ordered to prevent British reinforcements from the north reaching Dublin. Hence most of the action over the next three days was concentrated along the Navan Road at Dunboyne, Clonee, Dunshaughlin and, finally, from the vantage point of Tara Hill.

In his book *The Battle of the Hill of Tara*, Laurence J. Steen points out: 'The rebels had selected Tara as their gathering point before the revolution broke out. Tara was an excellent position as it was a hill with a good view of the surrounding countryside and was well situated for cutting off the Dublin-Navan road. It was easily defensible, with a complex of ancient earthen fortifications providing cover. It was also a symbol of independence being the ancient seat of the Irish High King.'[4]

By Friday, 25 May the complement of Meath, Westmeath and Kildare rebels assembled at Tara numbered 4,500. These young idealists became known as the 'Croppies' because of their short hair, and soon sections of the mounds on Tara would be renamed 'the Croppy graves'. But on this night before the fight hope of victory was high. Campfires once more flickered on the summit and, no doubt, around them heroic tales were recalled as this mixed band prepared for the battle that would surely come the next day.

It came all right, but it was preceded on the Saturday afternoon by a cunning move on Lord Fingall's part which was to have a huge effect on the outcome. He had at his disposal a large quantity of whiskey from a distiller in Navan. Knowing that on their way to Tara from Dunshaughlin the rebels had called at Dunsany Castle looking for ale, Lord Fingall sent three cart loads of the whiskey along the old Dublin-Navan Road which passed through his estate and up over Tara. Not surprisingly, the cargo was confiscated and

*Headstone placed on the King's Seat beside the Lia Fáil in June 1938 as a memorial to the fallen Irish revolutionaries in the 1798 Battle of Tara.*

Old ballad about the Battle of Tara:
*'Peace be round the Croppies grave*
*Peace to your souls, ye buried brave*
*Tara's Hill when crowned and free*
*Had never nobler guests than thee.'*

as a young rebel, Thomas Kiernan, reported: 'In a short time the boys began to carry away whiskey in cans, pitchers, noggins and all manner of vessels.'[5]

It would appear that by the time the yeomanry and British reinforcements arrived around 4.30 p.m. on the same day a good number of the insurgents were more under the influence of drink than under the command of their leaders and in no condition for disciplined warfare. Thomas Kiernan's account continues: 'Our headquarters were soon appraised to the approach of the King's forces. They immediately formed the men into lines. I should say, "they tried to do so" but the whiskey made them so ungovernable that the lines could not be formed. This state of confusion was kept up until our enemy opened fire on us.'

That 'enemy' was no more then five hundred strong. But among them were some superb horsemen, like Lord Fingall himself, who had fought abroad. Many were part of the hunting fraternity and knew the country well. They chose to attack on the most gradual of slopes, rising from Rath Maeve toward Rath Lóegaire.

In their lines they had Captain John Preston with the Navan and Kells Cavalry on the left flank, the Skryne Cavalry under Lord Fingall was on the right. The infantry and one cannon held the centre. In these disciplined ranks they advanced up the slope toward what had now become an unruly mob.

But the rebels were also full of fight and, instead of holding their commanding position on the crown of the hill, they charged with their pikes into the face of withering fire and the blades of

*Left: A commemorative scene from the 150th anniversary of the 1798 Battle of Tara.*

*Below: Also at the 1948 commemoration were Taoiseach John A. Costello (far left of picture), President Sean T. O'Ceallaigh (next figure to the right) and former and future Taoiseach and President, Eamon de Valera (centre of picture, holding hat).*

*'The strength and majority of the National Movement was never exhibited so imposingly as at this great meeting. The numbers exceed any that have ever before congregated in Ireland in peace or war.'*[7]

Daniel O'Connell's
monster meeting at Tara.

mounted horsemen. Though losses were great, they charged and recharged during the next two hours until at least four hundred of their number lay dead on the hill. British losses were put at no more than thirty.

The final part of the battle probably included the most disciplined and determined effort on the part of the United Irishmen. Marshalled by an incredibly brave young woman, Molly Weston (*see Chapter 3, Women of Tara*) a tight-knit band remained in the field until the last and came close to breaking the British military ranks. One British captain named Blanche, who commanded a group of Grenadiers at the heart of the fight, said of that final struggle: 'On approaching the churchyard gate we met the most daring and obstinate resistance.'[6]

But for Molly Weston and her band courage was not enough. It appears that she and four of her brothers all died and like many others are probably buried on the hill itself. To mark their graves, the ancient Lia Fáil was moved from near the Mound of the Hostages to Rath Cormac. Over the centuries further memorials have commemorated this tragic event – a headstone was placed near the Lia Fáil in 1938 and a Celtic cross, now standing west of the Mound of the Hostages, followed in 1948.

## Daniel O'Connell's Monster Meeting

In 1800 the British Prime Minister William Pitt, alarmed by the 1798 Rebellion, passed the Act of Union. As a result Ireland lost her parliament, which now sat at Westminster as part of the English parliament, and became part of the United Kingdom. After successfully achieving Catholic emancipation and the removal of the punitive Penal Laws during the first decades of the century, Daniel O'Connell, the Kerryman who became known as 'The Liberator', turned his attention to repeal of the Union. In 1843, to bring attention of the people of Ireland and the British government to the call for repeal, O'Connell organised a series of some forty huge rallies around the country. Aged sixty-nine, he travelled 5,000 miles by coach to address thirty-one of these meetings.

Conscious of the Ireland that pre-dated British rule, O'Connell punctuated the series of rallies with what were called 'monster meetings' at important historic and Celtic sites. Cashel and the Curragh both hosted gatherings of close on three hundred thousand. But Tara was to be the site of climactic moments in what, during that incredible year, had become the most fervent,

## REPEAL MEETING ON TARA HILL.

In the fulfilment of the promise made by us last week, we this day present our readers with an engraving of the "monster" repeal meeting, held on Tara Hill, a spot hallowed by historical associations in the minds of all Irishmen. Tara, or Teagh-mor, signifies the Great House, a name it derived from being to the end of the 6th century the place where was assembled the convocation of the states-general of Ireland every three years, for the deliberation and decision of civil and ecclesiastical matters, and also for the election and investiture with supreme authority of one chief, who was appointed sovereign of all Ireland.

homes. The Tara meeting exceeded in numbers that of Enniscorthy, which was estimated, not upon any vague idea arising from its imposing appearance, but from a measurement calculation, at upwards of 100,000 individuals, including, of course, both women and children, who congregated in considerable numbers (in both instances) along the roads and in the adjacent fields. The procession from Dunshaughlin, which conducted Mr. O'Connell, and which was the last to arrive, fully occupied a mile of road. The *programme* of the procession of Trim and its adjoining parishes will afford the best idea of the appearance as well as of the organized manner in which those processions are got up. "Trumpeter on horseback; harper in open carriage, four horses; Trim band in open carriage, six grey horses; members of committee in open carriage, four horses; footmen, six deep; carriages, cars, gigs, and carts; horsemen, four deep; the mounted marshals, distinguished by white rosettes worn on the left breast; the repeal committee of each parish, carrying white wands, along the line of procession, to preserve order."

There were no trades except from Dublin and Drogheda. Those from Drogheda, who were conveyed up the Boyne to Navan in lighters gratuitously offered for the purpose, marched up the hill about half-past eleven o'clock, bearing twenty-one very large and beautiful flags of various colours and emblematic of their respective crafts, and passing through the centre of the crowd, who vociferously cheered them, they proceeded across the hill as if by pre-arrangement to Rathna-Riagh, ascended the mound, and planted on its verge their twenty-one flags in such a manner as to form a circle

Four masses were celebrated in the open air before twelve o'clock, an altar and canopy having been erected for the purpose near the graves of the Croppies. Neither military or police were sent to the immediate vicinity of Tara-hill, no movement whatever having taken place on the part of the constabulary, and that of the military having been confined to the transfer of a troop of dragoons and two or three companies of infantry to Navan and Trim.

At half-past one o'clock Mr. O'Connell's carriage arrived at the place of meeting, and shortly after, though with considerable difficulty, reached the platform. As he passed at the top of the hill under a triumphal archway, on which was inscribed, in English and Irish, "Tara of the Kings hails the Liberator with 100,000 welcomes," he was heartily cheered by as many voices. He and his son Dan were seated in the dickey, Tom Steele sat behind waving an olive branch, while the inside was occupied by Mr. J. O'Connell, M.P., Mr. Barnet, of the *Pilot*, and Mr. Haverty, of the *Freeman's Journal.*

Mr. O'Connell, having taken the chair, came forward amidst the most enthusiastic cheering to address the meeting; but as it is impossible for us to devote space to even an outline of his speech, we will merely mention that it embraced the usual exciting topics, which were dwelt upon and enforced with more than ordinary eloquence and impressiveness. The following passage in his speech, however, is too significant to be overlooked, inasmuch as it has already become the theme of more than one newspaper disquisition :—

I come here not for the purpose of making a schoolboy's attempt at declamatory eloquence, not to exaggerate the historical importance of the spot on which we now stand, or endeavour to revive in your recollection any of those poetic imaginings respecting it which have been as familiar as household words; but this it is impossible to conceal or deny, that Tara is surrounded by historical reminiscences which give it an importance worthy of being considered by every one who approaches it for political purposes, and an elevation in the public mind which no other part of Ireland possesses. *We are standing upon Tara of the Kings, the spot where the monarchs of Ireland were elected, and where the chieftains of Ireland bound themselves by the solemn pledge of honour to protect their native land against the Dane and every stranger.* This was emphatically the spot from which emanated every social power and legal authority by which the force of the entire country was concentrated for the purposes of national defence. On this important spot I have an important duty to perform. I here protest, in the face of my country and my God, against the continuance of the union. (Cheers.) My proposition is, that the union is not binding on us in point of conscience; that it is void in principle, void as a matter of right, and void by constitutional law. I speak not of those details which render the union a mockery; my proposition is, that there was no authority vested in anybody to pass that act. I arraign the union, therefore, on the incompetency of the authority that nominally passed it. The Irish Parliament was elected to make laws, not legislatures, and had no right to usurp such an authority—an authority which the people of Ireland alone could exercise. As well might the servant usurp the dominion of the master. We it was who employed them; we were their masters, they were our servants, and they had no right to transfer us to any power on earth. That is a manifestly just doctrine, and would be deemed so by every body if applied to England, were the English Parliament to transfer their power to the legislative chambers of France, even though an instalment of their own members were to become part of those chambers.

*'On the 15th day of August in the year of '43,*
*This glorious day I well may say, recorded it*
*shall be,*
*On the Royal Hill of Tara, Irish thousands did*
*prevail,*
*In Union bands to join their hands with Dan,*
*for the Repeal.*
*There was Wexford, Wicklow and Kildare,*
*Dublin and Ardee,*
*Westmeath, King's County and Dundalk most*
*glorious for to see,*
*Cork, Limerick, Tuam and Waterford, Strabane*
*and sweet Kinsale,*
*On the Royal Hill of Tara stood to sign for the*
*Repeal.'*[8]

peaceful outpouring of Irish sentiment for Irish rule to ever occur on this island.

The Tara gathering was planned for the Feast of the Assumption of the Blessed Virgin Mary on 15 August. For up to three days prior to the meeting, people thronged to the hill from every direction. By carriage, horse and on foot they came from an eighty-kilometre radius and beyond to fill the roads leading to Tara and its surrounding fields, in an act of gathering reminiscent of the mythical hosting of King Eochaid for his battle with the Dé Danann.

On the day itself, bands, ceremonial floats and thousands of banners added extra colour and became as much a festival as a political rally. The fact that the gathering was held on the royal site of ancient Ireland must have added enormously to the fervour and the unity of purpose that imbued the meeting – the largest gathering ever to have assembled on this island. Great propagandist that he was, O'Connell estimated the numbers at one and a half million people. The nationalist newspaper, *The Nation*, said, 'Without the slightest fear of exaggeration there were three-quarters of a million people present.' Other more objective estimates put the figure at five hundred thousand, and even O'Connell's greatest journalistic enemy, *The Times*, recorded one million people.

The *Illustrated London News* reduced the number to one hundred thousand but still reported the event in rather glowing terms, saying that 'the procession from Dunshaughlin, which conducted Mr O'Connell, fully occupied a mile of road.' The procession included a trumpeter on horseback, drummers, a harper playing 'The Harp that Once through Tara's Halls' from atop an open carriage drawn by six grey horses, footmen six deep, horsemen four deep, and banners and flags bearing the emotive word 'Repeal'.

That morning, masses were celebrated on altars erected on the various mounds around the site. Two bishops and thirty-five priests were on hand and, for this span of time at least, the curse of St Ruadhán was forgotten. Soon after midday, O'Connell's carriage made its way up to the top of the hill through an archway that read 'Tara of the Kings hails the Liberator with 100,000 welcomes'.

When O'Connell spoke, it was said by one local observer, 'You'd hear his voice a mile away, like it was coming through honey.' And across the fields boomed the words, 'Tara is

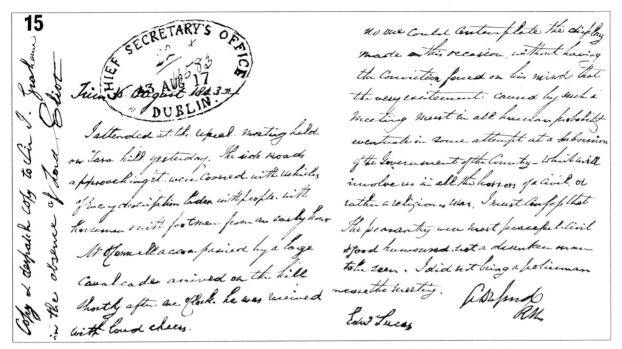

*Having witnessed the huge turnout at O'Connell's 1843 repeal meeting at Tara, Trim magistrate sent this worried dispatch to his superiors in Dublin Castle, expressing his concern that the movement might lead to subversion.*

surrounded by historical reminiscences which give it an importance worthy of being considered by everyone who approaches it for political purposes and an elevation in the public mind which no other part of Ireland possesses.' (It was held by local Tara people that O'Connell's words were relayed down the hill by officials assigned to that task.)

If, as many wanted at this time, Daniel O'Connell had been declared High King of Ireland, he certainly would have made Tara his seat.

O'Connell contined: 'We are standing upon Tara of the Kings, the spot where the monarchs of Ireland were elected, and where the chieftains of Ireland bound themselves by the solemn pledge of honour to protect their native land against Dane and every stranger. This was emphatically the spot from which emanated every social power and legal authority by which the force of the entire country was concentrated for national defence. On this important spot I have an important duty to perform. I here protest in the face of my country and my God against the continuance of the Union.'[9] ... 'The Repealers at Tara outnumber as three to one the Citizen Army of '82.'[10]

But the cheers that echoed across the plain of Meath in response to this speech were in fact ringing the death knell of O'Connell's popular movement. The fervour and size of the monster rally here did not go unnoticed by the government and pressure grew to put an end to such emotive gatherings. One local magistrate from Trim, reporting to his superiors in Dublin and London on the Tara meeting, wrote: 'Mr O'Connell accompanied by a large cavalcade arrived on the hill shortly after one o'clock. He was received with loud cheers. No one could contemplate the display made on this occasion without having the conviction forced on his mind that the very excitement caused by such a meeting must in all human probability eventuate in some attempt at a subversion of Government of the Country – which will involve us in all the horrors of a civil or either a religious war.'[11]

O'Connell must have feared the same outcome, for almost as an aside during his address he said, 'What could England effect against such a people so thoroughly aroused they rose out in rebellion? While I live such an uprising will never occur.'[12]

But the British government was not convinced and heeded the Trim magistrate's warnings. With the next monster meeting ready to go ahead in Clontarf, Prime Minister Sir Robert Peel issued a proclamation at the last moment banning the rally on the grounds that it would have a military character. The area was ringed by armed militia, and O'Connell was faced with a dilemma – confrontation or submission. Fearing bloodshed, he chose the latter course and messengers were sent along every road leading into Clontarf to turn the people back. It was a poignant and humiliating moment for 'the Liberator' and one from which he never recovered. Unlike his great victory in the fight for Catholic emancipation, this signalled a stinging defeat for the repeal effort. O'Connell was arrested, tried for 'conspiring to change the Constitution by illegal methods', and sent to prison. He was released a year later on appeal, but though he continued his campaign for appeal, his power to influence matters in London was gone.

It is interesting to note that a friend of his in the British government was Lord John Russell, who was actually owner of the land of Tara at the time of the rally. Whether he gave his permission for its use is not known. But under the laws that applied to Tara regarding access to the monuments, permission had to be accorded to the applicant 'subject to such reasonable conditions as the owner shall specify'. Obviously Lord John Russell did not apply any conditions. When he became British Prime Minister in 1846, Lord John did not give way to O'Connell's

Killeen Castle, Co. Meath.

*Killeen Castle, original seat of the de Cusacks just south of Tara. It dates back to 1181. The first owner, Geoffrey de Cusack, died in 1210. Through marriage it became seat of the Plunketts in 1403. Lucas Plunkett was named the 1st Earl Fingall in 1628. His son Christopher, the 2nd Earl, was on the nationalist side in the rebellion of 1641. He was part of a hosting at Tara on 7 December of that year. The 7th Earl, Arthur James, led the local yeomanry against the rebels in the 1798 Battle of Tara. James Horace, the 12th and last Earl Fingall, sold the land and moved out of Killeen in 1965. The castle was burned by the IRA in 1981 and has been in ruins ever since. A golf course is now planned for its lands.*

demands on behalf of Ireland. He presided ineffectually over some of the worst times the country had ever experienced, including the Great Famine, which raged during the latter part of the decade.

In 1847, the voice that had once rung out over Tara went silent forever – Daniel O'Connell died at Genoa on his way to Rome. There were many great moments in his seventy-two full years of life, and high among them was his monster meeting at Tara.

Regardless of the eventual political outcome, this hill had been the scene of another moment of glory which clearly demonstrated the power it still exercised on the minds of the Irish people of O'Connell's time. That power has never been tested since, and it may never be again. But one has the feeling that it still slumbers in the Otherworld that will always be at the heart of things Irish.

## The Last Hosting

At the beginning of the twentieth century, Tara took on a new literary life through the influential writings of members of the Irish Literary Revival, led by such people as W.B. Yeats and Lady Augusta Gregory. These writers deliberately sought to revive the spirit of Ireland's golden and mystical past. In his 1904 preface to Lady Gregory's book, *Gods and Fighting Men*, Yeats wrote of Tara:

1 Holinshed, Raphael, *Irish Chronicle*, 1577, republished in facsimile form by Liam Miller and Eileen Power, Dolmen edition, London 1979, p. 69.

2 Butler, Dean, *Notices of the Castle and Ecclesiastical Buildings of Trim*, p. 108.

3 Historical Manuscripts Commission, Report 1906, p. 208, quoted in Hayes-McCoy, *History of Irish Flags from the Earliest Times*, p. 43.

4 Steen, L.J. The Battle of the Hill of Tara, p.22.

5 ibid., p. 23.

6 ibid., p. 26.

7 Daniel O'Connell's speech at Tara, Tuesday, 15 August 1843, quoted in *The Green Flag*, Robert Kee, p. 209.

8 contemporary ballad, ibid., p. 208.

9 ibid, p. 209.

10 ibid, p. 209.

11 State Paper Office/Chief Secretary's Office/Registered Papers: 1843/15995 (courtesy of the RIA).

12 op. cit. O'Connell's speech.

13 Gregory, Lady, Preface I, *Gods and Fighting Men*, John Murray, 1904.

'The hill Teamhair, or Tara, as it is now called, with its green mounds and its partly wooded sides, and its gradual slope set among fat grazing lands, with great trees in the hedgerows, had brought before one imaginations ... of kings that lived brief and politic lives and the five white roads that carried their armies to the lesser kingdoms of Ireland, or brought to the great fair that had given Tara its sovereignty, all that sought justice or pleasure ...'[13]

Perhaps it was the importance given to Tara by these cultural nationalists, perhaps it was the strategic importance of the Hill of Tara with its commanding views, that led a small group of local Irish Volunteers to gather at Tara on the Sunday morning of the Easter Rising in 1916. They were to await orders that never came. Eoin Mac Néill, commander-in-chief of the rebel force, the Irish Volunteers, had sent countermanding orders from Dublin which in effect called off the insurrection for the country battalions. In Dublin, however, the Rising went ahead. A week of guns and shelling led to the execution of fifteen of the leaders of the Rising who instantly became transformed into national heroes of mythical status. The failed insurrection had achieved more than could ever have been hoped for – turning the tide of Irish opinion and sparking off the events that eventually led to Irish independence .

That day on the Hill of Tara the patient group of Volunteers had to return home to await another day. It was the last raising of the sword on the Hill of Tara. From that time on, all that hosted here have come in search of Yeats's second option – pleasure. The pleasure of a quiet moment, underpinned by vast ages of history and legend, surrounded by the same delightful view of 'great prospect' and near the same flowing wells that attracted the first settlers of this island to its wooded summit over 5,000 years ago.

# CHAPTER 13

# OWNERSHIP OF TARA

*'About this house away across Meath*
*were scattered the houses of Temair ...*
*The House of Temair, round which is the rath*
*from which is given to each his due;*
*honour still continues to such as them*
*at the courts of kings and princes ...'*

(Tenth-century poem by
Cinaeth Ua hArtacan)[1]

At the beginning Tara was of the people. Since then a Norman king has claimed it; knights, barons, lords, a duke, a world-famed philosopher, a British prime minister, a lord mayor of Dublin – all have called Tara their own down the centuries. Now Tara belongs to the people of Ireland once more. Ownership of the lands of Tara makes for a fascinating study and is almost as difficult to trace as its mythological pre-history.

The main monument site covers about 40.5 hectares of rich fertile land which since the earliest times has served as both sacred soil and fruitful pasture. The ancient legends about the hill abound with references to cattle and sheep while at the same time they speak with awe of the power in Tara's hidden strength – 'the secret place of the road of life'. Nor is it any different today. While flocks graze quietly on its crown, crowds climb its slopes seeking balm for their souls.

While preserved as a heritage centre by the government's Office of Public Works (OPW), Tara provides food each year for hundreds of lambs and the 'sweetest hay in Ireland' that sees a local farmer's cattle through the winter.

*While in the legends it is referred to as a* cahair *or 'city', in historic times Tara has never been more than a small rural hamlet. When Isaac Butler visited here in 1740 he noted that it had 'two tolerable inns', and when George Petrie wrote his book on Tara in 1839 there appear to have been seven houses. This Lawrence photograph shows those same thatched cottages. Their walls are part of the outbuildings that remain today, and the Maguire family now runs a shop in the largest of the houses. Other families that make up the small community include the Cassidys, Bolands, O'Reillys, Donnellys and Dowlings. Dr Austin Darragh now lives in a house just down from the hill which was originally built by Lord Powerscourt. In a 1989 development plan, the Meath County Council put the Tara area under 'special protection'. This prevents any further building within a wide radius of the hill. So the* cathair *of Tara is not likely to change very much in the next hundred years or, indeed, in the next thousand.*

In pre-Celtic and early Celtic times the land of Tara would have been in the common possession of the most powerful *tuatha* in the area. Later, branches of the southern Uí Néill controlled it. For example, during the sixth and seventh centuries, the Síl nÁedo Sláine, descendants of the last resident king, Diarmaid Mac Cerbaill, counted it within their territory.

Personal rather than communal ownership was the Norman norm. Not understanding or accepting this communal aspect of Celtic land use, the Normans seemed to think that the land of Meath had been the personal possession of former High King Muircheartach Mac Lochlainn. Henry II granted all of Meath in an 1172 Charter to his knight Hugh de Lacy.

During their conquest of the 'golden triangle' – that fertile area in the east midlands – the Normans hung the Celtic King of Meath and descendant of Malachy II, Magnus Ua Maelsechlainn, at their newly established stronghold of Trim. Under their regime, Tara was but another bundle of land in the hundreds of thousands of hectares that made up Hugh de Lacy's property. What became known as the Barony of Skryne was then parcelled up into a small slice of de Lacy's reward to his chief knight Adam de Feypo.

De Feipo in turn parcelled out segments of the barony to colonising families like the de Cusacks of Killeen (later the Plunketts) or the Barnwalls of Kilmessan or the Pentonys, who in the early centuries of Norman rule and right up until the time of Elizabeth I held the 'fee' of Tara as part of their 3,364 acres.

In Pearse Cusack's study of the area included in the *Records of the Meath Archaeological and Historical Society*, he says: 'By the reign of Elizabeth I almost all the ancient Skryne families had vanished. Pentony [Cabra in Tara parish] de Feypos and Kent in Danestown alone remained.'[2]

The Barnwalls got land between Tara and Killeen and founded a convent in the twelfth century for the Order of St Augustine – under the patronage of St Brighid in the townland of Odder on the south-western slope. Eventually the Order owned a large area that ran all the way over to the present-day Tara Stud at Collierstown (from *Baile na gCailleach*, 'town of the nuns' or 'the place of the women'). on the present Dublin to Navan road. In 1195 Pope Celestine III confirmed that religious orders could hold

*This document records the sale of sixty-four acres, eight perches of land on the southern half of the Hill of Tara in 1908. Lord John Russell (1792-1878), who was British Prime Minister during the Irish Famine, had inherited the southern half of the hill from the Duke of Bedford early in the nineteenth century. In 1908, under the new Irish Land Act of 1903, his son, the 2nd Earl Russell and father to famous philosopher Bertrand Russell, sold the land to the occupying tenants, Johanna and Hugh Cullen of Kilcarne, Navan. It remained in the Cullen name until reverting to state ownership in 1952.*

*Lismullen: During the civil war at the time of Sir John Fox Dillon's ownership, Lismullen House was burned down by the IRA. Having heard the raiders say that Killeen Castle was next on the arsonists' list, Sir John pencilled a note and sent a young boy running across the Hill of Tara with a warning to his friend, James Horace Plunkett, the 12th Earl of Fingall. Killeen was spared on that occasion but was later to be burned in the name of the IRA during the Maze Hunger Strike of 1981.*

*The mill at Lismullen continued to operate until 1883, when the last tenant refused to pay rent. As a result he was evicted and the mill was demolished. In the same vicinity, there was, up until recently, the Tara National School. Also at Lismullen a police barracks stood on what is called Soldier's Hill for up to a hundred years. It came under attack in the years prior to the 1916 Rising and was abandoned after Ireland achieved independence in 1922.*

*The last and 8th Baronet, Sir Robert Dillon, who was also a Baron of the Holy Roman Empire, sold Lismullen House and the lands at Lismullen to Opus Dei in 1966 and ever since it has been run as an international religious conference centre.*

possessions, and the nuns remained at Odder until Henry VIII confiscated their lands on 16 July 1539. Their 320 acres, along with a water mill on the stream that runs down from Rath Maeve, were given to a Richard Power and his heirs.

East of the hill at Lismullen, where on the river Nith, the first mill in Ireland was said to have been built by Cormac Mac Airt, Adam de Feypo gave land to his brother Thomas, who was a monk in a Dublin monastery. A nunnery was founded there in 1240 by Alicia de Cornere, a sister to the bishop of Meath. It, too, was for the canonesses of St Augustine and endured the same treatment from Henry VIII as its sister house at Odder. Closed on 15 June 1539, the lands and mill were granted to a Norman knight by the name of Thomas Cusack, who was Lord Chancellor of Ireland. Around 1650, a member of the Dillon family, who had lands south-west of Tara at Riverstown, married the heiress of Lismullen and it remained in the Dillon family name until the latter part of the twentieth century. William of Orange is said to have spent the night after his Battle of the Boyne victory, 2 July 1690, at Lismullen as a guest of Sir John Dillon. At the turn of the nineteenth century, Sir Charles Dillon kept a pack of hounds there and in 1832 he became Master of the Meath Hunt, which ever since has met near the Hill of Tara at least twice a year.

Over the centuries, for one reason or another, parts of the Irish countryside were confiscated by British rulers and later bestowed as rewards on someone who had rendered service to the Crown. There can be no doubt that Tara was part of lands taken over by Cromwell during his march from Drogheda to Trim in 1649, and as was his custom, the hill would then have been given to one of his favoured adventurers. It is recorded in Pococke that the original Tara Hall on the east slope was built by Cromwell's secretary Stopfords.

Many of Cromwell's adventurers had no inclination to stay in Ireland and thus sold their reward to the highest bidder. It was at this juncture that the name Preston became well-known in relation to Tara. The de Prestons were named as landowners in the area during the fifteenth century. We know that a relative to Lord Gormanston, Colonel Sir Thomas Preston, even though he had fought on the side of the King against Cromwell, later went to live in England and was made Viscount Tara in 1650. But it was a grandson of Jenico Preston, the third Viscount Gormanston, John

*Many Gaelic League meetings were held on the Hill of Tara in the early years of the twentieth century. They were attended by prominent figures like Sean T. Kelly, Easter Rising leader Thomas McDonagh, Máire Ní Chillin, Una Chaircheallaigh, Arthur Griffith and Douglas Hyde. A number of these gatherings were preserved on film by Peter Murray of Dunshaughlin, Co Meath.*

Preston, who was to determine the ownership of Tara from 1660 onwards.

John Preston came to Ireland in the mid-seventeenth century and established himself as a rich merchant in Dublin. He became Lord mayor of the city in 1653 and it is said that around this time he made large purchases of Meath land from Cromwell's soldiers. Included was a huge acreage that had been confiscated from the de Nangle family of Navan whose ancestors were among the original recipients of land grants from Hugh de Lacy.

By 1660, when Charles II was restored to the monarchy, John Preston of Navan was in possession of 7,854 acres at the heart of which was the Hill of Tara. He was elected Member of Parliament for Navan in 1661 and in that same year he married a daughter of Baron Nangle. In the Acts of Settlement of 1666 he was confirmed in ownership of his lands.

It appears that John Preston of Navan was very conscious of the significance of the Hill of Tara for he divided his property in half between two of his four sons. The southern half of twenty-two hectares was willed to his eldest son, Phineas. The northern section of about eighteen hectares went to his namesake, John. A third son, Samuel, got lands in Co Laois, while the fourth son, Nathaniel, inherited acreage south of Tara at Swainstown, Kilmessan, which still remain in the Preston name.

Ownership of the two halves of Tara over almost three hundred years from the time John Preston of Navan divided it between his sons John and Phineas around the year 1690, until the two sections were re-united under the ownership by the Irish government in 1974, makes for a fascinating story.

## Tara, the South

John Preston of Navan had left this portion of Tara – twenty-two hectares – along with the estates of Ardsallagh House on the Boyne to his eldest son, Phineas. *His* son, John Preston of Ardsallagh, in turn left it to his daughter, Mary. In 1710 Mary Preston married Meath Member of Parliament, Peter Ludlow, who was a grand-nephew to one of Cromwell's generals. Their daughter, Alice, married her cousin, John Preston of Bellinter, great-grandson of the original John Preston of Navan, and was mother to the Lord Tara of 1764-1821. But it was Peter and Mary Ludlow's son and Alice's brother, Peter, who inherited the Ardsallagh estates and the southern half of Tara.

He lived in England and was created 1st Earl Ludlow in 1760. His properties were first inherited by his eldest son, Augustus, who was then succeeded by another son, George James. This 3rd Earl Ludlow died without heir and left his Irish estates, including the historic sites on Tara, to a friend and political ally, the Duke of Bedford. The Duke passed them on to his brother, Lord John Russell, who was to become British Prime Minister during the Irish Famine years, 1845-1852. The last member of that family to hold title to Tara was the 2nd Earl Russell, John Francis, father of the philosopher Bertrand Russell who was born in 1872 and later became the 3rd Earl.

The Tara land remained in Russell ownership until 15 October 1908 when, under the 1903 Irish Land Act, it was sold to its tenants Johanna and Hugh Cullen for the sum of £1,985. The Cullen family were originally from Liscarton Castle near Navan and related to Cardinal Cullen, who was Archbishop of Dublin in the mid-nineteenth century.

In July of 1915 ownership passed to Margaret and Catherine Cullen. Then, under the new Free State, their vested interest was confirmed, 20 July 1922 at an annuity of £64.10s.4d. On that same date the Cullens were given the right to collect sixpence from every person visiting the monument site. Margaret and Catherine lived as tenants at Tara Hall until the late 1920s. They then took up residence with another sister, who was married to the well-to-do T. M. Reddy of Cullionmore, Mullingar. Catherine died in 1930 and Margaret in 1949; both are buried at Skryne in the Tara parish church of St Columcille, where a stained-glass window has been erected 'in memory of the Cullen family, Tara Hall'.

*Below: Bill Tormey, the last person to privately own the northern half of the Hill. His portion of the site was taken by eminent domain after a court case in 1974. Bill is an avid horseman, and during his term of ownership many children's drag hunts were run over the land. It also hosted a number of Tara Harrier point-to-point races.*

As of 3 December 1952, the Irish Land Commission became 'full owner' of the Cullen hectares on Tara. The southern half of the hill was back in the common ownership of the people of Ireland.

## Tara, the North

The young John Preston, who received eighteen hectares – the northern half of the hill – from his father, first lived at Lismullen and then purchased Balsoon House on the Boyne near Bective Abbey from Henry Ussher (the grandson of Archbishop Ussher of Armagh) in 1716. His son, also John, built Bellinter House further along the river in 1750. This lovely building, which faces directly toward Tara from the west, was designed by the great Richard Castle, who was also responsible for the present Irish parliament building, Leinster House. Bellinter remained the Preston family seat until 1893. *(Turn to the Table of Contents for a picture of Bellinter House.)*

On 30 July 1800, just two years after he had participated in the defeat of the United Irishmen in the Battle of Tara, the great-grandson of John Preston of Navan, Captain John Preston of Bellinter, was made Lord Tara by King George III. Since he had no direct heir, the title died with him in 1821.

Bellinter House and its lands went to Lord Tara's brother, Rev Joseph Preston of Galbally, Limerick. When the Reverend died in December 1839, the property passed to his eldest son, John Joseph. In Griffiths' Valuation of 1876 John Joseph Preston owned a total of 3,001 hectares, including the 324 hectares that swept directly up to Tara from in front of Bellinter House.

Since John Joseph's only child, Helen, died in 1873, he had no direct heir. Much of his huge acreage, some of it in Laois and Dublin, was sold off under the Landed Estates Court in 1878. The following year, John Joseph leased Bellinter House and its demesne, including the eighteen hectares on Tara, for a term of thirty-one years to his close friend, Gustavus Villiers, Briscoe who was son to the Revd Francis and Dorothea Briscoe of Kilmessan.

The Briscoe family had lands in Tipperary and Kilkenny. Francis, the second son of Henry Briscoe of Tinvane, Co Tipperary, was ordained a minister in 1841 and, having served as chaplain to the Lord Lieutenant of Ireland for a period, he became rector of the Kilmessan union of parishes in 1849, which included the church on Tara Hill. His son, Gustavus Villiers Briscoe, served in the Waterford Militia and was a good horseman. He hunted John

*The title 'Lord Tara': John Theodore Cuthbert Moore-Brabazon, who owned the once beautiful Tara Hall on the east slope of the hill, made an unsuccessful attempt in 1942 to revive the title when he was knighted for his aviation achievements and government ministerial service during the war. He was refused permission and had to be content with 'Lord Brabazon of Tara' – a title he holds to this day. Meantime, the title 'Lord Tara' still lies dormant and will probably remain so for ever. Its patent, granted to John Preston in 1800, is preserved by members of the Briscoe family, who inherited the Bellinter Estates in 1892.*

Joseph Preston's beloved Bellinter Harrier Hounds and eventually became heir to Bellinter itself in 1892.

John Joseph Preston died on 6 April of that year and although he had made four separate wills, it was G.V. Briscoe who inherited. John Joseph's niece Josephine Kennedy took legal action against 'G. V.' in relation to lands at Woodpark near Dunboyne and was granted an annuity of £400 in 1895. No further action was taken and in essence the will stood. G. V. Briscoe was then owner of Bellinter, its lands and the Bellinter Harriers, which he renamed 'the Tara Harriers'.

The land on Tara itself remained in the Briscoe name for the next thirty years. ' G.V.' died in 1907 and his heir was Henry Cecil Briscoe.

In 1923 Henry Cecil gave a large portion of the lands between Bellinter House and Tara for the creation of the Bellinter Park Golf Club. This is now called the Royal Tara and covers a total of eighty-one hectares along the river Skane. Bellinter House itself was sold in 1955 by Henry Cecil's son, George Briscoe, to William Holdsworth. The Land Commission bought it in the early sixties and in 1965 the house and close on five hectares was purchased by the Catholic order of nuns, the Daughters of Sion. They have used it as a conference centre since then – one of twenty-three such centres now run by them in countries all around the globe.

The nineteen hectares on Tara itself were disposed of by Henry Cecil Briscoe in the early 1920s. After passing through a number of owners in 1928 the land became the property of the Tormey family who for generations have farmed on the western side of the hill. Bill Tormey inherited the Tara land along with his part of the farm in September 1949 and held them for twenty-five years until the Office of Public Works took them over by compulsory purchase order in 1974.

All of the Hill of Tara, for the first time in nine hundred years, was again in the ownership of the Irish people.

During the years that followed, there were many calls on both the Office of Public Works and the Irish tourist board, Bord Fáilte, to develop the site for tourists, but little happened until the early 1990s. Yet without any development or publicity Tara quietly attracted an average of twenty thousand visitors a year from at home and abroad, who roamed its mounds and made up their own minds as to what all the monuments meant.

Having acquired the now deconsecrated Church of Ireland on the hill, the OPW converted it into a very informative and attractive interpretive centre in 1991.

## Tara Hall

Tara Hall is remembered locally as having 'one window for every day in the year and a brown harp over the door'. It had magnificent gardens and its own source of water, supplied by a ram pump that worked by force of gravity from the river Nith which runs past the Hall's southern wall.

In Sir Isaac Butler's report of his visit to Tara in 1740 he makes this note about Tara Hall: 'On ye North Side of ye Hill in a Bottom ye Earl of Meath has a large modern Seat, there is a fine Avenue from the Road to ye House wch with ye Rookery forms an agreeable prospect.' The house was built three hundred years ago in the latter half of the seventeenth century by Cromwell's secretary. Some time during the next fifty years it came to be owned by the Brabazons, the Earls of Meath since 1627. In 1786 it was in the possession of a Rev William Brabazon (2nd son of the 7th Earl of Meath) and was called New Hall, thus indicating that there may have been a prior dwelling on the site.

Tara Hall stayed in the Brabazon family name for two hundred years until it was taken over by the Land Commission in the 1940s. In 1938 a local man was offered the superb house and twenty-four hectares for the price of £600. In his 1956 book, *The Brabazon Story*, aviation hero and later British government minister, Lord Brabazon of Tara, gives this account of the late history of the house:

'On the death of my father, my elder brother lived there. Then the Irish government claimed the land under the Irish Land Act.

'As my brother had no children it was arranged that although most of the land was taken, I should come in as incoming tenant with about 60 acres around the house. I then became the owner. Actually I did this because I thought my brother wanted to live there, but no sooner had I done it than he decided to quit Ireland. The place then became uninhabited and soon uninhabitable. I sold it and the house was pulled down, thus saving rates.'[3]

Tara Hall came into the hands of a Scottish man named David Frame, and fell into ruin. It is said that Frame made enough money from the beech trees along the avenue to pay back what the house cost him. Its lands were purchased in 1944 by Frank Henry of

*Tara Hall: Many say that Thomas Moore, who appears to have been related to the Brabazon family, wrote his famous 'The Harp That Once Through Tara's Halls' at this house.*

'The Harp that once through Tara's halls
The soul of music shed
Now hangs as mute on Tara's walls
As if that soul were fled.
So sleeps the pride of former days
So glory's thrill is o'er
And hearts that once beat high for praise
Now feel that pulse no more.'

*Many of the legendary high kings of Tara were named for the horse god, Ec or Eocaid. It is interesting, therefore, to note that during the last thirty years some of Ireland's greatest horsemen have made their homes within a short distance of the hill: Paul Darragh to the east at the Ashbourne Road, Eddie Macken to the north at Kells, Comdt. Gerry Mullins to the south, Capt. Con Power, champion jockey Adrian Maguire and Capt. John Ledingham to the west. Kilcarne Stud, just over six kilometres to the north on the Boyne, has produced some of the world's most valuable thoroughbreds, including the great winning mare Flame of Tara and the Sadlers Wells colt Song of Tara.*

Navan. His son Philip Henry then owned them and he was followed by Tony Kennedy in 1955.

In June, 1968 'Tara Hall' and a total of forty-seven hectares were bought by Dan and Ann Pierse. The gardener's cottage was their home for a year until they built the neat two-storeyed house along the garden wall that they and their family have lived in since then. It is sad that the Hall is gone.

1 op. cit., Gwynn, Temair III, 10 & 150.
2 Cusack, Pearse, *Records of Meath Archaeological Society*, p. 9, Vol. 7, no. 1, 1980-81.
3 Lord Brabazon of Tara, *The Brabazon Story*, 1956.

CHART OF TARA LAND OWNERSHIP
Prior to Normans – communal ownership under local and high kings
1172 Part of Meath granted by Henry II to Hugh de Lacy
Part of Barony of Skryne given to Adam de Feypo
1649 Cromwellian confiscations
1666 John Preston of Navan confirmed in ownership
John Preston of Navan d. 1690; divided Tara between two sons Phineas and John

TARA SOUTH
Phineas Preston of Ardsallagh
John Preston of Ardsallagh
Mary Preston married to Peter Ludlow 1710
The Ludlows' son Peter made 1st Earl Ludlow 1760
Ludlow willed to his friend, Duke of Bedford – d. 1839
Bedford willed to his brother, Lord John Russell (British PM, 1846-52)
John Francis Russell – 2nd Earl – inherited 1882
1908 leased to Cullen family
1915 Margaret and Catherine Cullen
1922 Irish Free State confirms Cullen ownership
1952 ownership reverted to Irish Land Commission

TARA NORTH
John Preston of Balsoon b. 1677
John Preston of Bellinter b. 1720
John Preston (Lord Tara) b. 1784, d.1821
Lord Tara's brother Rev. Joseph Preston d. 1839
John Joseph Preston d. 1892
G.V. Briscoe – inherited 1892
Cecil Briscoe – inherited 1907
Bought by Tormey family 1928
Bill Tormey – inherited 1949
Office of Public Works wins court case and state assumes control 1974

Two parts of the sacred hill re-united in 1974

# CHAPTER 14

# THE TARA LANDSCAPE

*'There is a hill in this fair land*
*'Twas never owned and never can*
*From its prow the eye can see*
*The very ends of Inishfree*
*Here once stood the royal seat*
*And here once trod the Fianna feet*
*Silent now but not forlorn*
*For this is still the Ard Rí's home*
*Diarmaid, Gráinne, Cormac, Fionn*
*'Twas here they loved and lost and won*
*Their secrets lie 'neath Tara's soil*
*Known only to the Lia Fáil.'* [1]

The story of how Tara became such a unique prominence on Ireland's east midland landscape began 350 million years ago, when the landmass of Ireland lay under a tropical, life-filled sea. Over fifty million years, during the Carboniferous period, layer upon layer of sediment became solidified rock. Deposits measuring up to 1,220 metres of limestone, largely composed of the remains of decaying shellfish, were laid down. But an area within a radius of some five miles of where Tara now stands was then in the form of a basin. A mixture of mud, silt and decaying growth filled this basin and then hardened into a thick layer of shale above the limestone. While still under the sea, some 290 million years ago, the limestone and shale layers were squeezed into folds like a washboard by pressure from great mountain-building upheavals. An upward bent ridge on one of these folds now forms Tara and runs for about thirty-two

*This quarry, just four fields south of Tara at Swainstown, exposes the two-hundred-foot layer of shale which also lies beneath Tara and helps make it such a prominent hill on the landscape. The surrounding limestone decomposed more quickly than the shale, to leave Tara Hill standing at 155m high above the plain.*

kilometres from Skryne Hill to Gallow Hill near Kilcock.

The huge landmass known as the Laurasian Plate that underlay what is now all of Europe was then heaved upwards above the sea and exposed to the elements. During the next fifty million years a process of denudation, or the break-up of the rock surface, took place. A combination of wind, rain and frost gradually chewed away hundreds of metres from the upper limestone layer which covered the central part of Ireland and left an almost level surface. All except for the Hill of Tara. For reasons that are not clear – even to geologists – its thick cap of black/brown shale rock did not decompose as rapidly as the limestone. For Tara, the result of the difference between the rate of limestone decomposition and that of shale is its prominent height of 155 metres at the edge of the central plain. With the exception of its sister hill of Skryne, which underwent a similar development, there is no other prominence of that height for many kilometres in any direction.

Just about every metre of Tara's landscape is referred to in some ancient legend or ritual or by some mythical personage. Its outline in aerial photographs is utterly fascinating and distinctive. Some writers about Tara have expressed disappointment at what is to be seen on the ground – no castles, no houses, no banqueting hall – just mounds, deep trenches and, of course, the view over the plains of Meath. But there is more to it than that. When reading this landscape, various layers of knowledge about each site must be kept in mind – its naming in the ancient documents; references to it in legends about Tara; archaeological investigations; and historic events that took place here.

The best approach is to divide the fifty or so monuments that lie along the top of the Tara ridge into the following zones:

1 St Patrick's Well on the eastern slope

2 The outer ring of the hill fort

3 The Mound of the Hostages

4 Cormac's House and the Royal Seat

5 Rath Lóegaire on the southern slope

6 The Clóenfherta or Sloping Trenches on the western side

7 The Banqueting Hall/ Ceremonial Entrance

8 The Rath of the Synods and church

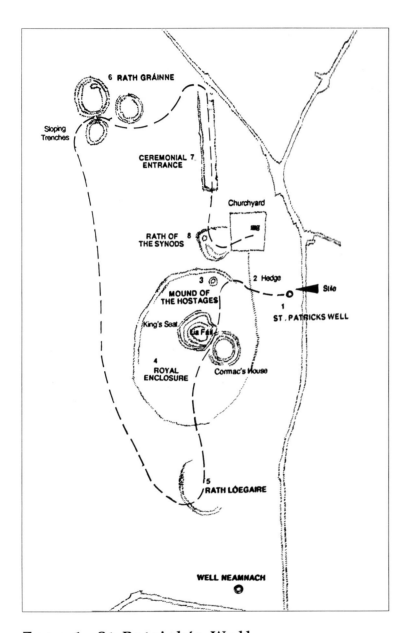

## Zone 1: St Patrick's Well

Running along the eastern slope of this 155-metre hill is a modern road which follows the route designated in the *Dindshenchas* as the Slí Dhála. Mid-way along the slope, there is a stile that leads to what is now named St Patrick's Well. This stile is one of ten on a path across the fields from the main Dublin to Navan road erected in the nineteenth century for local people making their way to the Tara church.

But one may also be walking in the footsteps of the very first settlers who may have taken this route around 3000BC when they followed the Gowra river to its source in one of Tara's wells. It and the other five named wells on the hill must have been prime attractions for these first settlers and have flowed here ever since the landscape of Tara took its final form during the last Ice Age.

## Tara and the Ice Age

In at least three advances during the past 200,000 years, huge ice sheets up to three hundred metres thick covered parts of Ireland. During the Munsterian advance (175,000 years ago) this frozen mass crept over hills and mountains to reach the southern tip of the island. The Midlandian surge of 75,000BC ground its way south to a line running from the Wicklow mountains to the Kerry highlands. Having retreated about 20,000 years ago, the ice sheet readvanced around 15,000BC. But this time it halted in a line that ran right along the north-west slope of Tara. There it remained stationary for some four thousand years before finally melting away by 11,000BC. As the ice retreated at the rate of a few metres a year it shaped the landscape. To the west of Tara lies an undulating plain, ribbed with long grass-covered ridges – the eskers. A row of eskers across the midlands from Dublin to Galway known as the 'Eiscir Riada' was later to be the dividing line which determined the two halves of the island ruled in the name of two sacred centres of Celtic Ireland – Cashel to the south and Tara to the north.

*Bronze Age burial urn found at the Mound of the Hostages, one of an estimated two hundred cremated burials in the mound.*

This best-known of Tara's wells has had a variety of names and meanings for the waves of settlers who have drunk its clear waters down through the millennia. Its alleged healing powers earned it the name 'Physician'; its connection with the earth mother goddess of Tara meant it was also known as the 'Well of the White Cow'; other names include 'Dark Eye' and 'Cormac's Well'. For many years up until the middle of the twentieth century it fed a horse trough on the roadside known as the 'Haw Haw'. It still supplies water to the people living in Tara.

One field further down the eastern slope stands the ruin of Tara Hall. In its grounds flows another well but it is not named in the

*The British Israelites at Tara.*

ancient documents. Both of these wells are closely related to that called 'Neamnach', about a third of a kilometre to the south where the Slí Dhála used to turn to the west and where the Odder Road now intersects with the Tara Road. The waters from all of these flows join up with streams from Lord Dunsany's land near Rath Maeve to form the sizeable and beautiful River Odder that runs down the glen to the right of Tara Hall. Cormac Mac Airt is supposed to have built the first mill in Ireland on this river for his lover Cernait. Directly across the hill from here is the Calf Well, which in legend is related to the Well of the White Cow. Another well named in the ancient documents is Tobar Finn or Finn's Well near Rath Gráinne to the north. A local family used water from this well right up to the middle of the twentieth century when some earth movement in the hill caused it to dry up. Two more wells on

*'There rise north of Temair
Adlaic and Diadlaic of the Host;
two springs flow diverse thence
down to the Carn of the Boys.'* [2]

the north-east slope can still be found in the fields between the Slí Mhídhluachra and Slí Asail.

Where the sixty-metre shale cap of Tara meets the underlying and more porous limestone on the west and east side of the hill, these wells emerge as strong clear flows which never run dry. Those on the eastern slope join up to become part of what we now call the Gowra River, which curves around the north-east side of the hill. The western side drains to the Skane, which meets the Gowra River just before entering the Boyne about three kilometres to the north-west of Tara at Dalgan Park.

Like a great moat, the Boyne holds Tara at the centre of its elbow as it arcs from the central plain to the sea. For some thirteen kilometres between the ancient monastic site of Bective and the modern town of Navan the Boyne flows never more than six kilometres from the hill. Just as the waters from the wells of this

*This picture, and that on the previous page, show the 'excavation' at the Rath of the Synods c.1899 by a group of devout Israelites from Britain. They were searching for the Ark of the Covenant, but all they found were some coins planted each night by local pranksters. What is perhaps a somewhat fanciful story about the event was included by Padraic Colum in his 1930 book,* The Road Around Ireland: *'A man who had some property rights on the Hill of Tara let his land to the British-Israelite Association. That curious association was about to begin digging operations... In Ireland at the time there was no public body that could take action to prevent such vandalism. A few writers determined that they would challenge the right of any man to deal destructively with an ancient monument: W.B. Yeats, George Moore, Douglas Hyde, Arthur Griffith, went up to Tara. The owner of the land ... sat on a ditch, grim and glowering, a gun across his knees, and challenged any of the gentlemen from Dublin to walk across his field. He would shoot the first one who would set foot on his property. Arthur Griffith stepped out and walked across the field. Not a shot was fired.'*

sacred hill mingle with the flow of this brooding, shimmering river, so too are Tara and the Boyne forever joined in the legends. Tara was the home of kings and heroes and gods in the ancient legends; the Boyne was one of their entrances to the Otherworld. When Tara became the inauguration place of kings, command over the fruitfulness of the Boyne was an important manifestation of royal power.

At some stage after the early hunter-gatherers reached Ireland some 9,000 years ago, they must have worked their way along this salmon-rich river, first discovering that there was a commanding hill in the district and then following the Skane or the Gowra from the Boyne up to the streams that lead to the wells of Tara itself. Here above the game-filled forest, close to the fish stocks of the Boyne, with fresh water in abundance and a commanding view of the country around, Tara became a chosen place.

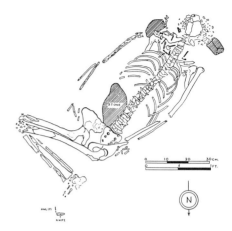

*Burial from the Mound of the Hostages, from Seán P. Ó Ríordáin's paper, 'A Burial with Faience Beads at Tara'.*

## Zone 2: The Outer Ring

At the top of the steep rise above St Patrick's Well, another stile leads into the royal enclosure of Tara itself. Here one gets the first impression of the main site. It is a large field dotted with banks and ditches. To the west is the dome-shaped Mound of the Hostages – about ninety metres away on the left are a series of grassy mounds topped by Tara's coronation stone, the Lia Fáil, and on the right is the church-yard wall. This is sacred ground.

The hedgerow through which the stile passes further south becomes part of the outside bank and ditch of the ancient ring fort. This outer ring of Rath na Ríg or the King's Fort encloses an oval area of about 70,000 square metres within which are the main earthworks of the site. The bank and ditch could date from between 200 and 300BC. A small section of it was excavated in 1956 by Seán Ó Ríordáin, who found that the actual fosse was cut into the underlying rock to a depth of over 3.4 metres below the surface. On the outside there would have been a wall created from the diggings of the wide fosse and inside that another trench. This arrangement of bank and fosse suggests that this outer ring surrounded a ritual rather than a fortified enclosure as defensive structures usually had the ditch on the outside and the bank inside. In this way it corresponds to other sacred Celtic sites such as Dún Ailinne in Co Kildare, Clogher in Co Tyrone and Emain Macha in Co Armagh. It is thought that the arrangement found at Tara was intended to keep out evil spirits rather than human enemies.

However, a 1993 survey by the Discovery Programme appears to have uncovered evidence that this outer ring was later modified to include a palisade. 'The addition of the palisade ... renders the enclosure more defensive, perhaps effecting a reversal of the role of the site. It is tempting to speculate on whether this turn-about might coincide with the building of Teach Chormac [Cormac's House], which is in all probability a ring fort.' [3]

During the same investigations, a funnel-shaped entrance through the eastern side of the outer bank was found which

*Seán P. Ó Riordáin's 1955*
*excavation at the Mound of the Hostages.*

appears to be aligned with an entrance through the circular banks and ditches of Cormac's House. Two other less elaborate entrances were found on the western and southern sides of the outer ring.

## Zone 3: The Mound of the Hostages

Inside the northern perimeter of the ring fort is the oldest and perhaps the most sacred monument on Tara – the Mound of the Hostages. Up until Ó Ríordáin's work here in the 1950s, the entrance to the passage-grave part of this large mound was

*'Behold the noble house of Mairise,*
*chief for beauty in Erin;*
*it is high to the west,*
*very high to the north,*
*level eastward of it –*
*it was a triumph of the mason.*
*It is there situated, the house,*
*on the margin of Nemnach;*
*about this house away across Meath*
*were scattered the houses of Temair.*
*Temair, whence Temair Breg is named*
*Rampart of Tea wife of the son of Miled,*
*Nemnach is east of it, a stream through the glen*
*on which Cormac set the first mill.'[4]*

covered in earth and bushes. But now you can look in and see the engravings on the large stone just left of the opening. These were created by some ancient craftsman or holy man over 5,000 years ago. They may have been part of a primitive calendar that used symbols of sun, moon and stars as markers – or they may have an even deeper religious meaning.

Under the flagstone floor of the chamber lie a great number of cremations. In fact, the remains of at least two hundred burials, dating back some 3,500 years, were found during the 1955-1959 excavations. The 0.6-metre clay layer of the mound covers a layer of stones which in turn cover the slabs that roof the passage. From atop this mound there is a splendid view that goes some way toward explaining why Tara had such a strategic importance. From this vantage point you can see land and hill features in up to half the counties of Ireland. Hence Tara's ancient name 'Temair' or 'place of great prospect'. The Dublin and Wicklow mountains are to the south; Mount Leinster in Carlow and Slieve Bloom in Laois are visible to the south-east; the prominence of Skryne and behind it, Pudden Hill, can be seen to the east; Slieve Gullion in Armagh, and Slane to the north-east; the sacred hills of Loughcrew near Oldcastle are to the west.

**Also from atop the Mound of the Hostages, visitors can get their bearings in relation to the other zones. Just to the north of it is the Rath of the Synods (Zone 8). As one views this mound it appears very disjointed. It was more symmetrical up until the end of the last century, when a group of devout Israelites dug it up in search of the Arc of the Covenant. They did not find the object of their search. But some ninety years earlier, in 1810, just beyond this mound, one of Ireland's most precious hordes of ancient gold was found. The Tara torcs are now in the National Museum of Ireland, and date from about 1000BC. North of the Rath of the Synods can be seen the beginning of a huge oblong earthworks. Up until recently these were thought to be the remains of the site on which the great assembly banquets of Tara took place during the triennial Feis. At the far north-west edge of the hill (Zone 6), is what might be called the 'feminine' side of Tara, for most of the monuments in that area – including the Clóenfherta or Sloping Trenches – bear relationships to women.**

## Zone 4: The King's Seat and Cormac's House

The walk across the green of Tara from the Mound of the Hostages to the two circular mounds, the Forradh, King's Seat or Place of Judgement on the right and Cormac's House on the left, is about ninety metres. Then, as one scrambles down three metres of bank – up and then down and then up again – the realisation dawns that this is a major piece of construction work. These ditches are hewn some 3.35 metres into the rock. It would be difficult enough with a motorised digger today but in the early centuries AD these earthworks were created with the most primitive iron and wooden tools.

The Forradh could have had a round wooden and thatched house at its centre. It may also have been used for burials and the fact that its outer bank bends in the north-east quadrant indicates that its planners were avoiding an earlier sacred mound of some sort. Somewhere underneath these banks and ditches, according to the *Dindshenchas*, is the 'Mound of Tea' called after the goddess Tea, wife of Eremón, the leader of the Milesians, and after whom, according to one tradition, Tara was named. Most recent studies indicate that the mound may have actually been built on top of three earlier mounds. Tea's grave could indeed be one of those.

Atop the mound stands the Lia Fáil, the Stone of Destiny, Ireland's coronation stone, said to have been brought here by the divine race of Danu, the Dé Danann. It roared when a rightful king touched it. Only about half the full length of Lia Fáil protrudes above ground. In total it is about 10 feet long, and has also been called the 'Penis Stone'. Composed of granular limestone, it certainly did not originate in the Tara district. Perhaps a receding glacier left it in its wake; perhaps it did come from a far-off land – it is a mystery just like Tara itself. There is also a strong tradition that a flat stone from Tara was taken to Scotland and used for coronation ceremonies there until Edward I confiscated it at the end of the thirteenth century. This is supposed to be the Stone of Scone, which now sits in Westminster Cathedral.

Next to the Lia Fáil is the gravestone and Gaelic inscription marking the burial place of the fallen of the 1798 Rebellion. The battle was fought mainly on the slope between here and the Odder road with mounted cavalry right and left of the advancing British military line of four hundred foot soldiers and cannon, coming to attack over four thousand revolutionaries positioned on the hill. It

*Conor Newman and Joe Fenwick of the Discovery Programme, investigating the Clóenferta or Sloping Trenches in 1993. Initiated by the then Taoiseach Charles Haughey in 1991, the Discovery Programme is presently undertaking a literary and archaeological study of Tara. In the* Discovery Programme Report 1 *(1993), Dr Edel Bhreathnach (Tara Research Fellow) outlines some of the questions being asked of the documentary evidence: 'Was Tara inhabited in historic times? If so, by whom and for what purpose? Were inauguration rites held at Tara in the historic period? Who physically held Tara and its hinterland at various periods? When were the various dynasties holding Tara pushed aside and by whom?' Although the Discovery Programme covers many sites around Ireland, its official logo is a representation of the sacred site at Tara.*

is difficult to imagine this now peaceful slope as a bloody battlefield.

For about a hundred years, from the end of the nineteenth century until 1992, when it was removed by the Office of Public Works, a rather unattractive but much loved statue of St Patrick stood just south of the gravestone. It was the work of a stonemason, William Curry of Navan, and was weathered in the Boyne before its erection on Tara. There is a local legend that a hunting man, who once shot off two of Patrick's cement fingers as a joke, later had two of his own fingers bitten off by a dog. Like many things regarding Patrick, any connection would be hard to prove, but such are the religious legends of Tara. Despite the statue's poor state of repair the people of Tara strongly objected to it being taken down and still want it replaced. The issue has yet to be decided. But Patrick will be back in one form or another – that much is certain.

The mound called Cormac's House, named for King Cormac Mac Airt, is similar in size to the Forradh (152.4 metres in diameter). Although there is as yet no historical proof that he ever existed, the time assigned to Cormac in the legends is the early part of the third century AD. His mound appears to differ little from the Forradh except that it has just one ditch between two banks rather than the latter's two. While this might not be important to us, it may well have had a sacred or royal significance to those who created the mound close on two thousand years ago. Neither of these mounds has as yet been excavated. It is thought that the lay-out of the ground on top of the mound indicates that it accommodated an oblong house.

Construction of the Forradh preceded that of Cormac's House, though both are dated to about AD200. Historians have argued about which mound corresponds with which in the ancient documents. The best guess, supported by the latest findings, is the mound called the Forradh to the west and Cormac's House to the east.

## Zone 5: Rath Lóegaire

Directly south from Cormac's House is the 130-metre-in-diameter ring fort of King Lóegaire, said to have been king at Tara when St Patrick arrived here. Lóegaire, legend maintains, was buried standing up facing his lifelong enemies, the Leinstermen of Dublin, Wicklow and Kildare, with his sword in his hand. Beyond Rath Lóegaire, a kilometre or so in the distance, is the much larger Rath of Queen Maeve who was so closely linked to the concept of sovereignty at Tara.

Nearer at hand in the south-east corner of the hill is the well of Neamnach, or the 'pearly one', already mentioned above. This flow of water from under Tara has worn a deep gully in the field as it heads down the valley to join the waters from other similar wells. It must have been a very sacred place and gets special mention in the ancient Tara poems as having houses built around it.

The walk from here to the Sloping Trenches (Zone 6) is about one kilometre and takes one along the western side of the Royal Enclosure. En route you pass the two-hectare field called Fodeen, in which the Calf Well still flows. Anyone looking for a shamrock at Tara may find it in the soil between the stones on the western side of this bank.

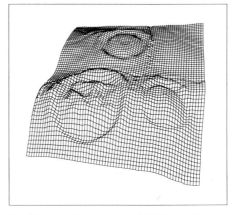

*The Discovery Programme's digital terrrain model of Rath Gráinne and the Sloping Trenches.*

## Zone 6: The Clóenfherta or Sloping Trenches

These Sloping Trenches look as if they were created as circular raths and then just slid down the hill. The first of the two is said to be the one in which the maidens of Tara – numbering 3,030 in the legends – were massacred by Dunlaing, King of Leinster in AD222. Some say this story points to there having been a college of vestal virgins at Tara and that this part of the hill would have been their *Grianán* or 'Sunny Place'. The second Sloping Trench is, according to legend, the site of the wise judgement by Cormac Mac Airt which led to his being recognised as the true king *(see Chapter 6, Priest Kings and Ancestors)*. The unfortunate King Lugaid Mac Con made a false judgement, and as a result the house he was in slid down the hill – hence the SlopingTrenches. From these banks there is a lovely view of the surrounding farmland, all of which at one time was part of Lord Tara's estate. In the glen below, a family of foxes make their home. No wonder the Preston coat of arms, which Lord Tara bore, has a fox as one of its features. The glen also provides a beautiful walk through groves of oak and chestnut.

Rath Gráinne is immediatley east of the Sloping Trenches and it recalls one of the most tragic love stories in all of Celtic literature – the forbidden love of Gráinne for Diarmaid; his daring elopement with her; the dogged pursuit of Fionn Mac Cumhail and the eventual tragedy of Diarmaid's death on Ben Bulben *(see Chapter 3, Women of Tara)*. Gráinne's rath measures about sixty metres in diameter and consists of a central mound surrounded by a ditch and an external bank. It incorporates a similar previous mound in its north-east quadrant, which in turn includes another mound. Investigation of this site has established this as a feature in the burial mounds of Tara, but as yet no explanation of its meaning has been found.

The ground between Rath Gráinne and the ceremonial entrance (Zone 7) covers an area which in the *Dindshenchas* had innumerable sites including: the Mounds of Dall and Dorcha; the Dwarf's Grave, the Stone of the Warriors; the Grave of Caelchu and his Ladder, the Cross of Fergus; Wall of the Three Battles; the Mound of the Monster. These were stone circles, burial mounds and the like, vaguely alluded to in ancient legends.

> **During 1992 and 1993 the most in-depth archeological study ever attempted at Tara was begun under the aegis of the Discovery Programme. Using state of the art survey equipment, researchers first created a new and detailed map of Tara, including subsoil features identified through geophyscial prospection (resistivity and geomagnetics). This has resulted in a doubling of the number of known monuments. By merging the various layers of information, archaeologists can now advance a detailed theory about how the complex developed, the order and function of the monuments. In 1992, for example, the Discovery team were able to report that they had found a number of circular features in the field between Zone 6 and Zone 7 for which there was no visible surface indication. The same techniques were applied to the areas of the Royal Enclosure with even more profitable results, such as the discovery of a funnel-shaped entrance feature through the outer bank near Cormac's House.**

It appears certain that any further findings will enhance rather than diminish Tara's reputation as a most important ritual and royal place.

## Zone 7: The Banqueting Hall/Ceremonial Entrance

On the north-east slope of Tara, running at a 45-degree angle to the present northern road and stretching for a distance of over two hundred metres, is the long trench that for centuries has been referred to as the *Tech Midchúarta* or the Banqueting Hall. Of all the places named in the ancient documents, this one receives the most detailed description. The *Books of Lecan* and of *Leinster* give diagrams showing seating arrangements and the portions that should be served at the great banquets of Tara.

However, it is now believed more likely that this banqueting hall was more of an *ad hoc* structure than a permanent building. Perhaps it was constructed of wood and thatch for each Samhain festival somewhere on the green of Tara and ritually burnt down when the celebration was over.

This long trench is thought to have been a ceremonial entrance to Tara from the point at which all of the five ancient roads of Ireland converged. Provincial kings would have made their way up this avenue after a long trek from Crúachain in Connacht; Ailech or Emain Macha in Ulaid; Uisneach in the midlands or Dún Ailinne in Kildare along the Slí Mór; the Slí Dhála, the Slí Cualann, Slí Mhídhluachra or Slí Asail.

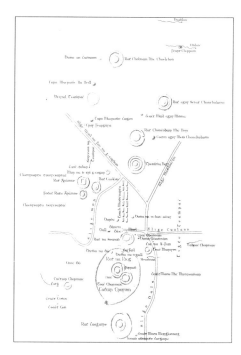

*Aerial drawing by George Petrie, showing the ancient roads of Tara and monuments on the hill, restored from ancient documents.*

> **The ancient roads of Ireland, said to have sprung into being at the birth of the ancestor of the Uí Néill, Conn of the Hundred Battles, were five in number: Slí Asail went north-west down the 'chariot slope', then west to Lough Owel, the Shannon and the north-west; Slí Mór was the mid-west road which ran along the rows of eskers that divided ancient Ireland in two; Slí Dhála, the south-west road, followed the same route as the present-day Tara road and then turned right on the Odder road to the south-west and the Slieve Bloom mountains. Slí Cualann went east for a time but then became the road south to Dublin and the Wicklow hills. Slí Mhídhluachra was the north road into Ulster and its capital, Emain Macha and Armagh.**

## Zone 8: The Rath of the Synods and the Church

A previous owner of this section of the hill once asked a diviner to check whether there was water near the Rath of the Synods. He was told that there was a lake under here but the theory has never been tested. This large rath was the first monument on the hill to be excavated by Professor Seán Ó Ríordáin back in the summer of 1952. A highly publicised dig here revealed this to be a

*'The Rath of the Synods, noble excellence,*
*lies north of the Precinct of Temair;*
*eastward from the Rath beside the Stone*
*in the house whence Benait escaped.*
*The Synod of Patrick was at the noble Rath,*
*The Synod of Brendan and of Ruadan,*
*The Synod of Adamnán thereafter,*
*assembled to curse Irgalach.'*[6]

multi-purpose site with ritual, domestic and industrial uses between AD100 and AD300. It is interesting to note that during that time a round house on the site had been built and re-built many times. A banqueting hall perhaps? We do not know. Evidence was found that these 'houses' were used for both domestic and ritual purposes. The post-holes that were discovered indicate a resemblance to the round, thatched reconstructions of similar finds at places like Lough Gur in Co Clare. Objects found at the site include a Roman lock and pottery which may date to AD200. Ó Ríordáin came to the following conclusions about his excavation work at the site: 'The dwellers at Tara were in touch with the Roman world. The site was inhabited and evidences were available of ordinary domestic and industrial activities – iron smelting and enamelling, for instance. But there are special features which suggest a ritual purpose and most remarkable are the re-buildings, each of which made the site larger and more impressive and which may have coincided with special events in the history of Tara.'[5]

At least three Church Synods are said to have taken place here and are referred to in a poem probably dating from the early eleventh century.

There is no record of when the first two meetings took place. But historians give a probable date of AD697 for the Synod of Adamnán, when Irgalach was king of the area around Tara. Prior to the erection of the church wall in the nineteenth century, the rath clearly extended into what is now the churchyard, and included in the list of monuments associated with this spot are a number that bore the name of St Adamnán, who was a powerful ecclesiastical personage of the seventh century and a biographer of St Columcille. The Tent of Adamnán, the Seat of Adamnán and the Mound of Adamnán – all were associated with the Rath of the Synods and with earthwork mounds that have been identified inside the cemetery area by aerial photography. The last monument, the Cross of Adamnán, is thought by some to refer to the tall standing stone on the left of the path through the church-yard. This ancient stone has the figure of a small child carved on it, and it could be the shaft of St Adamnán's 'cross'.

But it is also suggested that the figure is that of a continental Celtic deity known as Cernunnos, who was usually represented as seated in the Buddha position. The evidence seems to point toward this stone being of pagan rather than of Christian origin. And this belief would be reinforced by the presence of another standing stone, which may date back to the sacred stones of Blocc and Bluicne, mentioned in the ancient inaugural rituals on Tara. These stones moved to allow the chariot of the true king to drive between them. 'And there were two flag-stones in Tara: "Blocc" and "Bluicne"; when they accepted a man, they would open before him until the chariot went through. And Fál was there, the "stone penis" at the head of the chariot-course; when a man should have the kingship of Tara, it screeched against his chariot-axle, so as all might hear.'[7]

Also named in the *Dindshenchas* is a stone called 'Moel'. All three – Moel, Blocc and Bluicne – were called after three druids who may have been buried here:

> 'Westward from the Grave of the Dwarf
> are Moel, Blocc, and Bluicne – foolish their wisdom!
> over them are the three stones
> that the Prince of great Macha flung.'[8]

Near the stones of Blocc and Bluicne is a section of wall from the church that once stood here and that dated back to the Reformation. The earliest headstones in the church-yard are from the seventeenth century. In the nineteenth-century church itself there is a wall plaque from the earlier church dated 1595 in memory of Richard Dillon, whose family lived at Riverstown, Kilmessan, and were related to the Dillons of Lismullen House, Tara. Also preserved in the church is a beautiful stained-glass window by Irish artist Evie Hone. She loved Tara and used to visit by pony and trap with her sister, Mrs Nancy Connell of Leixlip, who was Master of the Meath Hunt from 1931 to 1952.

*Drawings by George Petrie of Adamnán's Cross and one of the golden torcs discovered at Tara.*

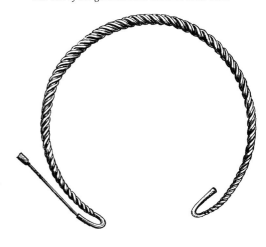

The church is now the property of the Office of Public Works and has been made into an Interpretive Centre. Surrounding the church, a two-hundred-year-old stand of twenty beech trees gives Tara its distinctive profile when viewed from a distance. The trees are home to a flock of crows that lend their own atmosphere to the hill. I like to think of them as the living descendants of the birds which lived here during the millennia covered by the legends. Perhaps they viewed from their lofty perches all that has passed here. Their story would fill a book much larger than mine – if they could but tell it.

1 Song about Tara by author.

2 op. cit., Gwynn, Temair III, p. 23.

3 Discovery Progress Reports 2, Projects Results 1993, RIA, Dublin, p. 67.

4 op. cit, Gwynn, Temair III, p. 21.

5 Ó Ríordáin, Seán, *Tara, The Monuments on the Hill*, Dundalgan Press, Dundalk, 1982, p. 26.

6 op. cit., Gwynn, Temair III, p. 21.

7 From the geological tract 'De Shil Chonairi Moir', in the *Book of Duald Mac Firbis*, and after a translation by Francis J. Byrne in *Irish Kings and High-Kings*, p. 63.

8 op cit., Gwynn, Temair III, p. 19.

# Bibliography

CHAPTER 1

*The Book of Invasions* or *Lebor Gabála Érenn* from *The Book of Leinster*, edited and translated with notes by Professor R. A. S. Macalister, Irish Texts Society, Dublin, Education Company of Ireland, 1938-1956.

Fitzpatrick, Jim, *The Book of Conquests*, Paper Tiger, Dublin 1978.

Gregory, Lady Augusta, *Gods and Fighting Men*, John Murray, Dublin 1904.

O'Faolain, Eileen, *Irish Sagas and Folk Tales*, Poolbeg Press, Dublin 1989.

Rolleston, T.W., *Myths and Legends of the Celtic Race*, Bracken Books, London 1934.

Smyth, Darragh, *A Guide to Irish Mythology*, Irish Academic Press, Dublin, 1988.

CHAPTER 2

Battersby, William, *The Three Sisters at the Well*, Navan 1991.

Brennan, Martin, *The Stars and the Stones*, Thames and Hudson, London 1983.

Concannon, T., *St Patrick*, Talbot Press, Dublin 1931.

Condren, Mary, *The Serpent and the Goddess: Women, Religion and Power in Celtic Ireland*, Harper and Row, San Francisco 1989.

Delaney, Frank, *Legends of the Celts*, Grafton, London 1989.

Foster, R. F. ed., *The Oxford Illustrated History of Ireland*, Oxford Press, Oxford 1989.

Healy, Elizabeth, *Literary Tour of Ireland*, Wolfhound Press, Dublin 1995.

Matthews, Caitlín, *The Celtic Tradition*, Element, Dorset 1989.

Matthews, John, *The Celtic Shaman*, Element, Dorset 1991.

McCone, Kim, *Pagan Past and Christian Present*, An Sagart, Maynooth 1990.

McKeever, Edward, *Bective Abbey*, Meath Chronicle, Navan 1992.

McMann, Jean, *Loughcrew, The Cairns*, After Hour Books, Oldcastle 1993.

Roe, Helen, *Medieval Fonts of Meath*, Meath Archaeological and Historical Society, 1968.

Stewart, R.J., *Celtic Gods and Goddesses*, Blandford 1990.

Young, Ella, *Celtic Wonder Tales*, Maunsel & Co., Dublin 1910.

CHAPTER 3

Archer, Patrick, *Fair Fingall*, An Taisce, Dublin 1975.

Best, Dr R.I. & Bergin, Dr Osborn, *Tochmarc Étaíne*, translation *Eriú XII, 1937*.

McDowell, Patricia, *Daughter of the Boyne*, Wolfhound Press, Dublin 1992.

McDowell, Patricia, *The Sorrows of Tara*, Wolfhound Press, Dublin, 1995.

O'Faolain, Eileen, *Irish Sagas and Folk Tales*, Poolbeg Press, Dublin 1954.

O'Rahilly, Cecile, *The Táin*, Dublin Institute of Advanced Studies, 1967.

Small, Brian, *The Horse in Ireland*, Wolfhound Press, Dublin 1991

CHAPTER 4

Carbery, Ethna, *In the Celtic Past*, Gill and Sons, 1904.

O'Connor, Ulick, *Irish Tales and Sagas*, Dragon, London 1981.

O'Faolain, Eileen, *Irish Sagas and Folk Tales*, Poolbeg Press, Dublin 1989.

Rolleston, T.W., *The Adventures of Fionn Mac Cumhal*, Mercier Press, Cork 1979.

Todd Lecture Series, Royal Irish Academy, Dublin 1903,.Vol VIII, Temair.

CHAPTER 5

Byrne, Francis J., *Irish Kings and High-Kings*, Dublin 1973.

Dillon, Myles, *The Cycles of the Kings*, Oxford 1946.

Dillon, Myles, *Early Irish Society*, Dublin 1954.

Mac Neill, Eoin, *Celtic Ireland*, Dublin 1921.

CHAPTER 6

Dillon, Myles, *The Cycles of the Kings*, Oxford University Press, 1946.

Delaney, Frank, *Legends of the Celts*, Grafton Books, London 1989.

Ó hÓgáin, Dr Dáithí, *Myth Legend and Romance: An Encyclopaedia of the Irish Folk Tradition*, Ryan Publishing, London 1990.

'A Window on the Past', Proceedings of Rathfeigh Historical Society, 1987 and 1983.

CHAPTER 7

Boylan, Henry, *A Valley of Kings, The Boyne*, The O'Brien Press.

Byrne, F.J., 'The Rise of the Uí Néill and the High Kingship of Ireland', O'Donnell Lecture, Dublin, 1970.

Cullen, L.M., *Life in Ireland*, B. T. Batsford Press, London 1968.

Hopkin, Alannah, *The Living Legend of St Patrick*, Grafton, London 1969.

Kennedy, Gerald Conan, *Irish Mythology, A Guide & Sourcebook*, Morrigan Books, 1991.

Mac Neill, Eoin, *Celtic Ireland*, Academy Press, Dublin, 1921.

Mac Niocaill, Gearoid, *Ireland before the Vikings*, The Gill History of Ireland 1, Gill and Macmillan, Dublin 1972.

Ray, James Charles, *The Road Wet, The Wind Close*, Celtic Ireland, Gill & Macmillan, Dublin 1945.

Wood-Martin, W. G., *The Lake Dwellings of Ireland*, Hodges Figgis, Dublin 1883 & 1986.

CHAPTER 8 AND 9

Andrews, John, *Ireland in Maps*, The Dolmen Press, 1961.

Mitchell, Frank, *Reading the Irish Landscape*, Michael Joseph, Country House, 1986.

Nolan, William, ed., *The Shaping of Ireland*, Mercier Press, Cork 1986.

CHAPTER 10

Chatterton, Roger Newman, *Brian Boru, King of Ireland*, Anvil Books, 1983.

Lydon, James, *Ireland in the Middle Ages*, The Gill History of Ireland, Gill and MacMillan, Dublin.

*The Metrical Dindshenchas*, Todd Lecture Series, Text Translation and Commentary, Edward Gwynn, Tara Poems, The Academy House, Dublin, 1903.

CHAPTER 11

Cogan, Revd A., *Diocese of Meath Ancient and Modern*, John Fowler, Dublin, 1862.

Gwynn, Aubry and Hadwick, R Neville, *Medieval Religious Houses of Ireland*, Longman, 1970.

Steen, L.J., *The Battle of the Hill of Tara*, Trim, 1991.

CHAPTER 12

Butler, Dean, *Notices of the Castle and Ecclesiastical Buildings of Trim, 1856*, Meath Archaeological Society, 1978.

Concannon, Mrs Thomas, *St Patrick: His Life and Mission*, Talbot Press.

Hayes-McCoy, G.A., *A History of Irish Flags from the Earliest Times*, Academy Press, Dublin 1979.

Lewis, Samuel, *Topographical Dictionary of Ireland*, London, 1837.

McKee, Robert, *The Green Flag*, Weidenfeld and Nicolson, London, 1972.

Rosse, Ann, *Everyday Life of the Pagan Celts*, London, 1970.

Trench, Charles Chenevix, *The Great Dan*, Jonathan Cape, London, 1984.

CHAPTER 13

*Dunsany 1894–1994*, David Lynch, John Donohoe, Michael Smith, Navan, 1994.

Carthy, Mary Rose, *History Of Killeen Castle*, Colour Books, Baldoyle, 1991.

*Proceedings Of Rathfeigh Historical Society*, 1987, 1993.

French, Noel E., *Bellinter House*, Trim Heritage Centre, 1993.

Lewis, Samuel, *Topographical Dictionary Of Ireland*, London, 1837.

Lord Brabazon of Tara, *The Brabazon Story*, Willian Heinemann, 1956.

CHAPTER 14

*The Boyne, 5,000 Years of History*, Navan, 1990.

Byrne, Francis J. *Irish Kings and High-Kings*, B.T. Batsford, London 1973.

Cone, Polly, ed., *The Treasures of Early Irish Art, 1500 BC to 1500 AD.*, Metropolitan Museum of Art, 1977.

Eoghan, George, *Catalogue of Irish Bronze Age Swords*, Stationary Office, Dublin, 1965.

Hickey, Elizabeth, *The Legend of Tara*, Dundalgan Press, Dundalk 1970, 1988.

McGowan, Kenneth, *The Hill of Tara*, Kamac, Dublin, 1979 and 1985.

*RIA Discovery Programme Reports 1 & 2, Dublin, Project Results* 1992–93.

## Picture Acknowledgements

BLACK AND WHITE: Courtesy of the artist, Sinead McCarthy: **map, Introduction; p.29; 149**. Courtesy of photographer, Robert Vance: **p.14; 18; 28 (top); 47; 82; 148**. From W.R. Wilde's *A Descriptive Catalogue of the Antiquities . . . in the Museum of the Royal Irish Academy*, M.H. Gill, Dublin 1857: **p.15; 16**. Courtesy of the Board of Trinity College Dublin: **p.17** (TCD MS 1289 p.87); **20** (TCD MS 58, fol.8r); **86** (TCD MS 58, fol.29r); **94 (bottom**; TCD MS 1318 cols 802-803). Courtesy of Bord Fáilte: **p.19; 48; 100**. Courtesy of the Royal Irish Academy: **p.21; 73**. From Helen M. Roe's *Medieval Fonts of Meath*, Meath Archaeological and Historical Society 1968: **p.23**. Drawing by Martin Brennan, from his *The Stars and the Stones: Ancient Art and Astronomy in Ireland*, Thames & Hudson 1983: **p.28 (bottom)**. Courtesy of photographer, Paul Caponigro: **p.30; 33; 35**. From G. Petrie, 1839: *On the history and antiquities of Tara Hill*, Transactions of the RIA 18, 25-232: **p.37; 76; 161; 163**. Courtesy of the *Meath Chronicle* (postcard in the 'Irish Monastic Series', Kamac Publications, Dublin): **p.135**. Courtesy of the National Library of Ireland: **p.39; 72; 120; 131; 133; 138**. Courtesy of the Office of Public Works: **p.42; 57; 90; 96; 97; 112; 115; 121; 150; 151; 154-5**. Courtesy of Louis Le Brocquy: **p. 71** (from *The Táin*, trans. Thomas Kinsella, OUP in ass. with The Dolmen Press, 1969). Courtesy of Desmond Kinney and the Irish Dairy Board: **p.44-45**. Courtesy of Navan Fort Interpretive Centre, Armagh: **p.46**. Courtesy of Waterford Crystal Ltd: **p.49**. Courtesy of Laurence Steen, Tara: **p.52**. From R.J. Stewart's *Celtic Gods, Celtic Goddesses*, Blandford 1990: **p.53**. Courtesy of Jim Fitzpatrick: **p. 58; 67**. Courtesy of the National Museum of Ireland: **p.59; 89; 100; 108; 109; 124**. Courtesy of the National Gallery of Ireland: **p.61**. Courtesy of the Donnelly family, Tara: **p.63**. Drawing by Stephen Conlin, courtesy of the Navan Fort Association: **p.66**. From Jean McCann's *Loughcrew: The Cairns*, After Hour books, 1993 (after Elizabeth Shee Twohig): **p.74**. Reproduced with the kind permission of the trustees of the Ulster Museum: **p.81**. From Roger Chatterton Newman's *Brian Boru: King of Ireland*, Anvil books, 1983: **p.84** (after MacNeill, *Celtic Ireland*, 1921); **114** (from drawing by T.J. Westropp); **116** (by H. Warren, from *History of Ireland*, vol. 1, by Thomas Wright, London [n.d]). Courtesy of the Meath Heritage Centre, Trim: **p.87**. Courtesy of Peter Gallagher, GPS Photography: **p.88; 127; 128**. Courtesy of the artist, Ann Fallon: **p.94 (top)**. Courtesy of the British Library, London (reproduced form *Treasures of Irish Art 1500BC-1500AD*, The Metropolitan Museum of Irish Art & Alfred A. Knopf, New York 1977: **p.98**. Woodcut from John Derricke, *Images of Ireland, 1581* (reproduced from *Life in Ireland*, L.M. Cullen, Batsford, London 1979): **p.101; 107**. Courtesy of the Geological Survey Office, Dublin: **p.102**. Courtesy of Tom Connachy, *Evening Herald*: **p.122**. From *Taylor and Skinner's Maps of the Roads of Ireland*, 1783: **p.126**. Courtesy of photographer, John Donohoe: **p.129**. Courtesy of the Land Commission Office, Dublin: **p.139**. Photographs by Peter Murray, courtesy of his son, Brendan Murray: **p.141**. Courtesy of the Tormey family: **p.142**. Courtesy of the Pierse family: **p.145**. From R.A.S. Macalister's *Tara: A Pagan Sanctuary of Ancient Ireland*, London 1931: **p.152**. From Seán P. Ó Ríordáin's paper, 'A Burial with Faience Beads at Tara', *The Prehistoric Society*, no.19, 1955: **p.153**. Courtesy of Michael Slavin: **p.158**. Reproduced courtesy of the Discovery Programme: **p.159**.

COLOUR: Courtesy of photographer, Robert Vance: **Section One, p.1, 2, 4, 7; Section Two, p.1, 3, 4 (main picture), 7 (main picture), 8; Section Three, p.1, 2 (main picture), 4 (centre), 6 (main picture), 7 (top), 8**. From R.J. Stewart's *Celtic Gods, Celtic Goddesses*, Blandford 1990: **Section 1, p.5**. Courtesy of Jim Fitzpatrick: **Section One, p.6; Section Two, p.2 (top); Section Three, p.3 (inset)**. Courtesy of the Board of Trinity College Dublin: **Section One, p.8; Section Two, p.2 (bottom)**. Courtesy of the National Museum of Ireland: **Section Two, p.5 (top), 6 (top & bottom); Section Three, p.5 (main picture)**. Courtesy of the Royal Irish Academy: **Section Two, p.5 (bottom)**. Courtesy of the Office of Public Works: **Section Three, p.4 (top)**. Courtesy of the Central Catholic Library: **Section Three, p.4 (bottom)**. Courtesy of Royal Tara Ireland Ltd: **Section Three, p.7 (bottom)**.

## A

Act of Union (1800), 130
Adamnán, Saint, 38, 98, 101-2, 162
Áed Allen, king of Tara, 103
Áed Mac Néill, king of Aileach, 108
Áed Oirdnide, 103-4, 105
Áed Sláine, 100
Áed (son of Ainmire), 100-101
Áedh Guaire, 97
Ailill Ane, king of Leinster, 75
Ailill Eochraid, 46
Ailill Mac Mata, 42, 44
Aillen of the Flaming Breath, 64-65
Alexander II, Pope, 118
Amorgen (son of Míl), 19, 21-22
*Annals of Clonmacnoise*, 77, 83, 84, 115
*Annals of Innisfallen*, 86
*Annals of the Four Masters*, 23, 34, 86, 87, 116
*Annals of Tigearnach*, 75, 86
*Annals of Ulster*, 86, 99, 101, 104
Aoife, 122
Aonghus, 92
Aonghus (love god), 22, 31, 46, 50
Aonghus (monk), 38
Aonghus Tuiremech, 77
Archer, Patrick, 52-53
Ardsallagh House (Co. Meath), 142
Art Mac Cuin, 30
Art Oenfer, 86, 87
Assembly of Tara – see Feis of Tara
Athboy (Co. Meath), 120
Augustinian Order, 139, 140

## B

Badb, 56
Baetan, 100
Balor of the Evil Eye, 18, 19, 57-58, 60, 62
Balsoon House (Co. Meath), 143
Banqueting Hall (Tech Midchurta, Tara), 31 (illus.), 160-61
Barnwall, Nicholas, Viscount Gormanston, 126
Barnwalls, 124, 138, 139
Battersby, William, 32
Battle of Achall (Skryne), 83
Battle of Belach Mugna, 109
Battle of Mag Tuired, 62
Battle of Moylena (13th-century text), 85
Battle of Tara (26 May 1798), 52-53, 127-30, 157
Battles of Moytura, 17, 19
Bealtaine (festival), 31
Bechulle (sorcerer), 61
Bective Abbey, 38, 143, 152
Bede, 104
Belach Mugna (Carlow), 109
Belgae, 15

Bellinter Harriers, 144
Bellinter House (Co. Meath), 143, 144
Bellinter Park Golf Club, 144
Belper (Tara), 29, 31
Ben Bulben (Co. Sligo), 48 (illus.)
Bhreathnach, Edel, 158
Blacar (Norse leader), 110
Blocc and Bluicne (sacred stones at Tara), 163
Bóinn (White Cow Goddess), 31
Bolgi, 15
*Book of Ballymote*, 69, 73, 79, 88, 121
*Book of Clonmacnoise*, 34
*Book of Glendalough*, 44-45
*Book of Kells*, 20 (illus.), 37
*Book of Lecan*, 83, 94, 161
*Book of Leinster*, 34, 41, 69, 73, 79, 83, 161
*The Book of Leinster*, 14
*Book of Rights*, 73 (illus.)
*Book of the Taking of Ireland* – see *Lebor Gabála Erenn*
boroimhe (tribute), 83, 85, 94
Boyne (river), 32, 85, 89, 152-53
Brabazon, Rev William, 145
Brabazon family, 145
Brabazon of Tara, Lord, 145
Bran Dub, king of Laigin, 101
Breas (Dé Danann warrior), 16, 17, 18, 56, 57, 60, 74, 78
Brehon Laws, 87, 123
Brennan, Martin, 28
Bresal Bo-Dibad, 77
Bri Leith, 46
Brian Boru, king of Munster, 25, 83, 93, 99, 109, 110
   conflict with Malachy II, 110, 111-18
   inauguration, 113-14
Brighid, Saint, 30
Brighid (fire goddess), 30-31
Briscoe, Rev Francis, 143
Briscoe, Gustavus Villiers, 143-44
Briscoe, Henry Cecil, 144
Briscoe family, 143
British-Israelite Association, 151 (illus.), 152 (illus.)
Brown Bull of Cooley, 43, 44
Brugh na Bóinne, 46
Butler, Sir Isaac, 145
Byrne, Francis J., 25, 35, 70, 99

## C

Cairenn, 92
Caoilte Mac Ronáin, 15, 67
Cashel, kings of, 105, 109 – see also Brian Boru
Cashel (Co. Tipperary), 85, 112 (illus.)
Castle, Richard, 143
Castleboy (Tara), 32

Cath Maighe Lena (Battle of Moylena), 85
Cathaoir Mór, king of Leinster, 49, 84, 88
Catholic Confederacy, 125-27
Cauldron of Plenty, 17, 18, 19, 62
Ceithlenn, 60
Celatin (druid), 44
Celestine III, Pope, 139-40
Celts, 24-25, 27, 72-73, 75
Cenel Conaill, 100
Cenel nEoghain, 100, 102, 103
Cerball Mac Donngaile, king of Leinster, 108
Cernait, 72, 88, 151
Charles II, 126, 141
Christianity, 24, 31, 37-39, 80, 89, 93, 94
   clerical immunity, disputes over, 96-97
   cursing of Tara, 97
   and Uí Néill kings, 94, 95-96, 103, 104
Cian (Dé Danann chieftain), 57, 58
Ciaran, Saint, 96
Cinaed Mac Conaing, 107
Claddy Bridge (near Bective Abbey), 106 (illus.)
Clann Cholmain of Uisneach, 92, 100, 108
Clóenfherta (Sloping Trenches or Crooked Mound of Tara), 35,87, 159-61
Clonard monastery, 23 (illus.), 38, 96, 103
Clonmacnoise, 19 (illus.), 96, 98, 106
Cobthach the Meagre, 75
*Collectio Canonum Hiberniensis*, 114
Collierstown (Co. Meath), 139
Colman Rimid, 100
Columcille, Saint, 14, 38, 96-97
Comhrag (huntsman), 67
Conaill Gulban, 92
Conaire Coem, 86
Conaire Mór, king of Tara, 77, 80-82
Conall, ruler of the west of Ireland, 84
Conall Err Breg, 92
Condren, Mary, 35-36
Congal, king of Tara, 102
Congalach Cnogba, 100
Congalach Cnogba Mac Maelmithig, 110

Conn Ceadchathach (Conn of the Hundred Battles), 62, 64, 65, 72, 77, 84-86
Connachta, 84, 91
Connell, Nancy (Leixlip), 163
Conor Mac Nessa, king of Ulster, 43
Cormac, king of Cashel, 109
Cormac Mac Airt, 30, 35, 49, 51, 67-68, 80, 86-89, 140, 151, 159
  compilation of Brehon Laws, 87-88
  psalter, 98 (illus.)
  "Teagasc na Riogh," 88
Cormac's House (Tara), 154, 155, 158
Corravilla (Co. Cavan) stone head, 89 (illus.)
Crimthann, 93
Cromwell, Oliver, 126, 140
Crooked Mound of Tara – see Clóenfherta
Croppies, 128
Cross of Adamnán (Tara), 38, 162, 163 (illus.)
Cross of Cong, 120
Crúachain (Rathcroghan, Co. Roscommon), 42
Cuchulainn, 43-45, 62
Cuchulainn's Shield (Tara), 45
Cúil Dreimne (Co. Sligo), 96
Cullen, Margaret and Catherine, 142
Cullen family (Tara Hall), 142
Cumhail, 63
Curry, William, 158
Cusack, Pearse, 138-39
Cusack, Thomas, Lord Chancellor, 140

D
Da Dearga's Hostel, 82
Daghdha (Dé Danann father-god), 17, 18, 22, 31, 46, 60, 62, 78
Daire of Cooley, 43
Daire (poet), 50
Dal Cais, 109 – see also Brian Boru
Dalgan Park (Co. Meath), 152
Dalny, 14
Daughters of Sion (Bellinter), 144
De Cornere, Alicia, 140
De Cusack, Geoffrey, 124
De Cusacks of Killeen, 138
Dé Danann, 16-19, 21-22, 24, 55-60, 72
de Feypo, Adam, 124, 138, 140
de Feypo, Thomas, 140
De Lacy, Hugh, 122 (illus.), 123-24, 138
De Nangle family, 141
De Prestons, 140
Defenders, 127-28
Dervorgilla, 121
Desa, 80
Dianan (sorcerer), 61
Diancecht, 60, 62

Diarmaid Mac Cerbaill, king of Tara, 14, 34, 101, 138
Diarmaid Mac Fergus Cerbaill, king of Tara, 95-98
Diarmaid (son of Duibhne), 50-51, 159
Dillon, Sir Charles (Lismullen), 140
Dillon, Sir James, 126
Dillon, Sir John, 140
Dillon, Sir John Fox, 140
Dillon, Ralph (Lismullen), 128
Dillon, Richard, 163
Dillon, Sir Robert, 140
Dillon family, 140
Dillons, 124
Dindshenchas Erenn, 18, 21 (illus.), 25, 31, 38, 87, 149, 157, 163
Discovery Programme, 11, 154, 158, 160
Domhnall, high king of Ireland, 101
Domhnall Ua Néill, king of Tara, 110
Donard (Co. Wicklow), 101
Donnchadh, high king of Ireland, 118, 119
Donnchadh, king of Uisneach, 103
Donnchadh Donn, king of Tara, 109-10
Druim Cain (Tara), 16, 19
Druim Ceit, 100
Drumree (Co. Meath), 107
Dubhtach (chief poet of Ireland), 37
Dublin (Viking settlement), 106
  subjugation by Malachy II, 114, 115
Dui Dallta Degaid, 77
Dunlaing, king of Leinster, 35, 83, 159
Dunsany, lords of, 124
Dunshaughlin (Co. Meath), 100

E
Eachlann (Laigin warrior), 84
Easter Rising (1916), 136
Eber (son of Mil), 22-23
Eilim Mac Conrach, 82, 83
Eiscir Riada, 85, 105, 108, 150
Eithne, 49, 82-83, 88
Elizabeth I, 139
Emain Macha (Co. Armagh), 29, 41, 46 (illus.), 92
Enda, 92
Enna Aighneach, king of Tara, 77
Enna Airgdech, 74
Eochaid Aireamh, king of Tara, 47, 48-49, 77
Eochaid Mac Erc, king of the Fir Bolg, 15, 16-17, 55, 56, 57, 72, 78
Eochaid Mugmedon, 92
Eochaidh Fiedhleach, 30
Eochu Apthach, king of Tara, 75
Eochu Edgathach, 74
Eochu Feidlech, 77
Eoganacht, 85, 108, 109, 113

Eoghan, 92
Eoghan Mór, 85, 86
Erainn, 82
Erc, Bishop of Slane, 95, 97
Eremon (son of Mil), 21, 22-33, 72, 73, 91
Eriu (wife of Mac Gréine), 22, 41
Étaín, 46-49, 80, 86, 87
Etar, king of Leinster, 46
Eterscele, king of Tara, 77, 80, 81
Ethlinn, 57-58, 63
Ethriel, 74

F
Faildergoit, 74
Feidhlimidh Mac Criomthain, king of Cashel, 105-6
Feidhlimidh Rechtmar, 84
Feis (Assembly) of Tara, 34-35, 36, 47, 83, 156
Fenwick, Joe, 158
Ferdia, 43-44, 57
Fiacha Ferwara, 77
Fiacha (warrior), 65
Fiachu Findiolches, king of Tara, 74, 82
Fiachu Finscothach, 34
Fianna, 49, 50, 51, 63, 64-68, 88
Findian of Mag Bile, 14
Fingall, earls of, 53, 124, 126, 128
Finghein Mac Luchta, 85
Finian, Saint, 38, 96
Finnegas (druid), 64
Fionn Mac Cumhail, 49-52, 63-68, 88
Fir Bolg, 15-17, 24, 55-57, 69, 72, 82
Flann Sinna, king of Tara, 108-9
Flatbertach, king of Tara, 102
Fomorians, 14-15, 17, 18, 19, 57, 58, 59, 60, 61
Forradh (Tara), 157, 158
Frame, David, 145
Fuamnach (goddess), 46
Furbaidhe, 45

G
Ga Bolga (Cuchulainn's spear), 43, 44
Gaelic League, 141
Gaels, 75
Gap of Ulster, 43
George III, 143
Giant's Causeway (Co. Antrim), 67
Giolla Comhgaill O'Sleibhin (chief bard of Ulster), 117
Glas Teamhrach (Tara), 31

*Glossary of King Cormac*, 30-31
Goibniu, 31, 60, 61
Goll Mac Morna, 63, 64, 65
Gormfhlaith (Kildare princess), 113, 115-16
Gormlaith, 106
Gowra (Co. Meath), 68
Gowra (river), 32, 150, 152, 153
Gráinne, 49-52, 67, 159
Great Famine, 135
Gregory, Lady Augusta, 135
Grianan of Aileach, 96 (illus.)
Griffith, Arthur, 152

**H**

Harp of Tara, 126
Harp of the Daghda, 18, 19
Harp of the Daghdha, 18, 62
Henry, Frank, 145-46
Henry, Philip, 146
Henry II, 123
  Treaty of Windsor (1175), 124
Henry VIII, 125, 140
Hickey, Elizabeth, 97
Hill of Allen, 66
Hill of the Cow (Tara), 31
Holdsworth, Henry, 144
Holinshed, Raphael, 125
Hone, Evie, 163

**I**

*Illustrated London News*, 132
Imbolg (festival), 29-31
Inber Cichmaine, 46
Inver Scéine, 22
Inver Sláine, 19
IRA, 140
Irish American Cultural Institute (St Paul, Minnesota), 27
Irish Literary Revival, 135
Irish Volunteers, 136

**J**

Jones, Colonel Michael, 126

**K**

Kells Cavalry (1798), 129
Kells (Co. Meath), 37
Kennedy, Josephine, 144
Kennedy, Tony, 146
Keshcorran (Co. Kerry), 51
Kiernan, Thomas, 129
Kilcarne Stud, 146
Killeen Castle (Co. Meath), 124, 126, 128, 135 (illus.)
King's Seat (Tara), 157, 158
Knowth (Co. Meath), 28, 107
  kerbstone, 35 (illus.)

Labhraidh Loingseach, king of Tara, 75
Laegh (druid), 43
Lagore (Dunshaughlin, Co. Meath) brooch, 100 (illus.)
Laigin (Leinstermen), 75, 80, 83, 84, 94, 101
Laigne (son of Eremon), 73
Leath Choinn, 85, 108
Leath Mhogha, 85, 108
*Lebor Gabala Erenn* (*Book of the Taking of Ireland*), 13-14, 16, 17, 17 (illus.), 18, 23, 24
Leinstermen – see Laigin
Len of Loch Lene, 65
Lia Fáil (Stone of Destiny), 17-18, 18 (illus.), 19, 35, 69, 81, 85, 130, 153, 157
Lismullen (Co. Meath), 38, 140
Lismullen House (Co. Meath), 140
Lóegaire, king of Tara, 24, 31, 34, 36-37, 83, 92, 93-94, 158
Lóegaire Lorc, king of Tara, 75
Loingsech Mac Oengusso, high king of Ireland, 101-2
Lough Ennell (Co. Westmeath), 104 (illus.), 108, 110
Lough Neagh, 67
Lough Owel, 107
Loughcrew (Co. Meath), 22, 28-29
  decorated stone, 33 (illus.)
  "Hag's Chair," 113 (illus.)
Lucat-moel (druid), 37
Luchta, 61-62
Ludlow, Peter, 142
Lugaid Mac Con, king of Tara, 86, 87, 159
Lugaidh, king of Tara, 94
Lugh, king of Tara, 78
Lugh of the Long Hand (mythical hero), 15, 19, 32, 43
Lugh (sun god), 57-63, 85, 86
Lughnasa (festival), 32
Lugna Fer Tri, 87
Luigne (son of Eremon), 73

**M**

Macalister, R. A. S., 34
Mac Ceacht (Dé Danann king), 21, 72, 82
McCone, Kim, *Pagan Past and Christian Present*, 24
Mac Cuill (Dé Danann king), 21, 72
MacGowan, Kenneth, *The Hill of Tara*, 39
Mac Gréine (Dé Danann king), 21, 22, 72
Macha, 29, 41, 43, 56
Mac Lochlainn, Domhnall, 119, 120
Mac Lochlainn, Muircheartach, 120, 122, 138
McMann, Jean, *Loughcrew, The Cairns*, 28-29

Mac Murrough, Diarmuid, king of Leinster, 121-22
Mac Néill, Eoin, 136
Mac Niocaill, Gearoid, *Ireland before the Vikings*, 91
Maeve, 29-30, 42-45, 86, 87, 159
Magnus Ua Maelsechlainn, 138
Maigh Adhair (Co. Clare), 114, 114 (illus.), 115 (illus.)
Malachy I (Maelsechlainn Mac Mael Ruanaid), 107-8
Malachy II (Maelsechnaill Mac Domhnaill), 25, 93, 99, 110
  conflict with Brian Boru, 110, 111-18
    re-assumption of high kingship, 118
  subjugation of Dublin Vikings, 114, 115
  surrender to Brian Boru, 117-18
Mamos (druid), 61
Manannan Mac Lir, 22, 58
Mathgamain, king of Cashel, 113
Mathgen (magician), 61
Meas Buachalla, 80
Meath County Council seal, 87 (illus.)
Meath Hunt, 140, 163
Melge, king of Tara, 75
Mellifont (Co. Louth), 38
Men of Erin, 43, 44, 47
Midhir the Proud, 22, 46, 48-49
Milesians, 19, 21-23, 24, 41, 72, 75
Moel (sacred stone at Tara), 163
Moire (Co. Down), 101
Monasterboice, 38
Mongfind, 92, 93
Moore, Thomas, 145
Moore-Brabazon, John Theodore Cuthbert, 143
Morrigu (war goddess), 56
Mound of the Cow (Tara), 31, 32
Mound of the Hostages (Tara), 28, 29, 130, 153, 155-56
  burial urn, 150 (illus.)
Mound of the Three Men (Tara), 16
Moynalty (Co. Meath), 15
Mugh Nuadhat, 85
Muimne (son of Eremon), 73
Muinemon, 74
Muircheartach Mac Earca, 94-95, 96
Muircheartach Mac Lochlainn, 120, 122, 138
Muircheartach (son of Niall Glundub), 109-10

Muircheartach the Great, high king of Ireland, 119
Muirchu, 36, 37
Muirne, 63
Muirthemne (Co. Down), 103
Mullaghmast (Co. Kildare), 94
Munster kings, 113 – see also Brian Boru
   challenge to Tara kingship, 105-6
   submission to Tara high-kingship, 108

N
Navan Cavalry (1798), 129
Neamnach, well of, 159
Neit, 21
Nemedians, 15
Nemglen, 81
Newgrange (Co. Meath), 22, 28, 30
   (illus.), 46, 47 (illus.), 89
Newman, Conor, 158
Newtown (Trim), 38
Niall Cáille, king of Tara, 105, 106-7
Niall Glundub Mac Áedo, 109
Niall Naoi-Ghiallach (Niall of the Nine
   Hostages), 91, 92, 95
Niav, 58
Nine Years War, 126
Normans, 121-24, 138
Nuadhu (Laigin warrior), 84
Nuadhu of the Silver Arm (king of the Dé
   Danann), 17, 18, 31, 57, 58, 59-60, 60, 62,
   78

O
Ochil (Hill of Skryne), 84
O'Connell, Daniel, 11
   monster meeting at Tara (1843), 130-35
O'Connor, Ruairi, high king of Ireland,
   120-23
   Treaty of Windsor (1175), 124
O'Connor, Turlough, 119-20
O'Connors of Connacht, 119-20, 121-22
Odder (river), 151
Odder (Tara, Co. Meath), 139, 140
Ó Domhnaill, Red Hugh, 126
O'Donovan, John
   aerial drawing of Tara, 92 (illus.)
Office of Public Works, 137, 144, 158
   Discovery Programme, 11, 154, 158, 160
Oisín, 50, 66, 67, 68
Olaf (Viking king), 113
Ollamh Fódla, king of Tara, 34, 36, 74
Ó Néill, Eoghan Rua, 126
Ó Néill, Sir Phelim, 126
Ó Néill kingship – see Uí Néill dynasty
O'Rahilly, Thomas F., Early Irish History
   and Mythology, 23, 75
Ó Riordáin, Sean, 153, 155, 161
O'Rourke, Tighernan, king of Breffni,

121-22
Oscar, 67, 68
Otherworld, 22, 27, 34, 46, 87, 89, 100, 153

P
Pale, the, 124
Parthalóns, 14-15
Patrick, Saint, 24, 31, 36, 37, 39, 92, 93
Peel, Sir Robert, 134
Pentonys, 124, 138
Petrie, George, 31, 95
   aerial drawing of Tara, 76 (illus.)
   ancient roads of Tara, 161 (illus.)
   Cross of Adamnan, 163 (illus.)
Pierse, Dan and Anne, 146
Pitt, William, 130
Plain of Teltown, 22
Plunkett, Arthur James, 8th Earl of
   Fingall, 128, 129
Plunkett, Christopher, 2nd Earl of
   Fingall, 126
Plunkett, James Horace, 12th Earl of
   Fingall, 140
Plunketts, 124, 138
Power, Richard, 140
Preston, George James, 3rd Earl Ludlow,
   142
Preston, John, Viscount Tara, 127, 128,
   129, 143
Preston, John (Ardsallagh), 142
Preston, John (Bellinter), 142, 143
Preston, John Joseph, 143, 144
Preston, John (Navan), 141, 142, 143
Preston, Rev Joseph, 143
Preston, Peter, 1st Earl Ludlow, 142
Preston, Phineas, 141, 142
Preston, Samuel, 141
Preston, Colonel Thomas, 126-27, 140
Preston family, 124, 140, 143

R
Rampart of Whisperings (Tara), 60
Rath Cormac (Tara), 130
Rath Gráinne (Tara), 151, 159-60
Rath Lóegaire (Tara), 93 (illus.), 158-59
Rath Maeve (Tara), 29, 31, 42 (illus.), 151
Rath na Rig (Tara), 153
Rath of the Synods (Tara), 38, 83, 156,
   161-63
   excavation by British Israelites, 151
   (illus.), 152 (illus.)
Rebellion of 1641, 125-27
Rebellion of 1798, 52
   Battle of Tara, 52-53, 127-30, 157
Records of the Meath Archaeological and
   Historical Society, 138-39
Red Branch Knights, 43
Reddy, T. M., 142

Reginald, first Norse king of
   Dublin, 109
Repeal movement
   monster meeting at Tara (1843),
   130-35
Riverstown (Co. Meath), 140
Rolleston, T. W., 22
Ros na Riogh (Slane), 89
Rothechtaid, 74
Royal Tara Golf Club, 144
Ruadhan, Saint, 38, 69, 97
Rudraige, king of Tara, 77
Russell, Bertrand, 142
Russell, Lord John, 134-35, 142
Russell, John Francis, 2nd Earl
   Russell, 142

S
St Patrick's Breastplate, 37
   (illus.)
St Patrick's Church (Tara), 39
   (illus.), 163
   graveyard, 127 (illus.)
St Patrick's statue (Tara), 38
   (illus.), 158
St Patrick's Well (Tara), 31,
   149-53
Salmon of Knowledge, 64
Samhain (festival), 34-39
Seat of Adamnan (Tara), 38
Setna Innarraid, king of Tara, 75
Sheen (Sin), 95
Sheerin, Paul, 27
Síl nÁedo Sláine, 100, 107, 138
Sirna Soegalach, king of Tara, 74
Sitric, king of Dublin, 113, 114
Skane (river), 32, 152, 153
Skryne Cavalry, 128, 129
Skryne (Co. Meath), 29, 37-38,
   84, 89
   Barony of, 124, 138
   Battle of Achall, 83
Sláine, king of the Fir Bolg,
   15-16, 72
Slane (Co. Meath), 15-16, 31, 97
   (illus.)
Slí Asail, 161
Slí Cualann, 161
Slí Dhala, 149, 151, 161
Slí Mhidhluachra, 161
Slí Mór, 161
Sliabh Gullion (Co. Armagh), 29
Sloping Trenches (Tara) – see
   Clóenfherta
Spear of Victory, 17, 18, 19
Sreng (Fir Bolg warrior), 16, 17,
   55-57

Steen, Laurence J., *The Battle of the Hill of Tara*, 128
Stewart, R. J., *Celtic Gods and Goddesses*, 27
Stone Heap of the One Man (Tara), 16
Stone of Destiny (Tara) – see Lia Fáil
Stone of Scone, 157
Stopfords (Cromwell's secretary), 140
Strongbow, Earl of Pembroke, 122-23
Suanach, 67
Summerhill (Co. Meath), 126
Swainstown (Kilmessan, Co. Meath), 141
Sword of Light, 17, 18, 86
Synod of Adamnan, 162

T
Tadg (son of Nuadhu), 63
Tailten Games, 15, 32, 41
Tailten (Teltown, Co. Meath), 15, 22, 29, 32, 83
  site of royal inaugurations, 104
Tailtiu, 15, 16, 29, 32, 41
Táin Bó Cuailgne (Cattle Raid of Cooley), 30, 42-45
Tairrdelbach, high king of Ireland, 119
Tallaght monastery, 104
Tara, Lord, 143
Tara Hall, 140, 145 (illus.), 145-46, 150-51
Tara Harriers, 144
Tara Interpretative Centre, 39
Tara National School, 140
Tara torcs, 156
Tara village (Co. Meath), 138 (illus.)
Tea (mother-goddess), 21, 157
Teach Chormac (Tara), 154, 155, 158
Tech Midchurta (Banqueting Hall, Tara), 160-61
Teltown (Co. Meath) – see Tailten

Tent of Adamnán (Tara), 38
*The Nation*, 132
*The Times*, 132
Tigernmas, 74
Tir Conaill, 92
Tir Eoghan, 92
Tir na nÓg (Land of Youth), 22, 46, 58, 68
Tireachan, 36
Tlachtga (Athboy, Co. Meath), 83
Tobar Finn (Finn's Well), 151
Tormey, Bill (Tara), 142 (illus.), 144
Tormey family, 144
Torna (poet), 92
Treaty of Windsor (1175), 124
Trim Castle (Co. Meath), 120-21 (illus.), 138
Tuan Mac Cairill, 14
Tuatha Dé Danann – see Dé Danann
Túathal Maolgharbh, 95-96
Túathal Techtmar, king of Tara, 34, 80, 82-84
Tuireann, sons of, 60, 62
Turges (Viking leader), 105, 106-7

U
Ua Lothchain, Cuan, 25
Ugoine Mór, king of Tara, 75, 80, 82
Uí Bhriain of Munster, 119
Uí Néill dynasty, 18, 23, 57, 70-72, 73, 75, 77, 80, 84, 86, 91-98
  abandonment of Tara, 97-98
  conflict with Christian church, 94-95, 104
  consolidation of power, 94, 99
  extension of rule to Munster, 108, 112
  northern Uí Néill, 92, 96, 100, 102, 103, 108

quest for high kingship, 99-104
  southern Uí Néill, 92, 103, 113, 138
Uisneach (Co. Westmeath), 83, 92
Ulaid (Ulstermen), 85, 86, 88, 92, 103, 117
United Irishmen, 11, 52
  Battle of Tara (1798), 52-53, 127-30, 157
Ussher, Henry, 143

V
Vikings, 104, 105, 106-7, 109-10, 113
  subjugation of Dublin Vikings by Malachy II, 114, 115

W
Well of the Calf (Tara), 31, 32, 151, 159
Well of the White Cow (Tara), 31-32, 150
Weston, Molly, 52-53, 130
William of Orange, 140
Woganstown (Co. Dublin), 52
Woodpark (Dunboyne, Co. Meath), 144

Y
Yeats, William Butler, 135-36
Yellow Book of Lecan, 79
Yellow Ford (Slane, Co. Meath), 43